Stochastic Operations Research

First Edition

Mark Huber

ISBN: 979-8-9927906-0-3

Cover art:
Eugène Boudin
Jetty and Wharf at Trouville
1863
Painting

Contents

Contents

Preface

Purpose This book covers a one semester course in stochastic operations research for students who have had an undergraduate, Calculus based course in Probability.

Organization The course begins with an introduction before moving on to the main topics.

- Queuing Networks.
- Simulation.
- Decisions.
- Models.

Why are all the numerical answers in problems and examples given to 4 significant digits? In my homework assignments to students I require that all noninteger answers be presented to four significant digits. There are several reasons why I do this.

The first is that it makes answers uniform. I do not have to worry if $1/(3+\sqrt{2}) = (3-\sqrt{2})/5$ or not if the answer given is 0.2265. The second is that it emphasizes to students that in most problems in applied mathematics the exact numbers are uncertain. The number $1/3$ is specific and exact, but not actually encountered outside of toy problems. Third, it builds numerical literacy (aka numeracy.) Seeing that $\exp(-2) \approx 13.53\%$ is a useful thing, as it makes it crystal clear that the answers are not mere abstractions, but give results that can be acted upon.

Part I

INTRODUCTION

Chapter 1

What is Stochastic Operations Research?

Question of the Day

What is stochastic operations research all about?

Summary

- The mathematical science of making optimal decisions with partial information is *Stochastic Operations Research.*
- *Logical statements* evaluate to be either true or false.
- The *indicator function* outputs 1 if the input is true and 0 if the input is false.
- *Probability functions* inputs events and return a number between 0 and 1 indicating the information present about the truth of the event. They obey three rules. 1) The probability of a true statement is 1. 2) The probability a statement is false is 1 minus the probability it is true. 3) The probability that any of a sequence of events is true where at most one event is true equals the sum of the probabilities that the individual events are true.
- *Densities* of random variables can be used to calculate the *distribution* of the random variable, which is the probability that the random variable falls into a measurable set.
- For *discrete* random variables X with density f_X, $\mathbb{P}(X \in A) = \sum_{a \in A} f_X(a)$. For *continuous* random variables, $\mathbb{P}(X \in A) = \int_{a \in A} f_X(a)\,da$.

- X is *exponential with rate* λ if it is continuous with density $f_X(a) = \lambda \exp(-\lambda a)\mathbb{1}(a \geq 0)$. Write $X \sim \mathsf{Exp}(\lambda)$.

Mathematics has been used since ancient times to make choices that were the best possible. Ancient Greeks such as Plato exhorted nobles to learn arithmetic (or logistics as he called it) so that they would be able to properly supply their soldiers during times of war.

World War II saw the apotheosis of this application, as massive numbers of people and great quantities of military supplies had to be transported around the globe. The British coined a new term, *operations research* (OR), to describe the science and mathematics of making optimal decisions.

After the war, those scientists and mathematicians who had developed the beginnings of OR took those ideas into government and industry. They revolutionized production and systems development. OR was so important that it gained several synonyms. The terms

- operational research,
- management science, and
- decision science

all refer to making decisions in an optimal fashion.

In most situations where a decision must be made, the parameters that inform that decision are typically not known completely. For instance, if we are designing a network of roads, we usually do not know ahead of time how many people will use the roads once the network is built.

But just because we do not know the exact numbers does not mean we know nothing about the situation. Often we have *partial information* about the numbers we need. It might be known, for instance, that it is more likely that fewer than 1000 people per hour will use a road network than 1000 or more people will use it.

The mathematics of partial information, how to model and calculate with it, is called *probability*. Synonyms for partial information include

- random,
- stochastic, and
- uncertain.

Definition 1
The mathematical science of making optimal decisions with partial information is **Stochastic Operations Research**.

In this text, we will look at the major models and methods associated with Stochastic OR. These include queuing networks, models of decision making, simulation, and forecasting.

1.1 Probability

Suppose I am waiting for a bus. Let A denote the time needed for the bus to arrive in minutes. Then either $A > 5$ is true, or $A > 5$ is false. After five minutes, I will know for sure.

Notation 1
Use T to stand for true, and F to stand for false.

Definition 2
A **logical statement** is a statement that is either true (T) or false (F).

Since computers operate in binary at their most basic levels, which only uses 0 and 1 for each binary digit (usually abbreviated as a *bit*). Use 1 to stand for true statements, and 0 to stand for false statements. This is encoded in the *indicator function*, which we denote using a blackboard boldface numeral one.

Definition 3
The **indicator function** is $\mathbb{1} : \{\mathsf{T}, \mathsf{F}\} \to \{0, 1\}$, where

$$\mathbb{1}(\mathsf{T}) = 1$$
$$\mathbb{1}(\mathsf{F}) = 0.$$

A *probability function* (or *probabilistic model*) extends this notion of true or false to allow for partial information. Probabilities measure how likely a statement is to be true given our current information. Use $\mathbb{P}(p)$ to represent the probability of a statement p being true by a number that lies in the interval $[0, 1]$.

Definition 4
A **probability function** (aka **probability measure**) satisfies the following rules.

- **True statements** The probability of a true statement is 1. ($\mathbb{P}(\mathsf{T}) = 1$).
- **Negation** Let $\neg p$ be the **negation** of p. So if p is T, $\neg p$ is F, and if p is F, $\neg p$ is T. Then
$$\mathbb{P}(\neg p) = 1 - \mathbb{P}(p).$$
- **Countable mutually exclusive statements** If the set $\{p_i\}$ is either a finite set or an infinite sequence of statements such that at most one of them is true at any time, we call the statements **disjoint** or **mutually exclusive**. If the $\{p_i\}$ are a sequence of disjoint statements, then
$$\mathbb{P}\left(\text{one of the } p_i \text{ is true}\right) = \sum_i \mathbb{P}(p_i).$$

Often probability functions are defined in terms of sets instead of logical statements. Both treatments can be made rigorous, however, the definition in terms of logic is how probability is usually treated in practice, hence we will use the logical approach from here on out.

The name probability measure is also used to refer to $\mathbb{P}$ because it measures how likely a statement is to be true given our current information. For example, suppose that I am waiting for a bus. I can let T denote the amount of time I have to wait until the bus arrives.

Then to determine if $T > 5$ is true, all I have to do is wait five minutes. If the bus arrives in 5 or fewer minutes, then the statement is true, and if it takes longer, then the statement is false.

But before I wait the five minutes, I only have partial information about $\mathbb{P}(T > 5)$. This partial information gives me a *stochastic model* of the bus. For instance, I might know that in the past, the bus (on average) came within 5 minutes only 10% of the time. So I might initially say that $\mathbb{P}(T > 5) = 0.9$ and $\mathbb{P}(T \leq 5) = 0.1$.

Sets and intervals

Here a brief review of sets and set notation is given.

Sets are mathematical objects that either contain other mathematical objects. That is, for a set S and object a, either a is in set S is true or false. If it is true, call a an *element* of the set S.

Notation 2
The following notation is useful.

- Write $a \in S$ if it is true that a is an element of the set S.
- Use brace notation to indicate exactly which statement are true. For instance $S = \{a, b\}$ means that $a \in S$ and $b \in S$ are both true statements, but for any c different from both a and b, $c \in S$ is false.
- Write $A \subseteq B$ for two sets A and B if for all a such that $a \in A$ is true, it also holds that $a \in B$ is true.
- The set of real numbers is denoted $\mathbb{R}$.

Note that $(a \in S) = \mathsf{T}$ and $(b \in S) = \mathsf{T}$ could also be written as $(b \in S) = \mathsf{T}$ and $(a \in S) = \mathsf{T}$. That is, there is no notion of order of the elements of a set. So $\{a, b\}$ and $\{b, a\}$ are the same set.

Intervals are special sets of real numbers given using parentheses, brackets, and the extended real numbers $-\infty$ and ∞. Some example include

$$\begin{aligned}
(x \in (3, 5]) &= (x > 3) \text{ and } (x \leq 5) \\
(x \in [3, 5)) &= (x \geq 3) \text{ and } (x < 5) \\
(x \in (-\infty, 5)) &= (x < 5) \\
(x \in [3, \infty)) &= (x \geq 3).
\end{aligned}$$

So a parenthesis in interval notation means strict inequality on the right hand side, so less than or greater than. A bracket in interval notation means less than or equal to or greater than or equal to. An infinity (on the right) or negative infinity (on the left) means there is no restriction on the number.

1.2 *Discrete and continuous random variables*

Sets are useful in describing random variables. Using interval and set notation,

$$\mathbb{P}(T \leq 5) = \mathbb{P}(T \in (-\infty, 5]).$$

More generally, a random variable X is a mathematical object where there exists sets A of real numbers such that $\mathbb{P}(X \in A)$ is defined for those sets. The collection of sets A where $\mathbb{P}(X \in A)$ is defined is called the sets *measurable* with respect to X. The function that takes a measurable set A and returns $\mathbb{P}(X \in A)$ is called the *distribution* of the random variable X.

Definition 5
For a random variable X, the **distribution of X** is defined for measurable $A \subseteq \mathbb{R}$ as

$$\mathbb{P}_X(A) = \mathbb{P}(X \in A).$$

So how do we go about calculating $\mathbb{P}(X \in A)$ for a random variable? That depends on the type of random variable. It turns out there are three types of random variables. The two most common types are *discrete* and *continuous.*

Definition 6
A random variable is **discrete** if it has a **probability density function (pdf)** f_X such that for all measurable subsets A,

$$\mathbb{P}(X \in A) = \sum_{i \in A} f_X(i).$$

This is sometimes called a *probability mass function.* However, this term is outdated, there is no mathematical reason to call the densities for discrete and continuous random variables anything other than densities.

Definition 7
A random variable is **continuous** if it has a **probability density function (pdf)** f_X such that for all measurable subsets A,

$$\mathbb{P}(X \in A) = \int_{a \in A} f_X(a)\, da.$$

So for discrete random variables, we find $\mathbb{P}(X \in A)$ by summing the density over elements of A. For continuous random variables, we find $\mathbb{P}(X \in A)$ by integrating the density over elements of A.

Technically, discrete random variables have a density with respect to *counting measure*, while continuous random variables have a density with respect to *Lebesgue measure.* However, these details will be unnecessary for what we want to do with random variables, and so we will not discuss them further. Instead, use the following fact to determine if a density is for a discrete or continuous random variable.

Fact 1
Suppose a random variable X has density f_X. Then X is discrete if and only if

$$\sum_{i:f_X(i)>0} f_X(i) = 1.$$

Also, X is continuous if and only if f_X is continuous at all but a set of places that is countable.

Recall that a set is *countable* if it can be placed in a sequence. So for instance, $0, 2, 4, 6, \ldots$ is a countable set of numbers because they can be placed in a sequence. The set of real numbers (or a subset like $[0, 1]$) is famously *uncountable* because there is no way to put all of these numbers in a sequence.

1.3 Named distributions

Several distributions are important enough to have their own names. The first distribution we will be using is the exponential distribution.

Definition 8
Say that X has the **exponential distribution with parameter λ** if $\lambda > 0$ and X has density

$$f_X(a) = \lambda \exp(-\lambda a)\mathbb{1}(a \geq 0).$$

Write $X \sim \text{Exp}(\lambda)$.

Note that we used the indicator function here for convenience. When a is at least 0, $\mathbb{1}(a \geq 0) = 1$ and $f_X(a) = \lambda \exp(-\lambda a)$. When a is less than 0, $\mathbb{1}(a \geq 0) = 0$, so $f_X(a) = 0$. Another way to say this is that for the density to be nonzero, we must have $a \geq 0$ be true.

Yet another way to write this is

$$\lambda \exp(-\lambda a)\mathbb{1}(a \geq 0) = \begin{cases} \lambda \exp(-\lambda a) & a \geq 0 \\ 0 & a < 0. \end{cases}$$

Graphing this density yields

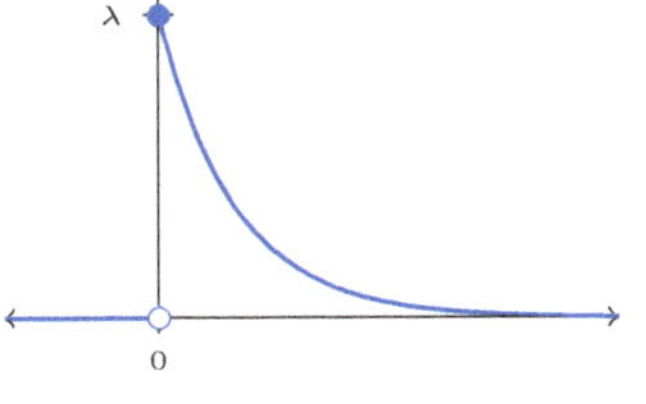

Call λ the *rate parameter*, as when it is higher, the random variable is more likely to be smaller.

Moreover, using indicator functions makes it easier to figure out how to find probabilities (and later in the course, expected value). That is because the indicator function in an integral (or a sum) tells us what the limits of integration (or summation) should be.

Example 1
Suppose $A \sim \text{Exp}(1.5)$. Find $\mathbb{P}(A > 1)$ and $\mathbb{P}(A \leq 1)$.

Answer For $\mathbb{P}(A > 1)$:

$$\begin{aligned}\mathbb{P}(A > 1) &= \int_{a\in[1,\infty)} 1.5\exp(-1.5a)\mathbb{1}(a \geq 0)\,da \\ &= \int_1^\infty 1.5\exp(-1.5a)\,da \\ &= -\exp(-a)|_1^\infty = 0 - (-\exp(-1.5)) = \boxed{0.2231\ldots}.\end{aligned}$$

Note that the $\mathbb{1}(a \geq 0)$ part of the integrand was redundant, since for $a \in [5, \infty)$, this was always true. For $\mathbb{P}(A \leq 1)$, we will use the indicator function in the density to change our limits of integration.

$$\begin{aligned}\mathbb{P}(A \leq 1) &= \int_{a\in(-\infty,1]} 1.5\exp(-1.5a)\mathbb{1}(a \geq 0)\,da \\ &= \int_0^1 1.5\exp(-1.5a)\,da \\ &= -\exp(-a)|_0^1 = -(-\exp(-1.5)) - (-\exp(0)) = 1 - \exp(-1.5) \\ &= \boxed{0.7768\ldots}.\end{aligned}$$

Note that the density is a continuous function except at a single point, making the random variable continuous.

Fact 2
Exponentially distributed random variables are continuous.

Problems

1.1 Which of the following are logical statements?

a) The capital of Iowa.

b) $4 > 6$.

c) $(\mathbb{1}(4 > 6) = 1)$.

d) The temperature at which water boils.

1.2 Which of the following are logical statements?

a) $3 = 7$

b) The capital of California is Sacramento.

c) What color is the Sun?

d) What year did the Battle of Hastings take place?

1.3 Evaluate the following.

a) $\mathbb{1}(3 = 4)$.

b) $\mathbb{1}(3 < 4)$.

c) $\mathbb{1}(4 < 3)$.

1.4 Evaluate the following.

a) $\mathbb{1}(7 = 7)$.

b) $\mathbb{1}(7 \leq 7)$.

c) $\mathbb{1}((\mathbb{1}(7 = 3) + \mathbb{1}(3 < 7)) \geq 1)$.

1.5 Given the density f_X of a random variable X, state whether X is discrete or continuous.

a) $f_X(2) = 0.3,\ f_X(4) = 0.7$.

b) $f_X(x) = \mathbb{1}(x \in [0, 1])$.

c) $f_X(0) = 1/3,\ f_X(1) = 1/3,\ f_X(2) = 1/3$.

d) $f_X(x) = \exp(-x)\mathbb{1}(x \geq 0)$.

1.6 Given the density f_Y of a random variable Y, state whether Y is discrete or continuous.

a) $f_Y(y) = (1/2)\mathbb{1}(x \in [0, 2])$.

b) $f_Y(1) = 0.8,\ f_Y(2) = 0.1,\ f_Y(3) = 0.1$.

c) $f_Y(0) = 0.5,\ f_Y(1) = 0.5$.

d) $f_Y(y) = 2\exp(-2y)\mathbb{1}(y \geq 0)$.

1.7 Suppose $X \sim \mathsf{Exp}(0.1)$.

a) Find $\mathbb{P}(X > 10)$.

b) Find $\mathbb{P}(X \leq 10)$.

1.8 Suppose $Y \sim \text{Exp}(1.3)$, and $W \sim \text{Exp}(2)$.

a) Find $\mathbb{P}(Y \in [0, 1])$.

b) Find $\mathbb{P}(W \in [0, 1])$.

c) Find $\mathbb{P}(Y \in [-1, 1])$.

Chapter 2

Conditional Probability

Question of the Day

Suppose $X \sim \text{Exp}(2)$. What is $\mathbb{P}(X > 2|X > 1)$?

Summary

- Write $X \sim Y$ if X and Y have the same distribution.
- A random variable X has a *cumulative distribution function* defined as $\text{cdf}_X(a) = \mathbb{P}(X \leq a)$. The Carathéodory extension theorem says that $X \sim Y$ if and only if $\text{cdf}_X = \text{cdf}_Y$.
- If X is continuous, then $\text{pdf}_X(a) = d\,\text{cdf}_X(a)/da$ wherever the cdf is differentiable. If X is discrete, then $\text{pdf}_X(i) = \lim_{\delta \to 0} \text{cdf}_X(i) - \text{cdf}_X(i - |\delta|)$.
- The *survival function* of random variable X is $\text{sur}_X(a) = \mathbb{P}(X > a)$ for real a. Note $\text{cdf}_X(a) = 1 - \text{sur}_X(a)$.
- For S a finite set with $\#(S)$ elements, say $X \sim \text{Unif}(S)$ if for all $i \in S$, $\mathbb{P}(X = i) = 1/\#(S)$.
- The conditional probability of event A being true given that event B is true is
$$\mathbb{P}(A|B) = \mathbb{P}(A \text{ and } B)/\mathbb{P}(B)$$
when $\mathbb{P}(B) > 0$.
- For $X \sim \text{Exp}(\lambda)$, the *memoryless property* says that for $s \geq 0$, $[X - s|X \geq s] \sim X$.

- Events A and B are independent if $\mathbb{P}(B = 0)$ or $\mathbb{P}(A|B) = \mathbb{P}(A)$. This holds iff $\mathbb{P}(AB) = \mathbb{P}(A)\mathbb{P}(B)$.
- A *stream* of random variables means for all i, given random variables $X_1, X_2, \ldots, X_i$ in the stream, there exists a random variable X_{i+1}.
- A stream of random variables is *independent, identically distributed* (iid for short) if for all i

$$[X_{i+1}|X_1, \ldots, X_i] \sim X_1.$$

2.1 Cumulative distribution function

Recall that the distribution of a random variable X is $\mathbb{P}_X(A) = \mathbb{P}(X \in A)$ for all measurable sets A.

Definition 9
Say that X and Y have the **same distribution** (write $X \sim Y$) if $\mathbb{P}_X = \mathbb{P}_Y$.

Because there are so many possible measurable sets A, it can be very difficult to ascertain if $\mathbb{P}_X$ and $\mathbb{P}_Y$ are the same. The *Carathéodory extension theorem* helps this process immensely, by stating that it suffices to check sets of the form $(-\infty, a]$. In other words, if $\mathbb{P}(X \leq a) = \mathbb{P}(Y \leq a)$ for all real a, then $X \sim Y$. Call $\text{cdf}_X(a) = \mathbb{P}(X \leq a)$ the *cumulative distribution function*, or cdf for short.

Definition 10
The **cumulative distribution function of X** (**cdf** for short) written $\text{cdf}_X(a) = F_X(a)$ has domain $\mathbb{R}$, codomain $[0, 1]$, and is defined as

$$\text{cdf}_X(a) = \mathbb{P}(X \leq a)$$

Theorem 1 (Carathéodory extension theorem)
If for all a, $\text{cdf}_X(a) = \text{cdf}_Y(a)$, then $X \sim Y$.

Some cdfs are easy to calculate.

Fact 3
If $X \sim \textsf{Exp}(\lambda)$, then $\text{cdf}_X(a) = (1 - \exp(-\lambda a))\mathbb{1}(a \geq 0)$.

The opposite of the cdf is the *survival function*.

Definition 11
The **survival function** of a random variable X is $\text{sur}_X(a) = 1 - \text{cdf}_X(a) = \mathbb{P}(X > a)$.

Fact 4
If $X \sim \mathsf{Exp}(\lambda)$, then $\text{sur}_X(t) = \exp(-\lambda t)$.

From the cdf of X, it is easy to find the density of X. That is, the pdf can be found from the cdf.

Fact 5
If X is a continuous random variable, then $\text{pdf}_X = [\text{cdf}_X]'$ wherever the cdf is differentiable.

If X is a discrete random variable, then

$$\text{pdf}_X(i) = \lim_{\delta \to 0} \text{cdf}_X(i) - \text{cdf}_X(i - |\delta|).$$

2.2 *Partial information*

What separates probability from other branches of mathematics is the notion of *conditioning*, or *partial information*. That is, the probability of events occurring can change as information is learned. Start with an example.

Notation 3
For a finite set S, $\#(S)$ is the number of elements of S.

For instance, $\#(\{a, b, c\}) = 3$, since there are three elements in S.

Definition 12
For a finite set S, say that X is **uniform** over S (write $X \sim \mathsf{Unif}(S)$) if for all $s \in S$, $\mathbb{P}(X = s) = 1/\#(S)$.

Definition 13
The **conditional probability** of A given B, written $\mathbb{P}(A|B)$ is the probability that A is true given that B is true.

Example 2
Suppose that X is the outcome of a roll of a six sided die. So $X \sim \mathsf{Unif}(\{1, 2, 3, 4, 5, 6\})$. So $\mathbb{P}(X = 1) = 1/6$. Now suppose the given information is that $X \leq 4$. Now either $X = 1$, $X = 2$, $X = 3$, or $X = 4$. Each is equally likely, so $\mathbb{P}(X = 1|X \leq 4) = 1/4$.

Definition 14
Let A and B be events where B has positive probability. Then

$$\mathbb{P}(A|B) = \frac{\mathbb{P}(AB)}{\mathbb{P}(B)}.$$

With this understanding of conditional probability, it is possible to solve the question of the day.

Example 3 (Question of the day)
For $X \sim \mathsf{Exp}(2)$, find $\mathbb{P}(X > 2|X > 1)$.

Answer By the conditional probability formula, this is

$$\begin{aligned}
\mathbb{P}(X > 2|X > 1) &= \frac{\mathbb{P}(X > 2, X > 1)}{\mathbb{P}(X > 1)} = \frac{\mathbb{P}(X > 2)}{\mathbb{P}(X > 1)} \\
&= \frac{\exp(-(2)(2))}{\exp(-(2)(1))} \\
&= \frac{\exp(-4)}{\exp(-2)} = \exp(-2) = \boxed{0.1353\ldots}.
\end{aligned}$$

More generally, *conditional distributions* describe how a random variable behaves conditioned on partial information about the random variable.

Definition 15
Let X be a random variable and A be a set where $\mathbb{P}(X \in A) > 0$. Then the **conditional distribution of X given $X \in A$** is $[X|X \in A]$, where $\mathbb{P}_{[X|X \in A]}(B) = \mathbb{P}(X \in B|X \in A) = \mathbb{P}(X \in AB)/\mathbb{P}(X \in A)$.

A uniform random variable over a set S will remain uniform when conditioned to lie in a smaller set $R \subseteq S$.

Fact 6
Suppose X is a random variable uniform over the finite set S. Let R be any subset of S. Then

$$[X|X \in R] \sim \mathsf{Unif}(R).$$

Proof. Let $r \in R$. Then

$$\mathbb{P}(X = r|X \in R) = \frac{\mathbb{P}(X = r, X \in R)}{\mathbb{P}(X \in R)} = \frac{\mathbb{P}(X = r)}{\mathbb{P}(X \in R)} = \frac{1/\#(S)}{\#(R)/\#(S)} = \frac{1}{\#(R)}$$

which is the desired result. □

Exponentials have a unique property among continuous random variables.

Fact 7
For $X \sim \text{Exp}(\lambda)$ and $s \geq 0$,

$$[X - s | X > s] \sim X.$$

This is called the **memoryless** property.

In other words, if T is an exponential random variable and it is known that $T > 3.4$, then it is like T starts over at 3.4. The time yet to wait, $T - 3.4$ has the same distribution as T itself! That is why exponential random variables are referred to as memoryless, as they are continually forgetting how much time has passed.

Proof. Let $s > 0$, $a \geq 0$. Then

$$\begin{aligned} \mathbb{P}(X - s > a | X > s) &= \frac{\mathbb{P}(X - s > a, X > s)}{\mathbb{P}(X > s)} \\ &= \frac{\exp(-\lambda(s + a)}{\exp(-\lambda s)} \\ &= \exp(-\lambda a). \end{aligned}$$

□

2.3 Independence

Two events are independent if knowing if one is true or false does not change the probabilities of the other event.

Definition 16
Two events A and B are **independent** if either $\mathbb{P}(B) = 0$ or $\mathbb{P}(A|B) = \mathbb{P}(A)$.

Another characterization is useful when dealing with independence.

Fact 8
Events A and B are independent if and only if $\mathbb{P}(A, B) = \mathbb{P}(A)\mathbb{P}(B)$.

A time evolving process can be modeled using a *stream*. A stream is similar to a sequence: it means that the first element of the stream exists, and given that the first n elements of the stream exist, then element number $n + 1$ of the stream exists.

Definition 17
A set of random variables is a **stream** if

- Begin with step 0 and the stream empty.
- At step i, given the i elements of the stream, the next element of the stream can be generated.

For example, suppose a fair coin is flipped once to start our stream. Given a finite number of flips, it is always possible to flip our coin one more time to generate a new random flip from the stream.

Definition 18
A stream $\{X_i\}$ of random variables is **independent, identically distributed** (**iid** for short) if for all n,

$$[X_n | X_1, \ldots, X_{n-1}] \sim X_1.$$

So X_n must be independent of $(X_1, \ldots, X_n)$ and must have the same distribution as X_1 for all n. Note that given the assumption of the induction axiom and the integer axioms, any stream of random variables yields a corresponding sequence, and so this term is often used instead. Here the term *stream* to emphasize that for operations research applications their is no assumption that all these random variables exist simultaneously, instead, they are generated from data or simulation only as needed, and after a finite number of steps is a finite set of random variables.

Problems

2.1 Suppose A occurs with probability 0.3, B occurs with probability 0.7, and both occur with probability 0.2.

a) Find $\mathbb{P}(A|B)$.

b) Find $\mathbb{P}(B|A)$.

2.2 Suppose A occurs with probability 0.4, B with probability 0.6, C with probability 0.7, AB with probability 0.1, AC with probability 0.4, and ABC with probability 0.1.

a) What is $\mathbb{P}(C|A)$?

b) What is $\mathbb{P}(C|A, B)$?

2.3 Suppose $D \sim \textsf{Unif}(\{1, \ldots, 100\})$.

a) Find $\mathbb{P}(D = 1 | D \leq 60)$.

b) Find $\mathbb{P}(D \leq 60 | D = 1)$.

2.4 Suppose $Y \sim \mathsf{Unif}(\{1, \ldots, 50\})$. What is $\mathbb{P}(Y \leq 30 | Y \text{ is even})$?

2.5 Let $X \sim \mathsf{Exp}(0.2)$.

a) What is the distribution of $[X - 3 | X > 3]$?

b) What is $\mathbb{P}(X > 5 | X > 3)$?

2.6 Let $Y \sim \mathsf{Exp}(3.2)$.

a) What is the distribution of $Y - 1$ given that $Y > 1$?

b) What is $\mathbb{P}(Y > 2 | Y > 1)$?

2.7 Let (B_1, B_2, B_3) be the first three draws from a stream of iid random variables where $\mathbb{P}(B_i = 1) = 0.3, \mathbb{P}(B_i = 0) = 0.7$ (write $B_i \sim \mathsf{Bern}(0.3)$ as this is a Bernoulli distribution.)

a) What is $\mathbb{P}(B_1 = 1, B_2 = 1)$?

b) Find $\mathbb{P}(B_1 + B_2 + B_3 = 1)$.

2.8 Let X_1, X_2, X_3 be the first three draws from a stream of iid random variables where $\mathbb{P}(X_i = j) = 1/4$ for $j \in \{1, 2, 3, 4\}$. Find $\mathbb{P}(X_1 + X_2 + X_3 = 11)$.

Part II

Queuing Networks

Chapter 3

Queues

Question of the Day

Customers arrive at a help desk according to a uniform distribution over $[0, 10]$. On average, what is the time between customer arrivals?

Summary

- **Queues** are composed of customers that are waiting for service. The number of customers waiting for service is the **queue length**. The **capacity** is the maximum value of the queue length. The **channels** of the queue is the number of servers that handle customers.

- **Queue discipline** is how the next customer is selected for service.

- Each arriving customer has an **arrival time**. The difference between two successive arrival times is called the **interarrival time**.

- The **service time** of a customer is the time between when a customer starts service and finishes service.

- Basic queue notation uses three symbols separated by slashes. These three symbols are the type of interarrival distribution, the type of service distribution, and the number of servers. M stands for a **memoryless** (aka exponential) distribution, G stands for a **general** distribution, and D means a **deterministic** value rather than a random one.

- The **arrival rate** is the multiplicative inverse of the average interarrival time. The **service rate** is the multiplicative inverse of the average service time.

Queues are a rich model in operations research. Many real life situations can be reduced to one or more queues working in unison.

At the simplest level, a queue consists of customers that are waiting for service. The term customer might refer to physical people waiting in line for service at a food truck, to packets of information traveling through the Internet, injuries at a crash awaiting medical care, theme park goers waiting to ride a roller coaster, inventory awaiting shipment, or computer searches awaiting resolution by a supercomputing cluster.

The notion of a queue is very general, which is why it is such a widely used model. Operations research deals with making decisions when resources are limited, and queues are an inevitable part of life with limited resources. The more servers that can be deployed, the faster customers will be served, but the more expensive it will be to maintain and run the queue.

Basic queuing models can be analyzed mathematically, while more complicated ones have behavior that is studied through simulation. We will start with the queues that we can analyze, and later on show how simulations can be used.

3.1 Queueing terms

Deciding which customer to serve next might be a matter of life and death if the queue is for treatment in an emergency room. In a more prosaic example, a supercomputer might decide to give priority to certain types of jobs that are more important. The way that a queue decides the next customer to serve is called the *queue discipline.*

Definition 19
The **queue discipline** describes how the customers in the queue are taken in for service. Three common methods of choosing which customer to service next are:

- FIFO (aka FCFS). This stands for *first in, first out* (or first come, first served) and means that the next customer to be served is the one that has been waiting in line the longest.
- LIFO. This stands for *last in, first out.* Here incoming customers are placed on a stack as they arrive, and the next free server picks from the top of the stack and works down to the bottom.
- Priority. Here each incoming customer is assigned a priority, and the highest priority customers are served first. This is typically the case in an Emergency Room, where patients needing immediate care are served first.

Many types of queue disciplines do not have names, and often real queues are a mix of FIFO and priority disciplines.

Definition 20
A **customer** refers to an entity that is awaiting a **service**. An entity performing a service is called a **server**.

An important factor in customer satisfaction is how many customers are waiting in line at any one time.

Definition 21
The number of customers waiting for service at a particular time is called the **queue length**.

It is easier to model queues when the number of customers that can wait is unbounded, but in the real world, there is a limit on the size of the queue.

Definition 22
The **capacity** of a queue is the maximum number of customers that can be waiting for service at any one time.

Definition 23
The **channels** of a queue refers to the number of servers that are available for servicing the customers.

Definition 24
The time needed for a server to service one customer is called a **service time**.

Service times are typically modeled using a distribution. Each service is then taken to be an independent draw from that distribution. The queue will serve customers faster if service times are small and the number of channels is high.

Definition 25
The time from the arrival of one customer until the arrival of the next customer in the queue is called the **interarrival time**.

A short interarrival time results in many customers arriving, and the length of the queue grows. The actual time the ith customer arrives to join the queue is called the *arrival time*.

Definition 26
The **arrival time** for the ith customer is the time that particular customer joins the queue.

Note that we can calculate the arrival times from the interarrival times.

Fact 9
If $A_1, \ldots, A_n$ are the first n interarrival times, then

$$T_n = A_1 + \cdots + A_n.$$

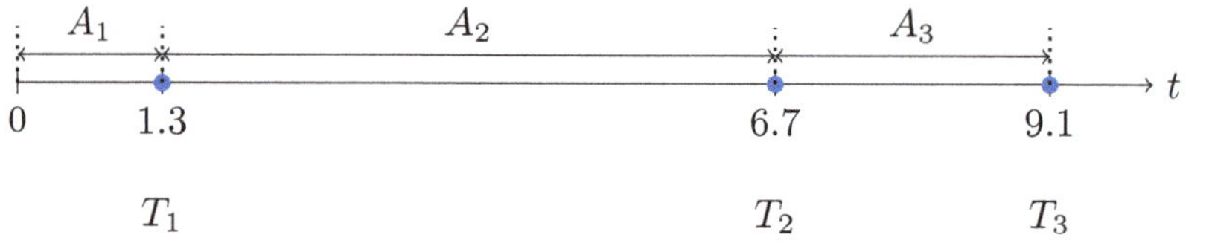

In the picture, $A_1 = 1.3$, $A_2 = 5.4$, and $A_3 = 2.4$. So that means $T_1 = A_1 = 1.3$, $T_2 = A_1 + A_2 = 6.7$, and $T_3 = A_1 + A_2 + A_3 = 9.1$.

3.2 Notation

To describe the queue, *queue notation* is used. The simplest form has three slots, for the arrival distribution, the service distribution, and the number of servers.

Notation 4
Queue notation has the form

$$*/*/*,$$

where the first entry indicates information about the arrival distribution, the second entry indicates information about the service distribution, and the third entry indicates the number of servers in the queue.

The information about distributions is either G for a *general* distribution, D for a constant time (D for *deterministic*), M for the exponential distribution (M for *memoryless* or *Markov*) and E_k for an *Erlang* distribution with shape parameter k.

Example 4
The queue notation

$$M/D/2,$$

means that interarrival times follow an exponential distribution, service takes a constant amount of time, and 2 servers work independently to clear customers from the queue.

The queue notation

$$G/G/1$$

means that their in one server, but the distribution of the arrival times and service times could be anything.

3.3 *Expected value*

The expected value of a random variable is a measure of central tendency. Not all random variables have an expected value, but when they do, the sample average of an iid stream of draws from the random variable will converge to this number.

Reminder 1
The **expected value** (aka **expectation** aka **average** aka **mean**) of $g(X)$ is

$$\mathbb{E}[g(X)] = \int_{\mathbb{R}} g(s) f_X(s)\, ds.$$

if X is a continuous random variable, and

$$\mathbb{E}[g(X)] = \sum_{\mathbb{R}} g(s) f_X(s)$$

if X is a discrete random variable.

Definition 27
If the expected value of X is a finite, real number, we say that X is **integrable**.

Example 5 (Question of the day)
If X is uniform over $[0, 10]$ minutes, then what is $\mathbb{E}[X]$?

Answer Write $X \sim \text{Unif}([0, 10])$ to indicate that X is uniform over $[0, 10]$. Then recall that the density of a uniform over an interval is the indicator of that interval divided by the length of the interval. That is,

$$f_X(s) = \frac{1}{10 - 0}\mathbb{1}(s \in [0, 10]).$$

Hence the expected value: $\mathbb{E}[X] = \mathbb{E}[g(X)]$ where $g(s) = s$ is:

$$\mathbb{E}[X] = \int_{\mathbb{R}} s\frac{1}{10}\mathbb{1}(s \in [0, 10])\, ds = \int_0^{10} \frac{s}{10}\, ds = \left.\frac{s^2}{2 \cdot 10}\right|_0^{10} = 5.$$

So the answer is $\boxed{5 \text{ minutes}}$.

Of course, it is not necessary to do this integral if the following fact is known.

Fact 10
For $X \sim \text{Unif}([a, b])$,

$$\mathbb{E}[X] = \frac{a + b}{2}.$$

Once we know the average time between arrivals, the **arrival rate** is just the inverse of that number.

Definition 28
The **arrival rate** for a queue is 1 over the average interarrival time.

A similar definition holds for services.

Definition 29
The **service rate** for a queue is 1 over the average service time.

Problems

3.1 Suppose customer 5 enters service at time 7.1 and finishes service at time 9.6. What is customer 5's service time?

3.2 Customer 1 in a queue starts service at time 0 and finishes at time 5.2. Customer 2 then immediately begins service and finishes at time 7.4. There is no one in the queue at this point, but Customer 3 arrives at time 9.5 and finishes service at time 11.6. What are the service times for the three customers?

3.3 Suppose three customers, a, b, and c arrive to a queue in that order.

a) Under a FIFO queue discipline, in what order are the customers served?

b) Under a LIFO queue discipline, in what order are the customers served?

3.4 A queue serves Gold status customers before Silver, which are served before Pearl. Otherwise the customers are served FIFO. Suppose we have a single server, and customer a (who is Pearl status) arrives first. While a is being served, b (who is also Pearl status) arrives next, followed by c (who is Gold status). Assuming all three of these customers are served before another customer arrives, what order are they served in?

3.5 If the first three interarrival times are $A_1 = 0.4$, $A_2 = 1.34$, and $A_3 = 0.013$, what are the first three arrival times?

3.6 Suppose the first three interarrival times are all 1.5, but then the fourth interarrival time is 2.6. What are the first four arrival times?

3.7 For interarrival times that are uniform over $[0, 2]$ hours, what is the arrival rate?

3.8 For service times that are uniform over $[3, 5]$ seconds, what is the service rate?

Chapter 4

Expectation and queues

Question of the Day

Suppose interarrival times are uniform over $[0, 10]$ minutes. Lower bound the average number of arrivals in the first hour.

Summary

Consider a queue with arrival rate λ.

1. **Wald's Equation** allows us to find the expected value of the sum of a random number T of iid random variables (sometimes). For T a stopping time with respect to iid $X_1, X_2, \ldots$ such that either the X_i are nonnegative or T has finite expected value,

$$\mathbb{E}\left[\sum_{i=1}^{T} X_i\right] = \mathbb{E}[T]\mathbb{E}[X_1].$$

2. Consider a $G/G/s$ queue. Let $\mathbb{E}[N_{[0,t]}]$ be the average number of arrivals over the time interval $[0, t]$. Then

$$\mathbb{E}[N_{[0,t]}] \geq \lambda t - 1.$$

If the interarrival times are at most m then

$$\mathbb{E}[N_{[0,t]}] \leq \lambda(t + m) - 1.$$

A very important fact about expectation is that it is a *linear operator*. That means (roughly speaking) that as an operator expectation distributes over addition and multiplication.

Fact 11
For any two integrable random variables X and Y and real numbers a and b,

$$\mathbb{E}[aX + bY] = a\mathbb{E}[X] + b\mathbb{E}[Y].$$

This can be extended by induction to any finite linear combination of random variables.

Fact 12
For any integrable random variables $X_1, \ldots, X_n$ and $a_1, \ldots, a_n \in \mathbb{R}$,

$$\mathbb{E}\left[\sum_{i=1}^{n} a_i X_i\right] = \sum_{i=1}^{n} a_i \mathbb{E}[X_i].$$

Since arrival times in a queue are just the sum of the interarrival times, this immediately gives the following.

Fact 13
For a $G/G/s$ queue with integrable interarrival times $\{A_i\}$, if T_i is the arrival time of the ith customer,

$$\mathbb{E}[T_i] = i\mathbb{E}[A_1].$$

Proof. If $A_1, \ldots, A_n$ are the first n interarrival times, then

$$\begin{aligned}\mathbb{E}[T_n] &= \mathbb{E}\left[\sum_{i=1}^{n} A_i\right] \\ &= \mathbb{E}[A_1] + \cdots + \mathbb{E}[A_i] \\ &= i\mathbb{E}[A_1].\end{aligned}$$

□

4.1 Stopping Times

Now suppose $T_1, T_2, T_3, \ldots$ is a stream of arrival times. For any given time t, there will be some of these times that are at most t, and some of these times that are greater than t.

For instance, if $(T_1, T_2, T_3, T_4) = (1.1, 2.0, 3.6, 4.7)$, then the set

$$\{i : T_i \leq 4\} = \{1, 2, 3\},$$

since the first three times are in t and the fourth time is greater than t. Similarly,

$$\{i : T_i > 4\} = \{4, 5, 6, \ldots\},$$

since the T_i form an increasing sequence.

The smallest number in a nonempty set $\{4, 5, 6, \ldots\}$ is called the *minimum* of the set. If the set is empty, then there is no minimum, which is why the minimum can be generalized to the *infimum* of a set.

Think of the infimum as the greater number which is still less than or equal to every element of a set. For a finite set, the infimum of the set is the same as the minimum. For an empty set, every number is less than or equal to all elements of the set, so make the infimum infinity. For a set with numbers that become arbitrarily small (like $\{-1, -2, -3, \ldots\}$, the infimum is taken to be minus infinity.

Say that a number is a *lower bound* for a set of real numbers if it is less than or equal to all the elements of the set.

Definition 30
A number a is a **lower bound** for $A \subseteq \mathbb{R}$ if

$$(\forall b \in A)(a \leq b).$$

Reminder 2
The symbol $\forall$ means **for all**, and means that what follows is true because, for any choice of $x > 4$, it holds that $x + 1 > 5$.

On the other hand, the statement $(\forall x > 4)(x > 6)$ is false because there is a choice of $x > 4$ (such as $x = 4.3$) which makes $x > 6$ false.

Formally, the infimum is defined as follows.

Definition 31
Given a subset of real numbers A, the **infimum** is

- $\inf(A) = \infty$ if $A = \emptyset$.
- If A has at least one lower bound, then $\inf(A)$ is the maximum of the set of lower bounds of A.
- $\inf(A) = -\infty$ if no lower bound exists.

In our example

$$\inf\{4, 5, 6, \ldots\} = 4.$$

That is, the infimum of a set is the largest number that is smaller than every other number in the set. In our example, 4 is less than or equal to every number in $\{4, 5, 6, \ldots\}$, and if I try to use a larger number like 4.1, it is not less than or equal to 4, so cannot be the infimum.

Example 6
Some examples of the infimum operator in action:

- $\inf(\emptyset) = \infty$.
- $\inf(\{4, 5, 6, \ldots\}) = 4$. Some lower bounds for this set include $-6, 3, 3.5, 3.9999, 4$, but the largest lower bound is 4, as anything bigger than 4 is not a lower bound.
- $\inf(\{\ldots, -3, -2, -1, 0, 1, 2, 3, \ldots\}) = -\infty$ since there is no lower bound, that is, there is no number that is less than or equal to every number in the set.

Now suppose that the stream of arrival times starts as:

$$T_1 = 1.2,\ T_2 = 3.6,\ T_3 = 6.1,\ T_4 = 6.5, \ldots$$

Then consider $A = \{n : T_n > 4\}$. This set will be $A = \{3, 4, 5, \ldots\}$ because $T_3, T_4, \ldots$ are all greater than 4, but T_1 and T_2 are not. Note that $\inf(\{3, 4, 5, \ldots\} = 3$, since that is the minimum value of the set.

In general, it holds that

$$M = \inf\{n : T_n > 4\},$$

is the number of the customer who is the first to arrive after time 4.

That makes T_M the first arrival time that is past time 4. In the example given above, $M = 3$, and $T_M = T_3 = 6.1$.

Because the arrival times $T_1, T_2, \ldots$ are random, the value of M will also be random. A random variable like M is called a *stopping time.*

Definition 32
Given a stream of random variables $X_1, X_2, \ldots$, a **stopping time** N is a random variable where the statement $N \leq n$ can be determined using only the first n values $X_1, \ldots, X_n$ of the stream.

Example 7
For arrival times T_i and nonnegative real number t, let

$$M = \inf\{n : T_n > t\}.$$

show that M is a stopping time.

Answer Let $n \in \{1, 2, \ldots\}$. Then $M \leq n$ if and only if $T_n > t$. This can be determined to be true or false using only $T_1, \ldots, T_n$, so M is a stopping time!

4.2 *Wald's Equation*

Linearity gives us that for a stream of integrable iid random variables $X_1, X_2, \ldots$,

$$\mathbb{E}\left[\sum_{i=1}^{n} X_i\right] = n\mathbb{E}[X_i].$$

How does that work with the sum of the X_i from 1 up to a stopping time N? *Wald's equation* tells us that it behaves much like the deterministic sum, as long as the random variables are somewhat nice.

Theorem 2 (Wald's Equation)
Let $X_1, X_2, \ldots$ be an iid stream of integrable random variables, and N a stopping time for the stream. Then if either

- $\mathbb{P}(X \geq 0) = 1$ (so the random variables are nonnegative) or
- N is integrable (so $\mathbb{E}[N] < \infty$), then

$$\mathbb{E}\left[\sum_{n=1}^{N} X_n\right] = \mathbb{E}[N]\mathbb{E}[X_1].$$

The arrival times can be found as the sum of the interarrival times. So

$$T_n = A_1 + \cdots + A_n.$$

That means

$$M = \inf\{n : A_1 + \cdots + A_n > t\},$$

and

$$\mathbb{E}\left[\sum_{i=1}^{M} A_n\right] = \mathbb{E}[M]\mathbb{E}[A_1].$$

By definition, $\sum_{i=1}^{M} A_n > t$, so

$$t < \mathbb{E}[M]\mathbb{E}[A_1],$$

and $\mathbb{E}[M - 1] > (t/\mathbb{E}[A_1]) - 1$. For a queue with arrival rate λ, this establishes the following:

Fact 14
For a $G/G/s$ queue, the expected number of customers that arrive in $[0, t]$ is at least

$$t\lambda - 1.$$

Example 8
Suppose interarrival times are uniform over $[0, 10]$ minutes. Lower bound the average number of arrivals in the first hour.

Answer An hour is $[0, 60]$ minutes. The arrival rate is one over the expected interarrival time, so $1/5$ per minute. Hence the expected number of customers is at least

$$\frac{1}{5 \text{ minutes}} \cdot 60 \text{ minutes} - 1 = \boxed{11}.$$

Note that if you tackle these problems correctly, the units of time should cancel, since the final result will be a unitless number.

In this case, because a uniform random variable over $[0, 10]$ is at most 10, it is possible to upper bound the expected number of customers in the first hour.

Example 9
Suppose interarrival times are uniform over $[0, 10]$ minutes. Upper bound the average number of arrivals in the first hour.

Answer Let M be $\inf\{n : A_1 + \cdots + A_n > 60 \text{ minutes}\}$. Then $\sum_{i=1}^{M} A_i \in [60, 70]$. So by Wald's Equation $\mathbb{E}[M]\mathbb{E}[A_1] \leq 70$, and since $\mathbb{E}[A_1]$ is 5 minutes,

$$\mathbb{E}[M] \leq \frac{70 \text{ minutes}}{5 \text{ minutes}} \leq 14.$$

That makes the average number of arrivals in the first hour $14 - 1 = \boxed{13}$.

This idea can be generalized to give the following fact.

Fact 15
For a $G/G/s$ queue with arrival rate λ, if the arrival times are at most m with probability 1, then the average number of arrivals in $[0, t]$ is at most

$$\lambda(t + m) - 1.$$

Problems

4.1 Suppose $\mathbb{E}[X] = 4.2$ and $\mathbb{E}[Y] = 5.6$. What is $\mathbb{E}[2X - 4Y]$?

4.2 Suppose that $X_1, X_2, \ldots$ are identically distributed random variables with mean 2.1.

a) Find $\mathbb{E}[X_1 + X_2 + X_3]$.

b) Find $\mathbb{E}\left[\sum_{i=1}^{12} X_i\right]$.

4.3 Find the infimum of the following sets.

a) $S_1 = \{1, 2, 3\}$.

b) $S_2 = \{1, 2, 3, \ldots\}$.

c) $S_3 = \{x : x > 0, x < 5\} =]0, 5[$.

4.4 Find the infimum of the following sets.

a) $A_1 = \{x : x \geq 3, x \leq 7\} = [3, 7]$.

b) $A_2 = \{x : x \geq 7, x \leq 3\}$.

c) $A_3 = \{2, 4, 6, \ldots\}$.

d) $A_4 = \{\ldots, -4, -2, 0\}$.

4.5 Say that interarrival times for a $G/G/2$ queue have density $20x^3(1 - x)\mathbb{1}(x \in [0, 1])$ when measured in minutes. Lower bound the expected number of customers to arrive in the first ten minutes.

4.6 Suppose that the interarrival times for a $G/G/3$ queue are $\text{Unif}([10, 20])$ seconds. Lower bound the expected number of customers to arrive in the first minute.

4.7 Suppose interarrival times for a $G/G/2$ queue are 1 minute with probability 0.3, 2 minutes with probability 0.6, and 3 minutes with probability 0.1.

a) Lower bound the expected number of customers to arrive in the first hour.

b) Lower bound the expected number of customers to arrive in the first two hours.

4.8 Suppose interarrival times for a $G/G/3$ queue are 5.2 minutes with probability 0.4, 1.6 minutes with probability 0.2, and 3.4 minutes with probability 0.4.

a) Lower bound the expected number of customers to arrive in the first thirty minutes.

b) Lower bound the expected number of customers to arrive in the first hour.

Chapter 5

Memoryless queues

Question of the Day

Consider an $M/G/2$ queue with arrival rate 2.4 per hour. What is the distribution of the number of arrivals in the first two hours?

Summary

Throughout this chapter, consider an $M/G/s$ queue with arrival rate λ.

- **Poisson** random variables with parameter μ (write $X \sim \text{Pois}(\mu)$) have $\mathbb{P}(X = i) = \exp(-\mu)\mu^i/i!$. The mean and variance of a Poisson random variable is also μ.
- The number of arrivals in the time interval $[a, b]$ has a Poisson distribution with parameter $\lambda(b - a)$.
- Say X is **Erlang** (aka **Gamma**) distributed with parameters k and λ if X has density

$$f_X(s) = \lambda \exp(-\lambda s)(\lambda s)^{k-1}/(k-1)!\mathbb{1}(s \geq 0).$$

- The arrival time of the kth customer is Erlang with parameters k and λ.

For $G/G/s$ queues, the value of $\mathbb{E}[T_n]$, the average time of the arrival of customer n, can be found exactly. It is also possible to lower bound the average number of customers that arrive in $[0, t]$.

For an $M/G/s$ queue, it is possible to do even more. For any n, it is possible to determine exactly the distribution of the arrival time of customer n. It is also possible to derive the distribution of the number of customers that arrive in $[0, t]$. For an $M/M/s$ queue, even more can be calculated, such as the steady state (aka long term) distribution of the number of people in the queue.

5.1 Number of customer arrivals for the $M/G/s$ queue

Suppose that the times between arrivals are exponential random variables with rate parameter λ. Then a special name is given to the set of arrival times. It is called a *Poisson point process*, or *PPP* for short.

It turns out that if we take a PPP and look at the number of points that fall in $[0, t]$ (so the number of customers that arrive in $[0, t]$) this will be a Poisson distributed random variable. (This is why it is called a Poisson point process.)

Definition 33
Say that X has a **Poisson distribution with parameter μ** if for $i \in \{0, 1, 2, \ldots\}$,

$$\mathbb{P}(X = i) = \frac{\mu^i}{i!} \exp(-\mu).$$

Write $X \sim \text{Pois}(\mu)$.

Poisson random variables are unitless numbers, and so X and X^2 have the same units. Compare this to something like L which measures length. In this case L might have units of meters and L^2 units of meters squared. Since Poisson random variables count things, they are pure numbers with no units.

Fact 16
For $X \sim \text{Pois}(\mu)$, $\mathbb{E}[X] = \mu$ and $\mathbb{V}[X] = \mu$.

Normally the mean of a random variable has the same units as the random variable, and the variance has units that are the square of the random variable. Poisson (being unitless) is one of the few random variables over the nonnegative integers with mean equal to the variance.

A PPP on $[0, \infty)$ has two great properties. The first is that the average number of points in $[0, t]$ is *exactly* λt. (Recall the earlier we could only lower bound it by $\lambda t - 1$.) The second is that for two time intervals $[a, b]$ and $[c, d]$ that do not overlap (so $b < c$), then the number of arrivals in the two intervals are independent of each other.

Even more amazing is that these two properties *define* what it means to be a Poisson point process of rate λ over $[0, \infty)$.

Definition 34
A **Poisson point process of rate λ on $[0, \infty)$** is $P \subseteq \mathbb{R}$ such that

- For all t, $\mathbb{E}[\#(P \cap [0, t])] = \lambda t$.
- For all $a < b < c < d$, $\#(P \cap [a, b])$ and $\#(P \cap [c, d])$ are independent random variables.

In words, a set of values is a Poisson point process if the values represent customer arrival times, the average number of customers that arrive in an interval has mean equal to the arrival rate times the length of the time interval, and for two intervals that do not overlap, the number of customer arrivals in one interval is independent of the number of customer arrivals in the other interval.

Fact 17
For a Poisson point process of rate λ on $[0, \infty)$,

$$\#(P \cap [0, t]) \sim \text{Pois}(\lambda t).$$

Example 10
Let P be a Poisson process on $[0, \infty)$ of rate 4. Then what is the chance that exactly 10 points fall in $[0, 2]$?

Answer The number of points that fall into $[0, 2]$ will be

$$\#(P \cap [0, 2]) \sim \text{Pois}(2 \cdot 4),$$

so the chance that this equals 10 is

$$\frac{8^{10}}{10!} \exp(-8) \approx \boxed{0.09926\ldots}.$$

Our big fact is that if you have a set of times with exponential interarrivals, then the result is a Poisson point process of rate λ.

Fact 18
Let $A_1, A_2, \ldots$ be an iid stream of $\text{Exp}(\lambda)$ random variables. Then

$$P = \{A_1, A_1 + A_2, A_1 + A_2 + A_3, \ldots\}$$

forms a Poisson point process of rate λ over $[0, \infty)$.

So for our $M/G/s$ queue, the times of the customer arrivals will be a Poisson point process.

Solving the Question of the Day

In the Question of the Day, an $M/G/2$ queue has rate 2.4 per hour. Therefore, in the first two hours, the number of arrivals $N_{[0,2]}$ has a Poisson distribution with parameter $2.4 \cdot 2 = 4.8$.

5.2 *Arrival times for the $M/G/s$ queue*

Recall that the arrival time of customer n is the sum of the first n interarrival times.

Reminder 3
If $A_1, \ldots, A_k$ are iid $\text{Exp}(\lambda)$, then the distribution of their sum is called gamma or Erlang with parameters k and λ.

Fact 19
The density of $X \sim \text{Erlang}(k, \lambda)$ is

$$f_X(s) = \frac{\lambda^k s^{k-1}}{(k-1)!} \exp(-\lambda s) \mathbb{1}(s \geq 0).$$

This allows us to calculate exactly the probability that a particular arrival time falls into a particular set.

Example 11
Suppose I have an $M/M/s$ queue with arrival rate 4 per minute. What is the chance that the fourth customer arrival comes in $[1, 1.1]$ minutes?

Answer Using the gamma distribution, this will be:

$$\begin{aligned}\mathbb{P}(T_4 \in [1, 1.1]) &= \int_1^{1.1} \frac{4^4}{3!} s^3 \exp(-4s)\, ds \\ &= \frac{4^4}{3!} \frac{-(3 + 12s + 24s^2 + 32s^3)}{128} \exp(-4s)|_1^{1.1} = \boxed{0.07402\ldots}.\end{aligned}$$

5.3 *Intuition behind the Poisson and Erlang distributions*

For a Poisson point process of rate λ, the average number of points that fall into an interval of length t is λt. When t is very small, it is likely that the number of points will either be 0 or 1.

Consider a differential interval of length dt, the probability that it contains a point will be $\lambda\, dt$.

What is the chance, then that all the other differential points will be empty? There are t/dt such intervals, each with a $1 - \lambda\, dt$ of being empty.

$$(1 - \lambda\, dt)^{t/dt} = \exp(-(\lambda dt)(t/dt)) = \exp(-\lambda t).$$

Hence if the goal is to find the chance that 3 points fall in interval $[0, t]$, it is necessary to integrate over all the differential intervals where the points might be. However, this overcounts things. A point set (x_1, x_2, x_3) will only be valid if $x_1 < x_2 < x_3$. If $x_2 < x_1 < x_3$ then these cannot be arrival times. Hence this number should be divided by the total number of orderings. That is,

$$\begin{aligned}
\mathbb{P}(\#(P \cap [0,t]) = 3) &= \int_{(x_1,x_2,x_3)\in[0,t]^3} \frac{1}{3!}(\lambda\, dt_1)(\lambda\, dt_2)(\lambda dt_3)\exp(-\lambda t) \\
&= \int_{x_1\in[0,t]} \int_{x_2\in[0,t]} \int_{x_3\in[0,t]} \frac{\lambda^3}{3!}\, dt_3\, dt_2\, dt_1 \exp(-\lambda t) \\
&= \frac{t^3}{3!}\exp(-\lambda t).
\end{aligned}$$

This argument was for three points but can be extended easily to an arbitrary number of points.

This is not a formal proof, but hopefully gives some intuition as to why the formula for the Poisson distribution is the way it is.

A similar analysis gives us the density of an Erlang. For the third customer arrival to fall in $[t, t+dt]$, there must be a point in $[t, t+dt]$ (this happens with probability $\lambda\, dt$), there must be two points in $[0,t]$ (this happens with probability $(\lambda t)^2/2! \exp(-\lambda t)$.

Also write $\mathbb{P}(X \in [t, t+dt])$ as $\mathbb{P}(X \in dt)$ where here dt refers to the interval of length dt around t. In terms of density,

$$\mathbb{P}(X \in dt) = f_X(t)\, dt.$$

Hence

$$\mathbb{P}(X \in [t, t+dt]) = f_X(t)\, dt = \frac{(\lambda t)^2}{2!}\exp(-\lambda t)(\lambda\, dt).$$

Problems

5.1 If P is a Poisson process of rate 2.5 per second over $[0, \infty)$, what is the chance that there are at most 3 points of P in the first 2 seconds?

5.2 Let Q be a Poisson point process of rate 5.2 per hour over $[0, \infty)$.

a) What is the average number of points of Q in $[0, 8]$?

b) What is the chance that the number of points equals $\lfloor \mathbb{E}[Q] \rfloor$?

5.3 Consider an $M/G/2$ queue with arrival rate 3 per minute.

a) What is the average number of arrivals in the first minute?

b) What is the chance that there are at least 3 arrivals in the first minute?

c) What is the chance of no arrivals in the first 1.5 minutes?

5.4 Consider an $M/M/3$ queue with arrival rate 1.8 per minute.

a) What is the average number of arrivals in the first minute?

b) What is the chance that there are at least 1.8 arrivals in the first minute?

c) What is the chance of no arrivals in the first 2.6 minutes?

5.5 If the interarrival times between customers are modeled as iid $\mathsf{Exp}(8.4/s)$, how many seconds (on average) are there between customer arrivals?

5.6 For service times that are modeled as iid $\mathsf{Exp}(2/\text{hr})$, what is the service rate?

5.7 For an $M/G/2$ queue of arrival rate λ, what is the distribution of the time of the third customer arrival?

5.8 For an $M/D/1$ queue with arrival rate 1 per minute, what is the chance the third arrival comes between time 3 minutes and 4 minutes?

Chapter 6

Queue capacity

Question of the Day

Suppose a single server averages 4.3 jobs per minute. How many servers are needed if the arrival rate is 13.4 per minute to keep the queue from exploding?

Summary

- For A_i iid and $T_n = \sum_{i=1}^{n} A_i$, call T_n a **renewal process**. The arrival times for a $G/G/s$ queue form a renewal process.
- The **Elementary Renewal Theorem** states that for a renewal process T_n with associated process $X_t = \#(n : T_n \leq t)$ the following holds

$$\lim_{t \to \infty} \frac{\mathbb{E}[X_t]}{t} = \frac{1}{\mathbb{E}[T_n - T_{n-1}]}.$$

- For $\mu < \lambda$, a queue will explode in length.
- For a $G/G/1$ queue with service rate μ, the queue $G/G/s$ with same arrival and service distributions has service rate $s\mu$.
- A **graph/network** consists of **nodes/vertices** connected by **edges/arcs** that connect two vertices. In **directed** graphs, the arcs have direction from one node to another, in **undirected** graphs they do not.
- A queue network **explodes** if for any integer n and probability $p < 1$, there is a time t such that there is at least a p chance that the number of customers in the network exceeds n.
- A **routing network** is a directed graph where nodes are queues, and the arcs tell you to which queue to go next. A **queuing network** consists of a routing network, an arrival arrow to a node, and an exit arrow.

- If there are multiple outputs from a queue, say that servers on the outputs are working in **parallel**. If there is a single output, the two nodes are working in **series**. For queues connected in series, the service rate is the minimum of the service rates of the servers. For queues connected in parallel, the service rate is the sum of the service rates of the servers.

- A server is a **bottleneck** if reducing the service rate of this server reduces the rate for the whole system.

- The **queue capacity** is the infimum of arrival rates for customers entering the queue that result in an explosion of the queue.

The worst thing that can happen in a queue is for the arrival rate to be faster than the service rate. It is at that point that the queue starts backing up and the customers waiting for service grows ever longer.

To see why, it is necessary to talk a bit about *renewal theory.*

Definition 35
If $A_1, A_2, \ldots$ are an iid stream of positive random variables, and $T_n = A_1 + \cdots + A_n$, then $\{T_n\}$ is a **renewal process**. Call the times $\{T_n\}$ **renewal times** (or more simply **renewals**.)

Example 12
The arrival times of a $G/G/s$ queue form a renewal process.

The name comes from the fact that since the A_i are independent, and T_n is known, then it is like the process starts over (renews) from there. The set of values $T_{n+1} - T_n, T_{n+2} - T_n, \ldots$ has the same distribution as $T_1, T_2, \ldots$. For any time t, let $X_t = \#\{n : T_n \leq t\}$ count the number of renewals in the interval $[0, t]$.

An important fact about renewal processes is the *Elementary Renewal Theorem.* It is similar to the Strong Law of Large Numbers and shows how the expected number of renewals in a finite time interval behaves.

Theorem 3 (Elementary Renewal Theorem)
For a renewal process $T_1, T_2, \ldots$, and $X_t = \#\{n : T_n \leq t\}$,

$$\lim_{t\to\infty} \frac{\mathbb{E}[X_t]}{t} = \frac{1}{\mathbb{E}[T_i - T_{i-1}]}.$$

For a $G/G/s$ queue with arrival rate λ, this says that the expected number of customer arrivals in $[0, t]$ divided by t converges to λ as t goes to infinity.

Note that both the interarrival and service times can be used to form a renewal process. Now consider the times when a customer completes service. Each of those times is preceded by a random draw from the service time distribution. But there could be times when the line of customers waiting for service is empty, so the number of services is at most the number of service time draws that fit into $[0, t]$. That is, if S_t is the number of services completed by time t,

$$\lim_{t \to \infty} \frac{\mathbb{E}[S_t]}{t} \geq \mu,$$

where μ is the service rate.

So what happens if the service rate is strictly smaller than the arrival rate? The number of customers waiting for service grows without bound!

Definition 36
Say that a queue system **explodes** if for any n there is a time t such that the expected number of customers waiting in line for service is at least n.

Fact 20
Suppose $\mu < \lambda$. Then the queue system explodes.

Proof. Let $\epsilon = (\lambda - \mu)/3$, N_t be the number of customers arriving in $[0, t]$, and S_t be the number of services in $[0, t]$. Then by the definition of limit, there exists t_1 such that for all $t \geq t_1$,

$$\frac{\mathbb{E}[N_t]}{t} \geq \lambda - \epsilon, \text{ and } \frac{\mathbb{E}[S_t]}{t} \leq \mu + \epsilon.$$

Hence for all $t \geq t_1$.

$$\mathbb{E}[N_t - S_t] \geq t(\lambda - \mu - 2\epsilon).$$

By our choice of ϵ, $\lambda - \mu - 2\epsilon > 0$. So set $t = \max\{n[(1-p)(\lambda - \mu - 2\epsilon)]^{-1}, t_1\}$ to complete the proof. □

So in designing queues that work, it is essential that the service rate always exceeds the arrival rate. Note that one simple way of doing this is increasing the number of servers.

Fact 21
Suppose a $G/G/1$ queue has service rate μ. Then a $G/G/s$ version of the queue has service rate $s\mu$.

Example 13 (Question of the Day)
Suppose a single server averages 4.3 jobs per minute. How many servers are needed if the arrival rate is 13.4 per minute to keep the queue from exploding?

Answer To make the queue not explode, it is necessary for $4.3s \geq 13.4$. Since $13.4/4.3 \geq 3.11$, this queue requires at least $\boxed{4}$ servers to make sure that the queue length does not explode.

6.1 *Queuing networks*

In the $G/G/s$ queue notation, the s servers are taken to be working in *parallel*. This means that as arrivals come in, they have a choice of which queue to move to. This can be represented by a *graph*.

Definition 37
A **graph** (aka **network**) consists of **nodes** (aka **vertices**) together with **edges** (aka **arcs**) that consist of two nodes. In a **directed graph** each edge is an ordered pair, and in an **undirected graph** each edge is a set of two nodes (so the nodes in the edge are unordered.)

Example 14
The following graph has four nodes $\{a, b, c, d\}$ and four edges $\{(a, b), (a, c), (b, d), (c, d)\}$.

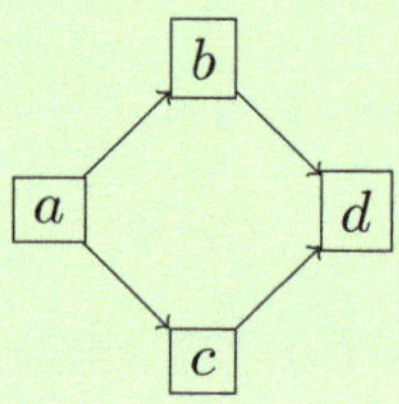

Remark Some authors reserve the word *graph* to mean objects where the edges have no direction, that is, they are subsets of nodes of size 2 rather than ordered pairs. For edges that are ordered pairs, they call it a *directed graph*.

Definition 38
Given a set of queues, a **routing network** tells us where customers serviced by one queue must go next.

Example 15
If the customers leaving Queue 1 and Queue 2 form the arrival process for Queue 3, then the routing network looks like

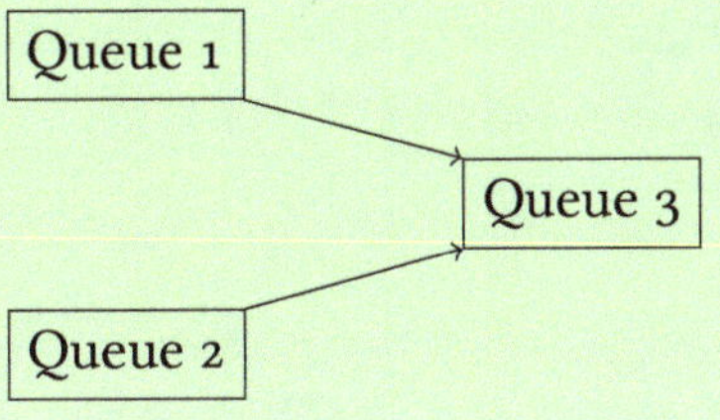

A *queueing network* feeds a routing network with arrivals and then has an edge representing customers leaving the system.

Definition 39
A **queueing network** consists of an *arrival arrow* followed by a set of queues connected by a routing network and completed by an *exit arrow*.

Example 16
Consider the following queue network:

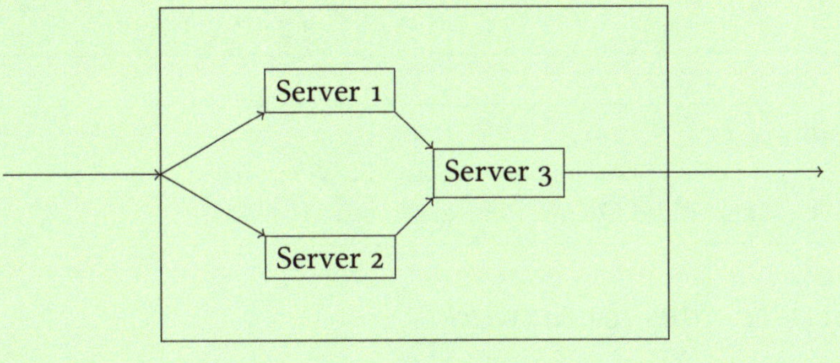

Here arriving customers go to either Server 1 or Server 2. Once they complete service there, they move to Server 3, and after completing that service, they exit. The part inside the rectangle is the routing network.

The previous example can also be written using subqueues.

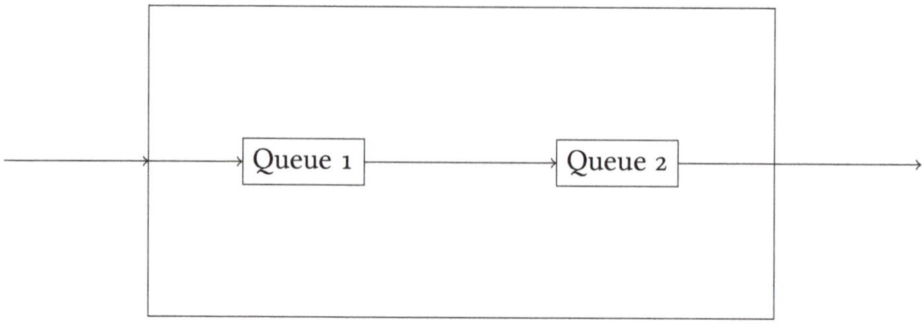

where the subqueues are

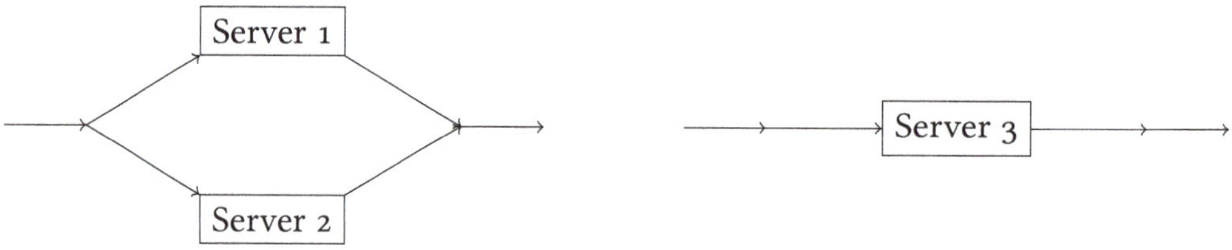

Queue 1 Queue 2

In the previous example, the arriving customers have a choice of moving to Server 1 or Server 2. Say that these two servers are in *parallel*.

Definition 40
In a routing network, if the output from a queue (or from the arrival process) has a choice of which server to take, say that the servers are arranged in **parallel**. If those customers exiting a queue immediately enter a second queue, say that the queues are arranged in **series**.

Example 17
In the previous example, Server 1 and Server 2 are arranged in parallel, while Queue 1 and Queue 2 are arranged in **series**.

6.2 Service rates for networks

A queueing network has an overall service rate called the *queue capacity*.

Definition 41
The **queue capacity** for a queuing network is the infimum of the set of arrival rates that cause the queue network to explode.

The overall service rate for a routing network is determined by *bottlenecks*.

Definition 42
A server in a queuing system is a **bottleneck** if reducing the service rate for this server reduces the service rate for the entire system.

For queues connected in series, it is the slowest (lowest service rate) queues that determine the overall service rate.

Fact 22
If queues Q_1, Q_2, ..., Q_n connected in series have service rates $\mu_1, \mu_2, \ldots, \mu_n$, then the overall service rate is

$$\min\{\mu_1, \ldots, \mu_n\}.$$

Any queue with $\mu_i = \mu$ is a bottleneck in the system.

Queues that are in parallel are much better for the customer. But then every queue is a bottleneck!

Fact 23
If queues $Q_1, Q_2, \ldots, Q_n$ connected in parallel have service rates $\mu_1, \ldots,$ μ_n, then the overall service rate is

$$\mu = \mu_1 + \cdots + \mu_n.$$

Every server in a queue connected in parallel is a bottleneck server.

Example 18

Suppose S_1, S_2, and S_3 connect in series to make Q_1, and S_4 and S_5 connect in series to make Q_2. Q_1 and Q_2 are then connected in parallel. The service rates are

$$\mu_1 = 1.2, \mu_2 = 4.2, \mu_3 = 1.2, \mu_4 = 2.3, \mu_5 = 1.2.$$

1. Draw the queuing system.
2. What is the overall service rate of the queuing system?
3. What are the bottlenecks of the system?

Answer

1. From the description, the queuing system looks like this:

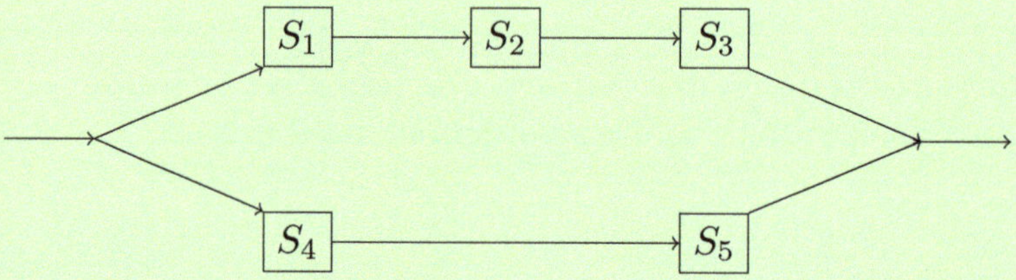

2. Q_1 has service rate $q_1 = \min\{1.2, 4.2, 1.2\} = 1.2$. Q_2 has service rate $q_2 = \min\{2.3, 1.2\} = 1.2$. Since Q_1 and Q_2 are in parallel, their overall service rate is $1.2 + 1.2 = \boxed{2.400}$.
3. The bottleneck is both Q_1 and Q_2 since they are in parallel. The bottlenecks inside Q_1 are S_1 and S_3, and inside Q_2 is S_5. So the bottlenecks are $\boxed{\{S_1, S_3, S_5\}}$. You can check that decreasing the service rate for any of these three nodes will decrease the rate of the overall system while decreasing the rate of S_2 or S_4 will not affect the overall service rate.

Problems

6.1 A queuing network's overall rate is limited by what type of server?

6.2 If a customer has a choice of servers, then the servers are arranged in ______________.

6.3 An entry ramp to the freeway uses a stoplight that lets traffic on at a rate of 2 cars every 3 seconds. If there are 24 cars waiting to get on the freeway, on average how long are you going to have to wait?

6.4 a) Consider the following queueing network. What is the overall system service rate?

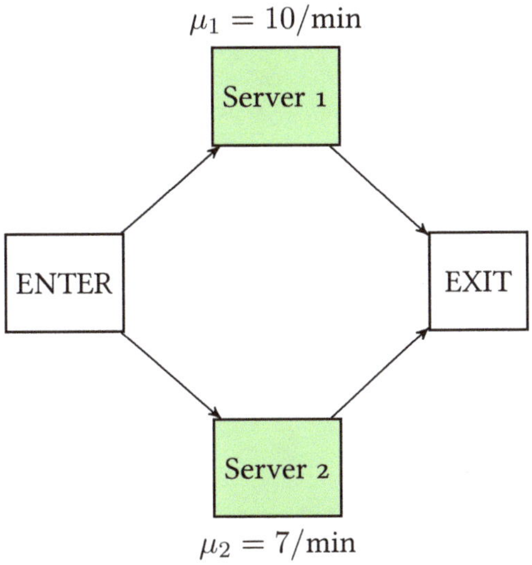

b) What is the overall service rate for the following network?

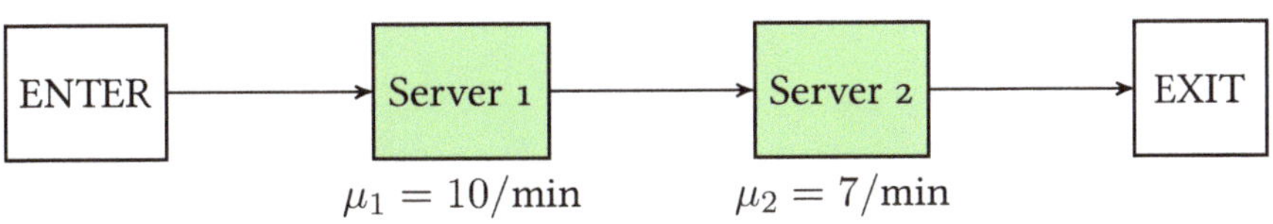

6.5 In the previous problem, what are the bottleneck servers?

6.6 What are the bottleneck servers of the following network?

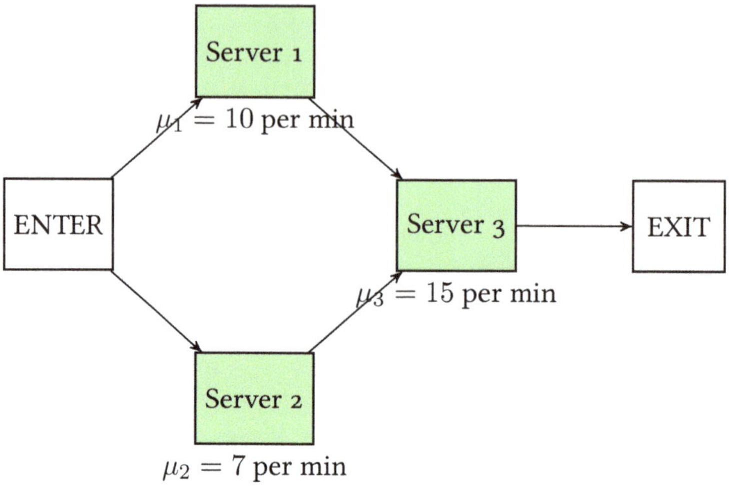

6.7 What is the capacity of the network in the previous problem? [In other words, what is the overall service rate of this network.]

6.8 Continuing the previous problem, if the bottleneck server (or servers) is (are) upgraded to serve at a rate 18 per minute, what is the overall service rate of this network?

Chapter 7

Little's Law

Question of the Day

Suppose that I buy four cans of tuna at the grocery store when it goes on sale every two weeks. I then consume the tuna at random iid intervals. After collecting data for six months I find that at home the average number of cans of tuna that I have is 7.3. On average, what is the time between when I purchase the tuna and the can of tuna is consumed?

Summary

- Consider a time interval $[0, t]$. During this interval, let L_t denote the average number of customers in a queuing system, let W_t denote the average time customers spend in the system, and λ_t be the initial number of customers in the system plus those that arrive in the interval all divided by t.

- Little's Law says that for any queuing network

$$L_t = \lambda_t W_t.$$

- These can be extended to an infinite time horizon. Let $\lambda_t = \lim_{t \to \infty} \lambda_t$, $L = \lim_{t \to \infty} L_t$. If R_i is the time in the system for customer i, let $W = \lim_{n \to \infty} (1/n) \sum_{i=1}^{n} R_i$.

- Little's Law says that for the infinite horizon,

$$L = \lambda W$$

  when these limits exist.

When entering a queue, the question of paramount importance to the customer is: How long until my service is complete? Call this the *time in system* for the customer.

Fortunately, there is a very general idea called *Little's law* that relates the arrival rate, the average size of the queue, and the average time that any particular customer spends in the system.

Theorem 4 (Little's Law)
Consider a queuing network over the time interval $[0, t]$. Let L_t denote the average number of customers in a queuing system, W_t denote the average time customers spend in the system, and λ_t be the initial number of customers in the system together with customer arrivals during $[0, t]$ divided by t.

$$L_t = \lambda_t W_t.$$

Example 19
Suppose for a $G/G/s$ the queue starts with one person in service. Another customer arrives at time 1.1, then the first customer finishes service at time 1.3. The second customer finishes service at time 2.7. A third customer arrives at time 3.3. Find L_4, W_4, λ_4, and verify Little's Law.

Answer The queuing network starts with 1 customer and two more arrive during the interval, so

$$\lambda_t = 3/4 = 0.75.$$

How long does each of the three customers spend in the system? Customer 1 is in the system over $[0, 1.3)$, Customer 2 is in the system over $[1.1, 1.3)$ and Customer 3 is in the system (during interval $[0, 4]$ over $[3.3, 4]$. Therefore, the average time customers spend in the system is

$$W_t = \frac{(1.3 - 0) + (2.7 - 1.1) + (4 - 3.3)}{3} = 1.2.$$

Finding L_t is a bit more complicated. In interval $[0, 1.1)$ there is one person in the system. In interval $[1.1, 1.3)$ there are two, then $[1.3, 2.7)$ there is one, $[2.7, 3.3)$ there are zero, and $[3.3, 4]$ there is one again. Hence the average number of customers in the system over $[0, 4]$ is

$$L_t = \frac{1(1.1 - 0) + 2(1.3 - 1.1) + 1(2.7 - 1.3) + 0(3.3 - 2.7) + 1(4 - 3.3)}{4 - 0}$$
$$= 0.9.$$

Now Little's Law can be verified: $(1.2)(0.75) = 0.9$. It is good!

The above example also shows why Little's Law is true. On the right hand side $\lambda_t W_t$ has the number of customers that arrive in both the numerator and the denominator, so they cancel out. The value λ_t also has the length of the interval in the denominator. This same length of the time interval is also in the denominator of L_t.

In the numerator, W_t has the sum of the lengths of the intervals. Notice that when the intervals overlap, the number of intervals that overlap for a particular subinterval is exactly the number of customers in the system. Customer 1 was in the system from 0 up to 1.3, and Customer 2 was in the system from 1.1 up to 2.7. So there were two customers in the system from 1.1 up to 1.3. That $2(1.3 - 1.1)$ was one of the terms in L_t.

Altogether, the numerator of L_t equals in value the numerator of W_t, they are just counting customers in two different ways. So Little's Law always holds!

7.1 Infinite time horizon

Often models operate over a finite time horizon, but it is good to understand whether this can be extended to the infinite time horizon case.

The limits of L_t and λ_t give rise to new parameters of the queuing network as $t \to \infty$.

Definition 43
Let

$$L = \lim_{t\to\infty} L_t,$$
$$\lambda = \lim_{t\to\infty} \lambda_t.$$

The fact that λ is used here when previously it was reserved for the arrival rate, is not a coincidence.

Fact 24
For an $G/G/s$ queue, the value of $\lambda = \lim_{t\to\infty} \lambda_t$ is the arrival rate of the queue.

This fact uses more renewal theory. A renewal here is a customer arrival–once a customer arrives, the time until the next arrival in a $G/G/s$ queue is independent of the previous arrival. In renewal theory, this fact follows from the Elementary Renewal Theorem and is very useful in understanding how these processes behave.

Let R_i denote the waiting time for customer i. Then the average waiting time becomes as follows.

Definition 44
If R_i is the time in the system for customer i, let

$$W = \lim_{n\to\infty} \frac{1}{n} \sum_{i=1}^{n} R_i.$$

Theorem 5 (Little's law, infinite time)
For any queuing network where the limits W and λ exist, L exists as well, and

$$L = \lambda W.$$

This theorem is quite amazing for several reasons. First, it makes virtually no assumptions about the nature of the system. This is a *universal law* that works regardless of the shape or characteristics of the network. It also does not depend in any way on the distribution of the arrival times or the service times. And yet, despite the universality of the result, it is surprisingly powerful.

In a typical application of Little's Law, two out of the three of L, λ, W are known and the goal is to calculate the third.

Example 20 (Question of the Day)
In this situation, 4 cans of tuna are bought every two weeks. Therefore, the arrival rate of the customers (which in this case are cans of tuna) is λ is 4 cans per 2 weeks which equals 2 cans per week. The average number of cans in the system is 7.3. Hence

$$7.3 \text{ cans} = W(2 \text{ cans/week}),$$

so

$$W = \boxed{3.650 \text{ weeks}}.$$

That is, on average any individual can stays 3.65 weeks in the system.

Note that the queue discipline was not important here! If I adopt a FIFO system and eat the cans purchased the earliest first, then the average time I have a can is 3.65 weeks. If I adopt a LIFO system and eat the cans purchased most recently first (and just to be clear, do not try this at home) then the average time a can is in the system is 3.65 weeks. Some cans will be eaten much earlier with this system, and some much later, but the overall average will be the same.

Example 21
A manager wants to keep the average wait time for jobs in a supercomputing cluster below 0.1 seconds. If jobs arrive on average at 10^5 per second, what must the average number of jobs in the system be kept below to accomplish this?

Answer The goal is an average wait time below 0.1 seconds and the arrival rate is 10^5, that gives the number of customers in the system as

$$L = (0.1 \text{ s})(10^5/\text{s}) = \boxed{10^4}.$$

7.2 *Proof of Little's Law*

Let $n(s)$ denote the number of customers in the system (either waiting for service or in service) at any particular time s. Then the graph of the function $n(s)$ over $[0, t]$ might look something like this.

Each time a customer arrives, $n(s)$ increases by 1, and each time a customer is served, $n(s)$ decreases by 1.

The rest of our notation is as follows.

λ_t	Arrival rate of customers in time $[0, t]$.
N_t	The number of customers in the system at time 0 plus those that arrive in time $[0, t]$.
L_t	The average number of customers in the system over $[0, t]$.
W_t	The average time customers spend in the system over $[0, t]$.
A_t	The area under the $n(s)$ for $s \in [0, t]$.

Using integral notation,

$$A_t = \int_0^t n(s)\, ds.$$

The proof of the finite version of Little's law comes down to looking at the area under the $n(s)$ curve in two different ways.

Proof of Little's law. The way you find the average height of a function like $n(t)$ is to find the integral over an interval and then divide by the length of the interval. In this case, this means

$$L_t = \frac{A_t}{t - 0} = A_t/t.$$

The average arrival rate over the interval $[0, t]$ is similarly N_t/t.

Let t_w denote the total time that customers are waiting in the system over $[0, t]$. Note that when a customer arrives at time T_i, the graph of $n(t)$ jumps up 1. If that customer stays in the system until time t, then the waiting time of that customer would be $(1)(t - T_i)$.

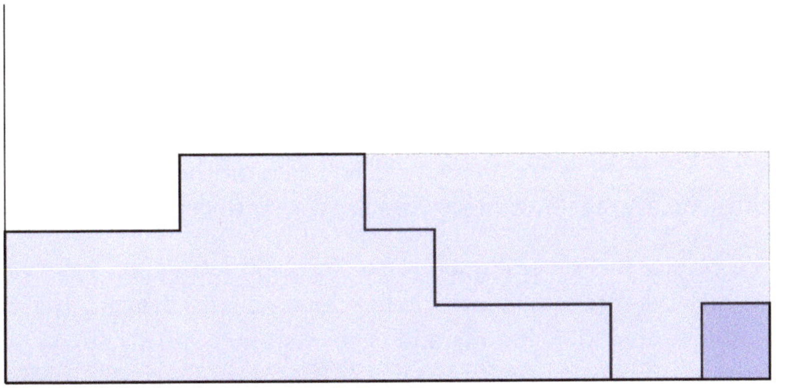

Note that if a point is to the right of two places where the function is increasing, it is counted twice, and so on.

However, at some time values customers are leaving the system. If at time t_ℓ a customer leaves the system, then that removes times $t - t_\ell$ from the overall waiting time of all customers.

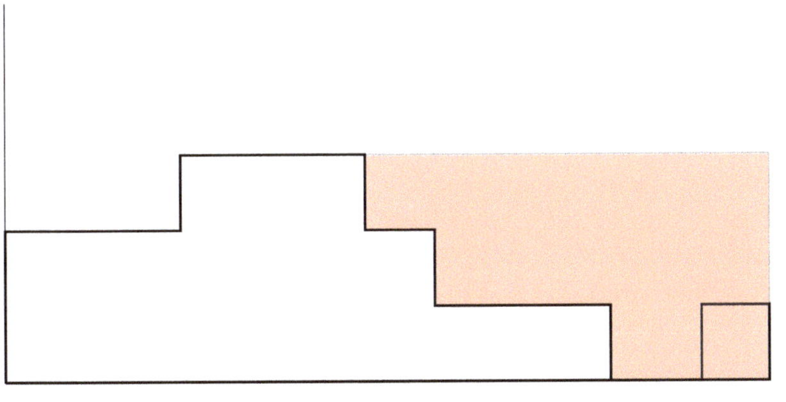

Therefore, the total waiting time is the area to the right of the curve when the curve is increasing, minus the area to the right of the curve when the curve is decreasing. But subtracting one from the other just leaves exactly the area underneath the curve. That is, $t_w = A_t$.

So the average waiting time is exactly A_t/N_t, the total waiting time of customers divided by the number of customers in $[0, t]$. Hence

$$\lambda_t W_t = \frac{N_t}{t} \cdot \frac{A_t}{N_t} = \frac{A_t}{t} = L_t.$$

□

Problems

7.1 The long term time customers spend waiting in a $G/G/5$ queue is 15 minutes, and the average long term queue length is 18.4.

a) What is the arrival rate to this queue?

b) What is the expected time between arrivals in this queue?

7.2 A road network has cars spending 28.2 minutes leaving City A and arriving at City B. If there are on average 500 cars on the road between the two cities, on average how many cars are trying to get from City A to City B?

7.3 A cafeteria has several queues (for food gathering and payment). If the average number of customers in the cafeteria is 20.3 during the lunch hour (call this time $[0, 1]$ hours), and each customer spends an average of ten minutes in the cafeteria, what is λ_1?

7.4 If a queuing system has a long-term average of 13.1 jobs in the queue, and each job waits an average of 1.1 days, what is the arrival rate?

7.5 Let $n(s)$ denote the number of customers in a queuing system. Suppose that the system starts with 2 customers. Customer 1 finishes service at time 0.8, Customer 3 arrives at time 1.4, Customer 4 arrives at time 1.8, Customer 2 finishes service at time 3.3, and Customer 3 immediately enters service but does not finish before time 5.

Draw a graph of $n(s)$ for $s \in [0, 5]$.

7.6 Let $n(t)$ denote the number of customers in a queue with one server at time t. The queue starts with no customers, and then there are customer arrivals at times $1.5, 2.1, 2.9, 3.4$. The time needed to service the first four customers are $1.2, 2.2, 0.8, 1.4$. Graph $n(t)$ over $[0, 4]$.

7.7 Jobs arrive at a computer server at 11.4 per second. If the average number of jobs waiting at any moment is 14.2, what is the average amount of time a job waits before being served?

7.8 A construction site is getting bricks delivered at rate 4000 per day. If the average number of bricks on site not yet set in a wall is 12300, what is the average amount of time a brick waits at the site before being set in a wall?

Chapter 8

Idle time for $G/G/s$ queues

Question of the Day

A Google server receives on average 200 requests a second, each of which takes on average 0.001 seconds to resolve. What percentage of time is the server idle?

Summary

- Idle time for $G/G/s$ queue is the long term average the queue has no customers.
- Jump processes are stochastic processes that jump from one state to another at discrete times.
- Continuous time Markov chains are jump processes where the time between jumps are independent, and exponentially distributed with parameter that only depends on the current state.

When dealing with queuing networks, when the arrival rate exceeds the service rate, the length of the queue explodes. What happens when the arrival rate is lower than the service rate?

8.1 Capacity Utilization

Suppose that for the Question of the Day, the interval of time under consideration in $[0, t]$. Since requests are coming in at 200 per second, assuming t is measured in seconds, the average number of requests in the interval $[0, t]$ will be $200t$.

Each of these (on average) $200t$ requests takes time (on average) 0.001 sections to resolve. By Wald's Equality, the time to resolve the average of $200t$ requests that each take an average of 0.001 time requires (on average) $(200t)(0.001) = 0.2t$ time.

So (on average) $0.2t$ time out of the $[0, t]$ interval is spent resolving requests. In other words, 20% of the time in the interval $[0, t]$, the computer is busy, and 80% of the time it is idle.

This is not a rigorous derivation because it assumes that all of the service jobs that arrived in the interval $[0, t]$ were actually serviced in $[0, t]$. This might not be true. For example, the arrivals and service times might have looked something like this:

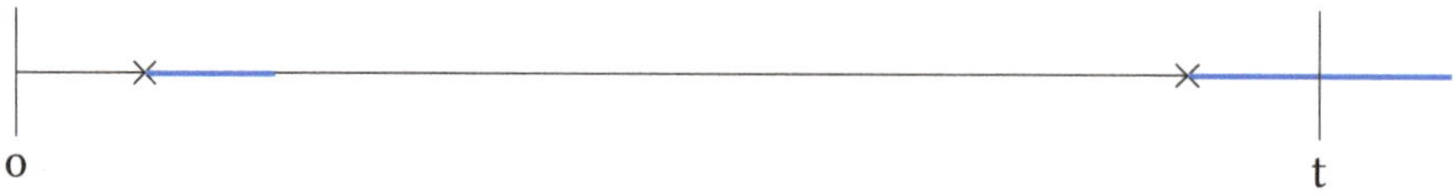

That being said, when t large, that extra bit of service on the end is negligible compared to the size of t.

The percentage of time that the server was busy was found by multiplying the arrival rate times the average time of service. The average time of service is one over the service rate. So the average percentage of time that the server is busy will be (for large times) the arrival rate divided by the service rate.

Recall that for queues with s servers that each have service rate μ, the overall service rate of the network is $\mu \cdot s$.

Definition 45
For a $G/G/s$ queue, the **capacity utilization** is

$$\rho = \frac{\lambda}{\mu \cdot s}.$$

When the capacity utilization is less than 1, the queue is capable of serving its customers at a rate faster than they arrive. But for capacity utilization greater than 1, the arrival rate is faster than the service rate, so the queue will grow on average to be infinitely long.

Definition 46
For a statistic S_t that refers to the queue over time $[0, t]$, if $S = \lim_{t\to\infty} S_t$ exists with probability 1, then S is the **long term** (aka **long run** aka **steady state**) value of the statistic.

These long run statistics were seen earlier in describing Little's Law over the infinite time horizon. The long run average queue length is the limit of the average queue length over $[0, t]$, and the arrival rate is the long term statistic of the arrival rate over $[0, t]$.

Fact 25
For a $G/G/s$ queue with finite expected service and interarrival times, and $\rho < 1$, the long run (steady state) busy time is ρ.

Definition 47
The **idle time** for a queue is the long term fraction of time there are no customers in the system.

When a queue is not busy, it is idle.

Fact 26
The long run idle time is $1 - \rho$.

For a single server, the busy time is the percentage of time the server is expected to be servicing a customer. For multiple servers, the busy time is the percentage of servers that are expected to be occupied at any particular time.

Proof idea For any given interval of time $[0, t]$ some of the time will be spent serving customers, and some of the time the system will be idle.

In time $[0, t]$, the average number of customers that arrive is the arrival rate times the time, or λt. Since the service rate is μs, on average each one of these customers takes takes service time (on average) of $1/(s\mu)$. Hence the time blocked out by services is roughly $\lambda t/(s\mu)$. That is, $\lambda/(s\mu)$ percent of the time is occupied by services.

8.2 *Stochastic Processes*

The number of customers in the system at time t is an example of a stochastic process.

Definition 48
A collection of random variables $\{X_t\}$ is called a **stochastic process**. The subscript t is the **index** of the variables.

Often the index $t \in [0, \infty)$ for a process that varies in time.

The idle time is measuring the time that the length of the queue is spending in state 0. More generally, indicator functions can be used to measure the time spent in other states.

Definition 49
For a stochastic process $\{X_t\}_{t\geq 0}$, the **fractional time spent in state i** is
$$\frac{1}{t}\int_{s\in[0,t]} \mathbb{1}(X_t = i)\, ds.$$

Of course, that makes the steady state time spent in state i
$$\lim_{t\to\infty} \frac{1}{t}\int_0^t \mathbb{1}(X_s = i)\, ds.$$

So see how this works in practice, consider an example.

Example 22
Suppose the process X_0 starts in state a, spends 1.5 seconds in state 0 and then jumps to state b, where it spends 1 second before jumping back to a. The process then repeats. The process X_0 looks like:

Then $Y_s = \mathbb{1}(X_s = a)$ picks out those times the state of X_s is a, and replaces them with a 1.

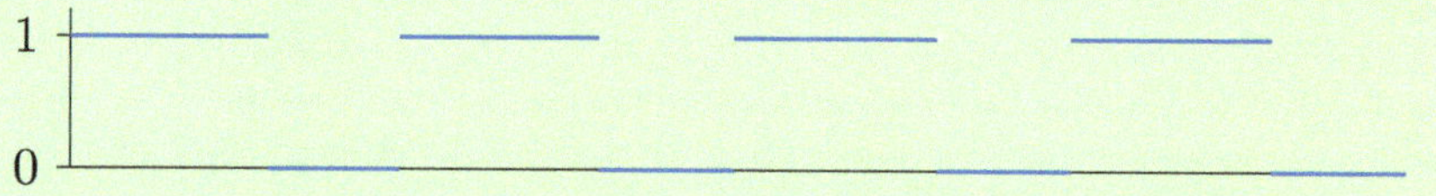

The average time spent in state a is then just the average of Y_s over $[0, t]$. In the limit as t goes to infinity, this converges to 0.6.

The process X_t is an example of a *jump process*. At a countable number of times in $[0, \infty)$, it jumps from one state to another.

Definition 50
A stochastic process $\{X_t\}_{t\geq 0}$ is a **jump process** if the path $t \mapsto X_t$ is constant with a number of discontinuities that is countably infinite with probability 1.

Recall that a set of values is countably infinite if it is finite, or infinite and can be placed into a sequence $d_1, d_2, \ldots$. So a stochastic process is a jump process if the times at which it jumps is either finite or can be placed into a sequence of times.

8.3 Continuous time Markov chains

If the time between jumps is memoryless (exponential) where the parameter only depends on the current state, then call the process a *continuous time Markov chain* or *CTMC* for short.

Definition 51
A stochastic process over state space Ω is a **continuous time Markov chain** (**CTMC** for short) if it is a memoryless jump process. This means there is a function $\lambda : \Omega \to [0, \infty)$ where at time t, given $\{X_{t'}\}_{t' \leq t}$, the time τ of the next jump satisfies $\tau - t \sim \text{Exp}(\lambda(X_t))$, and the distribution of X_τ only depends on X_t.

A nice fact about exponentials is that the minimum of two exponentials is still exponential.

Fact 27
Suppose $X \sim \text{Exp}(\lambda_X)$ and $Y \sim \text{Exp}(\lambda_Y)$ are independent. Then $\min\{X, Y\} \sim \text{Exp}(\lambda_X + \lambda_Y)$.

Proof. Recall that $A \sim \text{Exp}(\lambda)$ if and only if $\mathbb{P}(A > a) = \exp(-\lambda a)$. So

$$\begin{aligned}
\mathbb{P}(\min\{X, Y\} > a) &= \mathbb{P}(X > a, Y > a) \\
&= \mathbb{P}(X > a)\mathbb{P}(Y > a)[\text{independent}] \\
&= \exp(-\lambda_X a)\exp(-\lambda_Y a) \\
&= \exp(-[\lambda_X + \lambda_Y]a)
\end{aligned}$$

which means $\min\{X, Y\} \sim \text{Exp}(\lambda_X + \lambda_Y)$. □

Consider the $M/M/1$ queue. There is an exponential amount of time until the next arrival, and an exponential amount of time until the next service. So the next time of either an arrival or service will also be exponential since it is the minimum of two exponentials. This gives us the following result.

Fact 28
Let X_t be the number of customers in an $M/M/1$ queue at time t. Then $\{X_t\}$ is a continuous time Markov chain.

When the state space Ω is discrete, a continuous time Markov chains can be represented using an arc labeled directed graph.

- Nodes are states the chain can be in.
- Arcs are labeled with rate of jump between states.

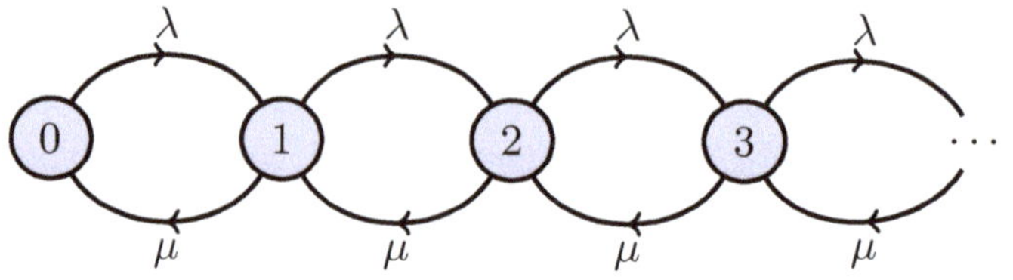

Problems

8.1 The capacity utilization is usually denoted by what symbol?

8.2 Fill in the blank: the value of the capacity utilization is an example of a ______________ run statistic of the queue.

8.3 For a $G/G/4$ queue with capacity utilization 65%, what is the long run idle time?

8.4 If a queue has capacity utilization 30%, what is the long run idle time?

8.5 Suppose a $G/G/4$ queue has arrival rate 4 per min, and the average service time for a single server is 0.8 minutes. What is the capacity utilization for the queue?

8.6 Suppose a $G/D/3$ queue has arrival rate 3.2 per min, and the time to service a single job is 27.2 seconds. What is the capacity utilization for the queue?

8.7 For a $G/G/s$ queue with arrival rate 4.2 per second and the expected time for a single server to serve a customer of 1.9 seconds, what is the maximum number of servers we can have and still have less than 50% long run idle time?

8.8 For a $G/G/3$ queue, if the service time of a single server is 3.2 minutes on average and the capacity utilization is 80%, what is the arrival rate of jobs?

Chapter 9

Long term behavior of a CTMC

Question of the Day

In an $M/M/1$ queue with average wait between arrivals of 1 min and average service time for each server of 0.75 min, what is the long term percentage of time the system has at most 3 customers?

Summary

- The **Ergodic Theorem** says the following. For a countable state space continuous time Markov chain, Ω the states with positive probability of being reached from the starting state, and π a probability distribution over Ω such that for all states $i \in \Omega$,

$$\sum_{j \in \Omega} \pi(i)\lambda(i,j) = \sum_{k \in \Omega} \pi(k)\lambda(k,i),$$

  the steady state amount of time spent in state i is $\pi(i)$.

- Taken together for all $i \in \Omega$, these are called the **balance equations**.

- For the $M/M/s$ queue it is possible to analytically solve the detailed balance equations.

An $M/M/1$ queue is a continuous time Markov chain. To understand how these chains evolve, consider the following example of a CTMC.

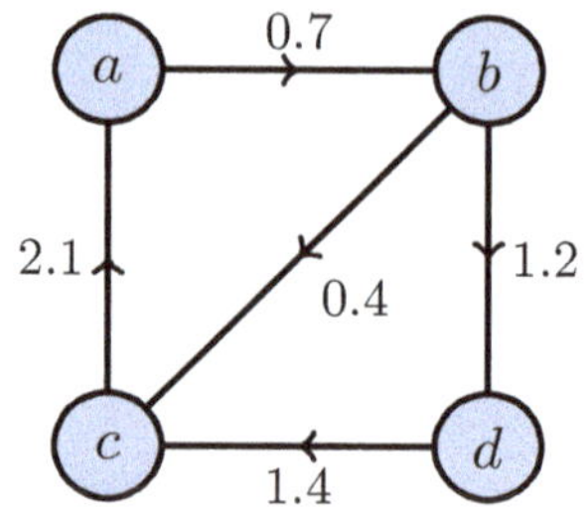

If the chain begins in state a at time 0, this can represented using a probability vector $p_0 = (1, 0, 0, 0)$. This means that the probability of being in state a is 1 and the probability of being in state b, c, or d is 0. Now consider the probability vector for times $t > 0$. The following shows how this vector evolves over time.

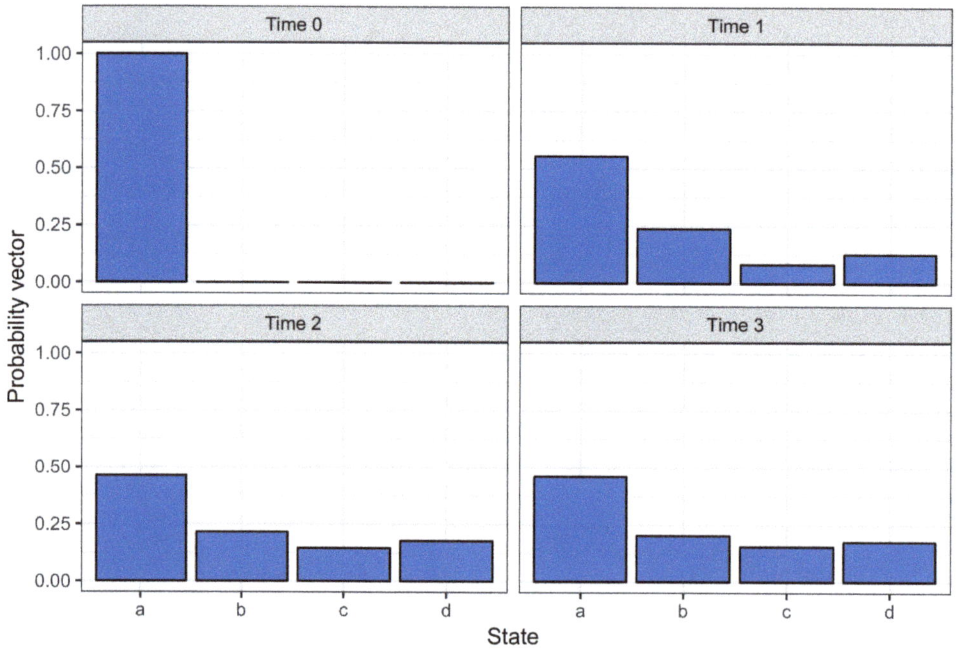

Note that by time 3 the chain has already *mixed*, that is, the probability vector is not changing much at this point. It is very close to

$$p_\infty = (0.4660\ldots, 0.2038\ldots, 0.1553\ldots, 0.1747\ldots).$$

This is the *steady state probability distribution*. The natural question is how to calculate this distribution (if it even exists). The answer lies in the *balance equations*.

9.1 Balance

Think of the Markov chain as a series of pipes. The pipes reflect the rate at which probability is flowing from one state to another. For instance, probability in state a flows out to state b at rate 0.7.

Say that the probability distribution is in *balance* if the flow out of the state exactly matches the flow into the state.

Let $\lambda(i, j)$ be the rate at which state i jumps to state j. In the example above, for instance, $\lambda(c, a) = 2.1$. The *Ergodic Theorem* states that for a countable state space Ω CTMC, if the flow is balanced at a certain distribution, then that distribution is unique, and will also be the steady state distribution.

Theorem 6 (Ergodic Theorem)
For a countable state space Markov chain, let Ω denote the states with positive probability of being reached from the starting state of the chain. Further, suppose there exists a probability distribution π over Ω such that for all $i \in \Omega$

$$\sum_{j \in \Omega} \pi(i)\lambda(i, j) = \sum_{k \in \Omega} \pi(k)\lambda(k, i).$$

Then the steady state amount of time spent in state i is $\pi(i)$.

Definition 52
The set of equations

$$\sum_{j \in \Omega} \pi(i)\lambda(i, j) = \sum_{k \in \Omega} \pi(k)\lambda(k, i).$$

for all states i are called the **balance equations**.

For the CTMC from earlier, there are 4 states, and so 4 balance equations. They are

$$\begin{aligned} 0.7\pi(a) &= 2.1\pi(c) \\ [0.4 + 1.2]\pi(b) &= 0.7\pi(a) \\ 2.1\pi(c) &= 0.4\pi(b) + 1.4\pi(d) \\ 1.4\pi(d) &= 1.2\pi(b). \end{aligned}$$

This system of equations is underdetermined. So the best that can be done is to solve them to say something like:

$$(\pi(a), \pi(b), \pi(c), \pi(d)) = \pi(a)\left(1, \frac{7}{16}, \frac{1}{3}, \frac{3}{8}\right).$$

Recall that probabilities always add to 1. This gives one additional equation:

$$\pi(a) + \pi(b) + \pi(c) + \pi(d) = 1.$$

Then we get

$$(\pi(a), \pi(b), \pi(c), \pi(d)) = \frac{1}{103}(48, 21, 16, 18).$$

This solution looks like

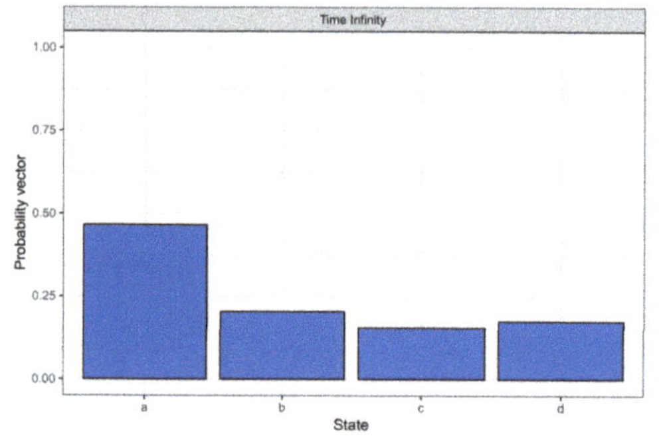

which is the same as the limiting behavior

9.2 *Limiting behavior for the $M/M/1$ queue*

For the $M/M/1$ queue, let N_t be the number of jobs in the system at time t (including the one being serviced) and N_∞ a draw from the steady state distribution. Recall that our CTMC looks like:

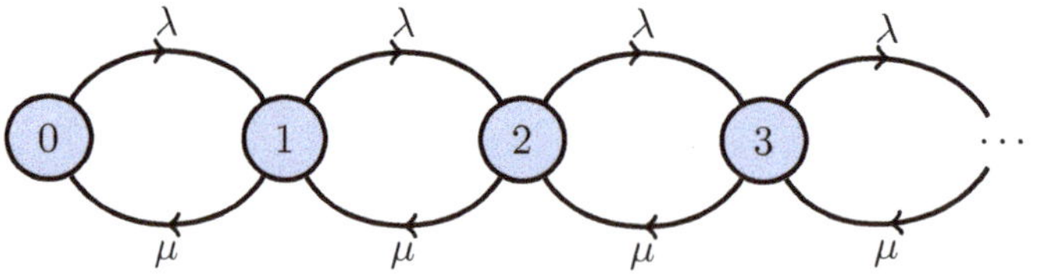

It turns out we can write down explicitly what the steady state distribution is!

Fact 29
For the $M/M/1$ queue,

$$\pi(i) = (1 - \rho)\rho^i$$

satisfies the balance equations.

Proof. Start with state 0:

$$\pi(0)\lambda(0, 1) = \lambda(1 - \rho) = (\lambda/\mu)\mu(1 - \rho) = \pi(1)\lambda(1, 0).$$

Now suppose $i > 0$:

$$\begin{aligned}\pi(i)\lambda(i,i+1) + \pi(i)\lambda(i,i-1) &= (1-\rho)[(\lambda/\mu)^i\lambda + (\lambda/\mu)^i\mu] \\ &= (1-\rho)[\lambda^{i+1}/\mu^i + \lambda^i/\mu^{i-1}]\end{aligned}$$

and

$$\begin{aligned}\pi(i+1)\lambda(i+1,i) + \pi(i-1)\lambda(i-1,i) &= (1-\rho)[(\lambda/\mu)^{i+1}\mu + (\lambda/\mu)^{i-1}\lambda] \\ &= (1-\rho)[\lambda^{i+1}/\mu^i + \lambda^i/\mu^{i-1}].\end{aligned}$$

So the balance equations hold! □

This should look familiar!

Fact 30
Let π be the steady state distribution of an $M/M/1$ queue. Then for $L = L_\infty \sim \pi$, the steady state line length satisfies

$$L_\infty + 1 \sim \text{Geo}(1-\rho).$$

In particular the average steady state line length is $L = \mathbb{E}[L_\infty] = \rho/(1-\rho)$.

Example 23 (Question of the day)
Given an $M/M/1$ queue with average wait between arrivals of 1 min and average service time of 0.75 min, what is the percentage of time there are at most three customers in the queue?

Answer Since we are not given the starting value, we should take this question to mean the steady state probability that there are at most three customers in the queue. From our steady state distribution for the $M/M/1$ queue, this will be

$$(1-\rho) + \rho(1-\rho) + \rho^2(1-\rho) + \rho^3(1-\rho).$$

Here $\rho = (1/1)/(1/0.75) = 0.75$, making the chance

$$0.25[1 + 0.75 + 0.75^2 + 0.75^3] = \boxed{0.6835\ldots}.$$

Little's Law can then be used to calculate expected wait time.

Example 24
Suppose we have a Google server $\lambda = 200$ thousand per second, $\mu = 1000$ thousand per second that is modeled as an $M/M/1$ queue. What is the average time a job spends in the queue for the server?

$$L_\infty + 1 \sim \text{Geo}(1 - 200/1000),$$

so

$$\mathbb{E}[L+1] = 1/.8 = 1.25 \Rightarrow \mathbb{E}[L] = 0.25.$$

By Little's law:

$$L = \lambda \cdot W \Rightarrow 0.25 = 200\,000W \Rightarrow W = \boxed{1.250 \cdot 10^{-6} \text{ seconds}}.$$

9.3 *Modeling the $M/M/2$ queue*

Now consider what happens when there are two servers working in parallel.

- Let N_t by the number of customers in the system at time t.
  - When $N \geq 2$ both servers are working.
  - When $N = 1$ one server is working.
  - When $N = 0$ no servers are working.
- The key difference is that when both servers are working, the service rate doubles to 2μ because they are working in parallel.

The graph of the CTMC is as follows.

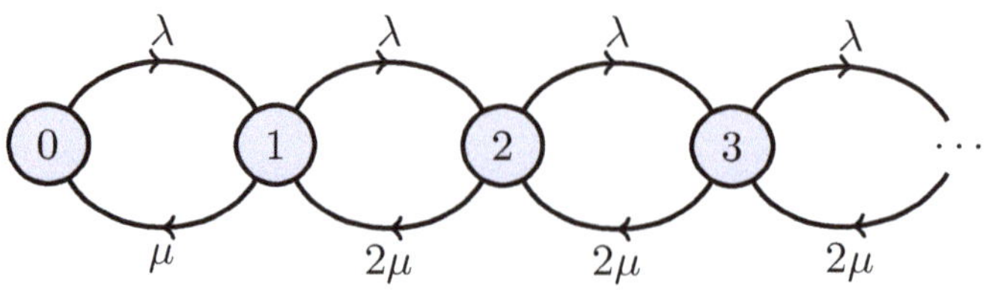

Fact 31
For the $M/M/2$ queue with $\rho = \lambda(2\mu)^{-1} < 1$, the steady state distribution is

$$\pi(0) = \frac{1-\rho}{1+\rho}$$
$$\pi(i) = 2\rho^i \frac{1-\rho}{1+\rho} \qquad i \geq 1.$$

and the expected steady state line length is

$$\frac{2\rho}{1-\rho^2}.$$

To prove this just verify that the balance equations are satisfied.
Note as $\rho \to 1$, the expected line length goes to infinity.

Problems

9.1 For an $M/M/1$ queue with arrival rate 3 per minute and service rate 5 per minute, what is the steady state length of the queue?

9.2 A food stand models their customers as an $M/M/1$ queue. If the servers can serve on average 12 customers in an hour, and on average 8 customers arrive in an hour, what is the average length of the queue?

9.3 For an $M/M/1$ queue with arrival rate 3 per minute and service rate 5 per minute, what is the steady state probability there are two or fewer jobs in the system?

9.4 A help desk is modeled using an $M/M/1$ queue with arrival rate 20 per hour and service rate 25 per hour. What is the steady state probability that there are four or more customers in the queue?

9.5 The help desk from the last problem upgrades to two servers (each has the 25 per hour service rate). Now what is the probability that there are four or more customers in the queue?

9.6 Consider an $M/M/2$ queue with arrival rate 3 per minute and service rate per server of 5 per minute.

- What is the long term probability that exactly one of the servers is idle?
- What is the long term probability that both of the servers are idle?
- What is the long term average number of servers that are idle?

9.7 Draw a graphical model of the continuous time Markov chain that models the $M/M/3$ queue with arrival rate λ and single server service rate μ.

9.8 Write down the balance equations for the $M/M/3$ queue.

Chapter 10

Studying data

Question of the Day

Douglas Consulting records queue length at 5 times during the day of $17, 21, 8, 7, 14$. What is the average queue length? What is the standard deviation?

Summary

- Given a dataset $X_1, \ldots, X_n$, basic statistics include the **sample average**

  $$\bar{X} = \frac{1}{n}\sum_{i=1}^{n} X_i,$$

  and the **sample standard deviation**

  $$\bar{\sigma} = \text{sqrt}\left(\frac{1}{n-1}\sum_{i=1}^{n}(X_i - \bar{X})^2\right).$$

- **R** is an open source statistical toolkit and a programming language that can calculate these statistics.

- Useful commands in R include `c` for making a vector, `mean` for finding the sample average of the values of a vector, and `sd` for finding the sample standard deviation of the values of a vector.

10.1 Statistics

Statistics is the science of collecting and analyzing data in order to make informed decisions. Often the mathematics used in building statistical models involve the use of probability, and so that subject is seen as being very closely related.

One of the most important theorems from probability is essential to building statistical estimators, the Strong Law of Large Numbers. This theorem says that for an iid stream of random variables, the sample average converges to the expected value of each random variable.

Definition 53
Let $X_1, \ldots, X_n$ be random variables. Then

$$\hat{\mu} = \frac{X_1 + \cdots + X_n}{n}$$

is the **sample average** of the data.

Often, the adjective sample is dropped, and this is called the *average* of the random variables. It is important to be careful though, you do not want to confuse the average of a set of numbers (which is a statistic) with the average of a random variable (which is an integral or summation depending on the type of random variable.)

The sample average is an example of a *statistic*.

Definition 54
Given data $(X_1, \ldots, X_n)$, a **statistic** is any function of the data.

For the sample average, the function is

$$\hat{\mu}(X_1, \ldots, X_n) = \frac{X_1 + \cdots + X_n}{n}.$$

The symbol μ (when not being used for the service rate of a queue) often represents the average of a random variable X_1. Note that $\hat{\mu}$ has a circumflex symbol above it. That indicates that $\hat{\mu}$ is an *estimate* for μ. Because the word "circumflex" is hard to say, statisticians use a simpler term, reading $\hat{\mu}$ as "hat mu".

One of the hallmarks of a good estimate is that when more data is given, the statistic is closer to the true value of a parameter. This idea is called *consistency*.

Consistent estimators

Definition 55
A sequence of estimates $(\hat{\theta}_1, \hat{\theta}_2, \ldots)$ is **consistent** for parameter θ if

$$\mathbb{P}\left(\lim_{n\to\infty} \theta_n = \theta\right) = 1.$$

Given a probabilistic model, it is impossible to guarantee that an estimate will converge to the right answer. But for a consistent estimator, it is possible to guarantee that convergence will happen with probability 1. The Strong Law of Large Numbers essentially says that the sample average of iid data gives a consistent sequence of estimators for the mean of the distribution the data is drawn from.

Theorem 7 (Strong Law of Large Numbers)
For $X_1, X_2, \ldots$ iid with finite mean,

$$\mathbb{P}\left(\lim_{n\to\infty} \frac{X_1 + \cdots + X_n}{n} = \mathbb{E}[X_i]\right) = 1.$$

In words, this says that the sample averages from an iid stream of data form a consistent estimate for the expected values.

Standard deviation

Another important statistic is the *sample standard deviation.*

Recall that the *standard deviation* of a random variable is a measure of the spread of the random variable away from its mean.

Definition 56
The **standard deviation** of a random variable X is

$$\sqrt{\mathbb{E}[(X - \mathbb{E}(X))^2]}.$$

Given a set of data, the value of $\mathbb{E}(X)$ is unknown. So use $\hat{\mu}_n$ to estimate that, then find (almost) the sample average of $(X_i - \hat{\mu}_n)$, then take the square root of the whole thing to get the sample standard deviation.

Definition 57
Given a set of data $X_1, \ldots, X_n$, the **sample standard deviation** is

$$\hat{\sigma} = \sqrt{\frac{\sum_{i=1}^{n}(X_i - \hat{\mu}_n)^2}{n-1}}.$$

Why divide by $n-1$ instead of n? The purpose of this is so that $\mathbb{E}(\hat{\sigma}_n^2) = \text{SD}(X)^2$. Practically, it is a reminder that the spread of a random variable cannot be estimated with only a single sample! At least two draws from the distribution are needed before it makes sense to talk about estimating the spread of the random variable.

Fact 32
The $\hat{\sigma}_n$ statistic is consistent for $\text{SD}(X_1)$.

10.2 Using R to calculate estimates

R is a statistical computing environment. That means that it contains built in functions for calculating the most common statistics, and also has a programming language that you can use to accomplish tasks that are not built in.

R is open source, which means that it is free to download and use. The examples here will be written using RStudio, which is an *integrated development environment* (or IDE) for working with R. The steps to download R and RStudio are as follows.

To install R

- Navigate your web browser to r-project.org.
- In the first paragraph of the Getting Started section of the webpage, click the link to download R.
- Click the link to a mirror (a repository where the R software can be downloaded) in a place near you.
- You will be taken to a page with three options: download R for Linux, download R for Mac, download R for Windows. Click the link appropriate for your system.

To install RStudio The instructions for downloading R have not changed much, since this is open source software. For the IDE RStudio, the instructions have changed over the years. Googling "how to download RStudio" is the best way to get to the current page for downloading the software. As of 2024, the company that makes RStudio is called *Posit*, so look for that name in the website you are downloading from.

When RStudio is first opened on a system, the screen will look something like this.

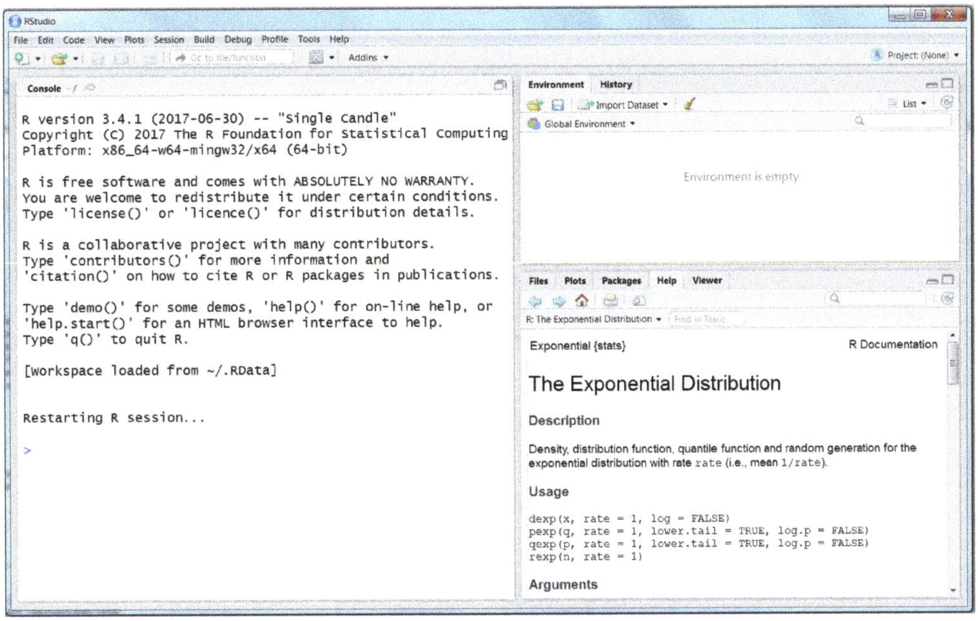

The program consists of a window that is divided into *panes*. One pane should be labeled *console*.

Start by typing some instructions into the console. You will see a > symbol next to a blinking cursor. Try typing

```
3
```

into the console at the cursor and hit return. R should return with just 3. It will display

```
[1] 3
```

where the [1] indicates that the result starts with the first number in the vector containing only the number 3.

To enter our data from the Question of the Day, use the *concatenate* function in R, which uses c as an abbreviation. Try entering

```
c(17, 21, 8, 7, 14)
```

into the console. The result should be

```
[1] 17 21  8  7 14
```

This data will be used more than once. So it makes sense to give this data a name. That is, the data should be *assigned* to a variable. To accomplish this, use the *assignment operator* in R, which looks like an arrow formed from the less than symbol and a hyphen. Try the following command in the console.

```
x <- c(17, 21, 8, 7, 14)
x
```

You should get the same result as before when you just typed in the data directly. Now, whenever the data is needed, it can be recalled by using its name `x`.

In particular, calculate the sample average of the data by using the `mean` function in R.

```
mean(x)
```

returns

```
[1] 13.4
```

The sample standard deviation can be calculated using the `sd` function in R. That is,

```
sd(x)
```

returns

```
[1] 5.94138
```

Both `mean` and `sd` are examples of *vector operations*, as they take a vector of data and return a single real value.

Problems

10.1 Suppose that data are stored in $X_1, X_2, \ldots, X_n$.

a) The function $M = \max(X_1, \ldots, X_n)$ is an example of a ____________.

b) For $(X_1, X_2, X_3) = (4.2, 5.1, -1.6)$, find M.

10.2 For $m = \min(X_1, \ldots, X_n)$ and data $(X_1, X_2, X_3) = (4.2, 5.1, -1.6)$, what is m?

10.3 Try out the following commands in R, and record the final result.

```
a <- c(4.2, 5.1, -1.6)
mean(a)
```

10.4 Try the following commands in R, and record the final result.

```
a <- c(4.2, 5.1, -1.6)
max(a)
```

10.5 Write an R command to put the following data

$$(2.3, 1.7, 2.3, 0.6)$$

into a vector named `data`.

10.6 Write an R command to put the following data

$$(-6.2, 4.1, 0.7)$$

as a vector into a variable named `x`.

10.7 Consider data $\{2.3, 1.7, 2.3, 0.6\}$.

a) Find the sample average by hand.
b) Find the sample average using R.
c) Find the sample standard deviation using R.

10.8 A farmer studying crop yield finds the four different places on the farm has yields of 410, 286, 317, and 422 bushels per acre of corn.

a) What is the sample average of the yield?
b) What is the sample standard deviation of the yield?

Part III

Simulation

Chapter 11

Discrete Event Simulation

Question of the Day

How can queues and queuing networks be efficiently simulated and visualized?

Summary

- **Simulation** creates random runs of a stochastic process on a computer to understand the average behavior.
- **Discrete event simulation** (DES) is a specific type of simulation where the state of the system changes at a discrete set of times.
- An **event representation graph** (ERG) is a graph where nodes represent events, and an edge from i to j indicates that executing event i might schedule event j. These edges can be adorned with times, distribution for times, and/or conditions for scheduling.

Modeling and simulation Models more complicated than a $M/M/1$ queue are difficult to analyze completely.

For instance, suppose interarrival times at a queue are $\textsf{Unif}([0,2])$ while service times follow a $\textsf{Unif}([0,1])$ distribution. Since the service rate is faster than the arrival rate, the queue will not become unbounded in length. What is the long term average waiting time of a customer?

Even the $G/G/1$ queue will not have an exact solution for fairly simple arrival and service distributions (although asymptotic analysis is possible in this case). When queues are connected in series or parallel in a routing network, the situation becomes far worse.

In these cases, *simulation* provides an easier approach to understanding the long-term behavior of the queue. In a simulation approach, a random instance of the queue is generated by a computer program. The output from such a random draw can then be analyzed using statistical tools to estimate the true average.

A computer program that has a random output is called a *Monte Carlo* algorithm, after the famed casino located in Monte Carlo, Monaco. Side note: the English spelling of Monte Carlo has no hyphen, whereas the French spelling does. Typically Monte Carlo in relation to algorithms uses the English spelling, but not always!

Types of simulation There are multiple ways of performing such Monte Carlo simulations. One way is to track each entity (and customer) as it moves through the system. Some examples of this entity based type of simulation include

- particle simulations;
- traffic simulations;
- airplane boarding.

One the other hand, some simulations track only the *state* of the system, a simplified version that only maintains information that is necessary to update the system. Consider a queue system with 10 customers in it.

- The entity approach would keep track of all ten customers individually. Each customer is updated individually as they move through the queue.
- The state approach just records that there are ten customers in the state of the system. Events such as a service or an arrival change the overall state of the system.

The state approach can use far less memory and be much faster in practice than the entity approach. On the other hand it can also be more difficult to design the model in the first place, and then program the model.

$G/G/1$ **queue** As an example, consider again the $G/G/1$ queue. For this queue, the state of the system can be entirely described by the following quantities:

- length of the queue;
- current time;
- next arrival time;
- free/busy status of the server;
- next finish of service for a busy server.

Definition 58
An **event** in a simulation is anything that changes the state of a system.

Note that this has nothing to do with an event in the probability sense of the term! There are three types of events in the $G/G/1$ queue.

- A start service event moves the server to the busy status and reduces the queue length by 1.
- An arrival event increases the queue length by 1 and might trigger a start service event if the server is free.
- A finish service event frees up the server, and might trigger a start service event if there are customers waiting in the queue.

11.1 Discrete Event Simulation

A particular type of simulation that is useful for these types of models is *Discrete Event Simulation*, or DES for short.

Definition 59
A **Discrete Event Simulation (DES)** is a type of simulation which focuses on the events that change the state of the system. The key component is an **event list** which holds all currently scheduled events and the times they occur.

This is a particular type of programming called *event driven programming*. Often this type of programming is used for writing graphical user interfaces where the events (such as mouse clicks) are generated by the user. Here, all of our events will be generated randomly by the simulation itself.

The event list must keep track of

- the clock (current time),
- the current state of the system,
- the list of events and the times that are scheduled to occur.

When an event is scheduled to occur, it is *executed*. During execution, an event can do either one or both of the following.

- Change the state.
- Schedule other events, that is, add events to the event list.

Graphical representation A *directed graph* is a mathematical object consisting of nodes and arcs that move from one node to another. Formally, we say $G = (V, E)$, where V is a set of nodes (aka vertices) and $E \subseteq V \times V$ is a set of ordered pairs of the form (i, j) where the order between i and j matters. We say that the arc (i, j) travels from i to j.

Definition 60
An **event representation graph** (ERG) for a DES uses nodes to represent events. Below each node, the states that event makes to the system are written. An arc from i to j represents that event i schedules node j. The label on the arc represents the time between when event i is executed and event j is scheduled, and the label can be a random variable indicating that each time the new event is scheduled, an independent random variable with that distribution is drawn. Arcs (i, j) can also be marked with a condition, in which case event i schedules event j if and only if the condition is met.

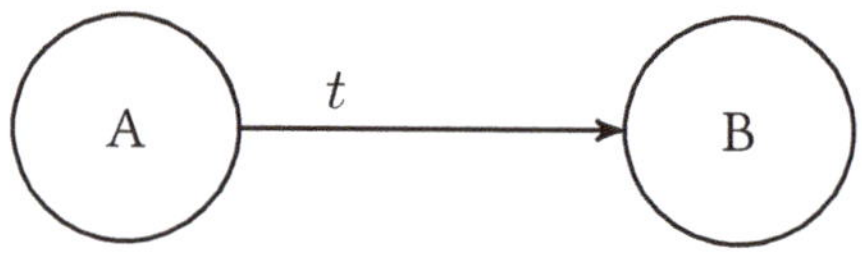

Event A schedules event B after t time has passed.

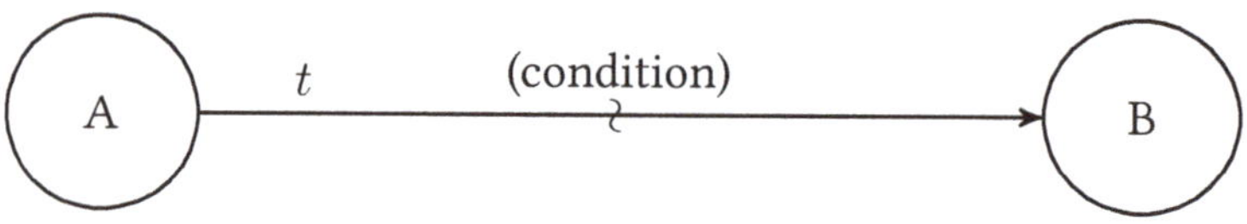

Event A schedules event B after t time has passed only if condition is true.

11.2 *A DES and ERG for the $G/G/1$ queue*

The Question of the Day asks about a $G/G/1$ queue. Earlier, three types of events were noted for this queue: start service, arrival, and finish service. It helps to add one more event that begins the whole process. All DES simulations will have this event, called a *Run* event.

The state of the system can be described using two variables. Let Q be the number of customers waiting in line to enter service, and S be the number of servers that are idle. Now examine each of the four events in turn.

Run event What the run event does is tell the system that there are no customers waiting originally, and one server is free to serve customers. After a random amount of time t_a, the first customer will arrive.

- Initializes $Q \leftarrow 0$, $S \leftarrow 1$
- Schedules the first arrival.
- In graph form, this event is represented as follows.

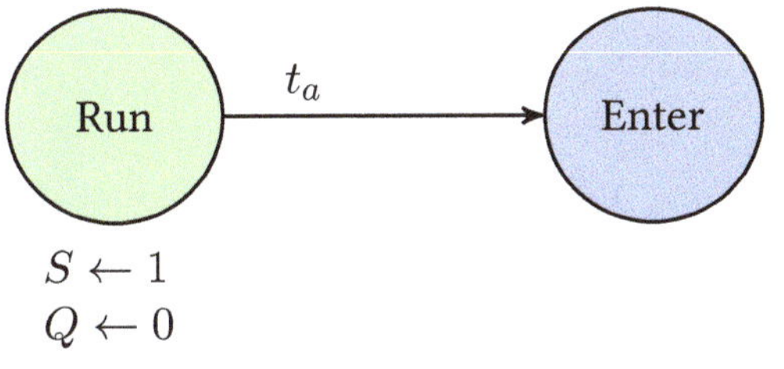

$t_a \sim \text{Unif}([0,2])$

Enter event The enter event will increase the queue by 1. If there is a server is free, it also schedules a start of service. After a random amount of time given by the interarrival distribution, it schedules another entry by a customer to the queue.

- Increases the queue by 1.
- If a server is free, schedules a start of service.
- Schedule the next arrival after a random amount of time.

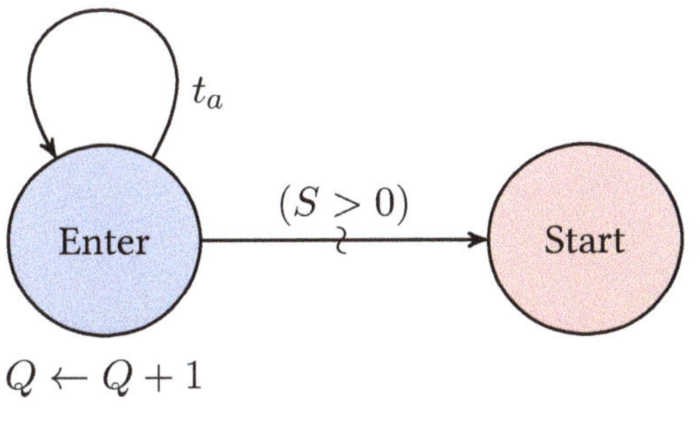

$t_a \sim \text{Unif}([0,2])$

Since there is no time on the edge from Enter to Start, the time of the start of service is the same time that the enter event was executed.

Start event When service begins, it takes a customer from the queue, takes a server from the available pool of servers, and decides how long service will take by scheduling a Leave (as in leave service) event.

- Decreases the queue by 1.
- Decreases the available servers by 1.

- Schedules the end of service, that is, a leave event.

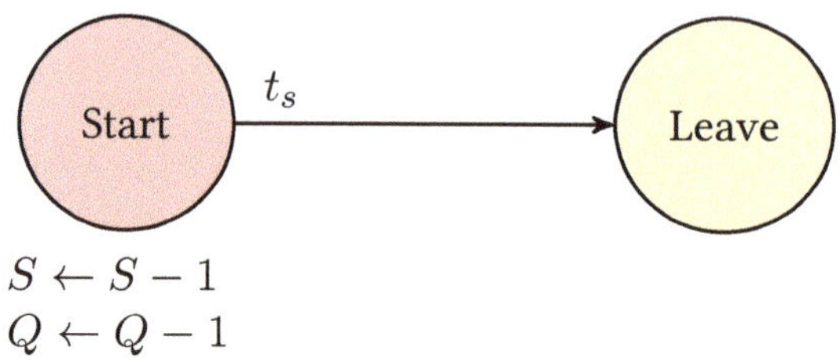

$t_s \sim \mathsf{Unif}([0,1])$

Leave event A customer finishing service frees up a server, and if there are more customers waiting in the queue, should trigger another start service event.

- Frees up a server,.

- If the queue is nonempty, should schedule a new service.

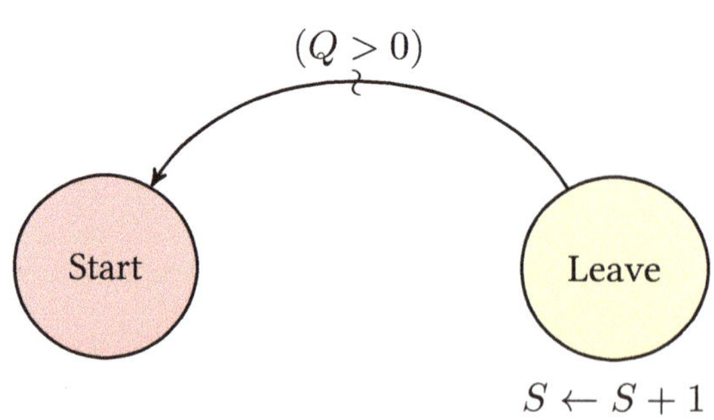

$t_s \sim \mathsf{Unif}([0,1])$

Putting everything together Drawing all four of these events together gives the following graphical representation of the DES for the $G/G/1$ queue.

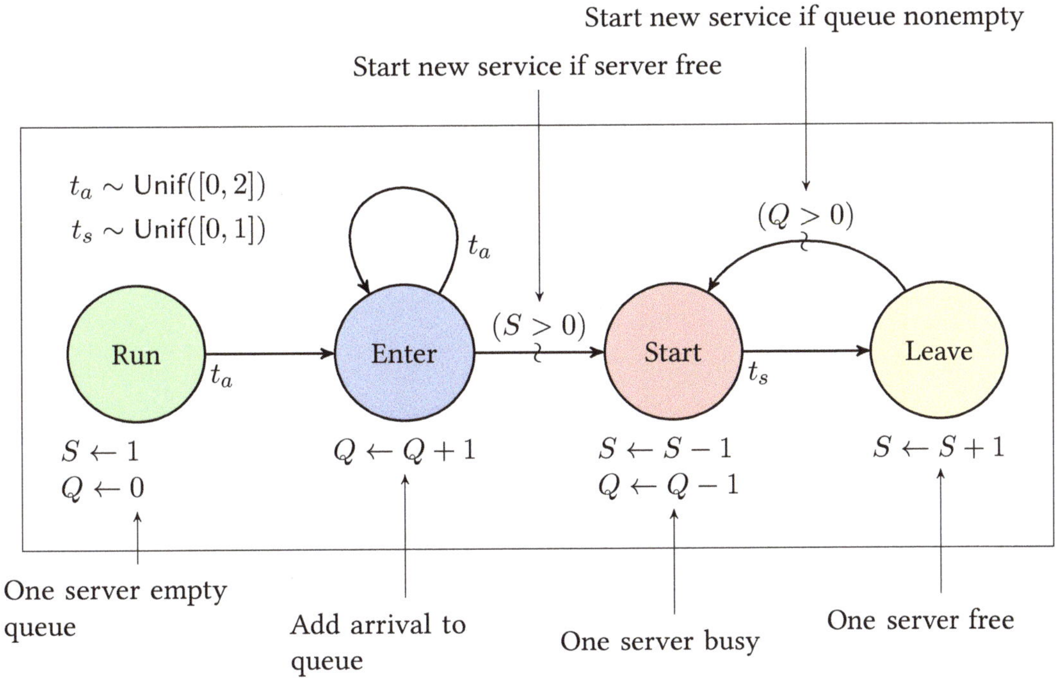

Problems

11.1 In an event representation graph, what do nodes represent?

11.2 In an ERG, what does a directed edge from i to j represent?

11.3 In the $G/G/1$ queue above:

a) What event(s) can the Enter event schedule?

b) What event(s) can the Start event schedule?

11.4 In the $G/G/1$ queue above:

a) What event(s) can the Run event schedule?

b) What event(s) can the Leave event schedule?

11.5 Events change the ______________ of the system in a Discrete Event Simulation.

11.6 For the following ERG for a simple DES, if t_s is drawn to be 3.4, and event A executes at time 2.2, what time is event B scheduled to occur?

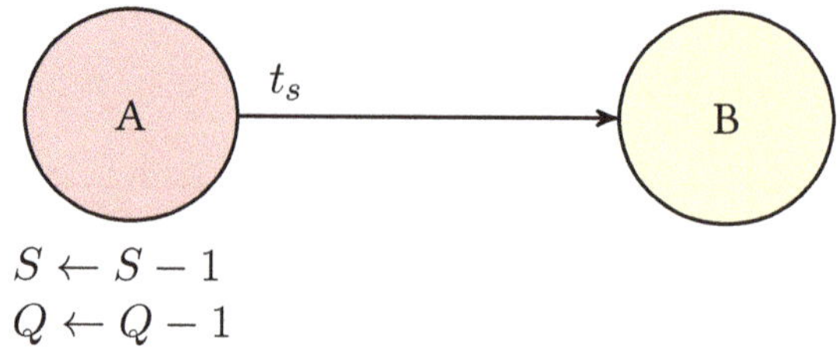

11.7 Suppose in the DES for the $G/G/1$ queue above, $t_a \sim \mathsf{Unif}([0, 4])$ and $t_s \sim \mathsf{Unif}([1, 2])$ are both in terms of minutes

a) What is the arrival rate?

b) What is the service rate?

c) What is the capacity utilization?

11.8 How would you modify the system above to model a $G/G/s$ queue?

Chapter 12

Flowchart for Discrete Event Simulation

Question of the Day

How should ties be resolved in a DES?

Summary

- The **master flowchart** for DES tells us how to implement a simulation in software.
- **Ties** and **deadlocks** can lead to unwanted behavior in the simulation if not dealt with carefully.

Last time an event representation graph (ERG) for a $G/G/1$ queue was built.

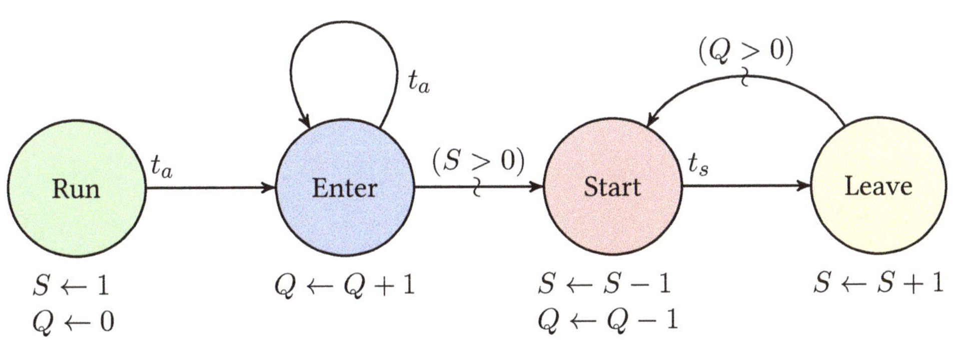

12.1 Watching the event list evolve

As events are executed, the event list, the current state, and the clock all change. Consider starting the DES for the $G/G/1$ queue.

- The event list at the beginning just consists of a Run event at time 0. The initial state has the number of customers waiting for service at $Q = 0$, and the number of available servers $S = 1$. So the state is $(Q, S) = (0, 1)$. The current clock time is $t = 0$.

t	state	type of event
0.00	$(0, 1)$	Run

- In the event list, the Run event occurs at the earliest time. So the first thing to do is execute this event at $t = 0$.
    - There is an arc leaving Run labeled t_a. So roll a value for t_a. Suppose the roll is $t_a = 0.12$. Then since the current time is 0.00, the Enter event will be scheduled at time 0.12.
    - Next, remove Run from the event list.

  The event of executing the Run event is that the event list looks like this.

t	state	type of event
0.12	$(0, 1)$	Enter

- The next event to occur must occur at time $t = 0.12$. So do the following.
    - Advance the clock time to 0.12.
    - Increase Q by 1.
    - Since $(S > 0)$ is true, schedule a Start event for the current time 0.12.
    - Generate a value for t_a. Suppose $t_a = 1.2$.
    - Schedule the next Enter event at time $0.12 + 1.2 = 1.32$.

  The resulting event list is as follows.

t	state	type of event
0.12	$(1, 1)$	Start
1.32		Enter

- The clock is still at 0.12. The next event to occur is the Start event at $t = 0.12$. The steps are

  - Update the state: $S \leftarrow S - 1, Q \leftarrow Q - 1$.
  - Roll $t_s \leftarrow 0.93$.
  - Schedule a Leave event at $0.12 + 0.93 = 1.05$.
  - Remove the Start from the event list.

t	state	type of event
1.05	$(0, 0)$	Leave
1.32		Enter

- Execute Leave event at $t = 1.05$:
  - Release our server to be available again: $S \leftarrow S + 1$.
  - Since $Q = 0$, do not schedule a Start. Note that for conditions like this, this is the only time the event scheduling can be activated.
  -

t	state	type of event
1.32		Enter

Some things to note.

- Because the first Run event schedules an Enter event, and each Enter event schedules a single Enter event before being destroyed, there will always be exactly one Enter event.
- Usually in practice, the simulations quits (ends) after t greater than some fixed t_{end}.

12.2 The Event Scheduling Flowchart

Event-driven programming In the event driven programming paradigm, the central object is the event list. It has certain properties for a DES.

- Each row of the event list is a time for an event and an event name.
- To run a DES, event list must be updated properly.

The following flowchart describes how the event list should be updated.

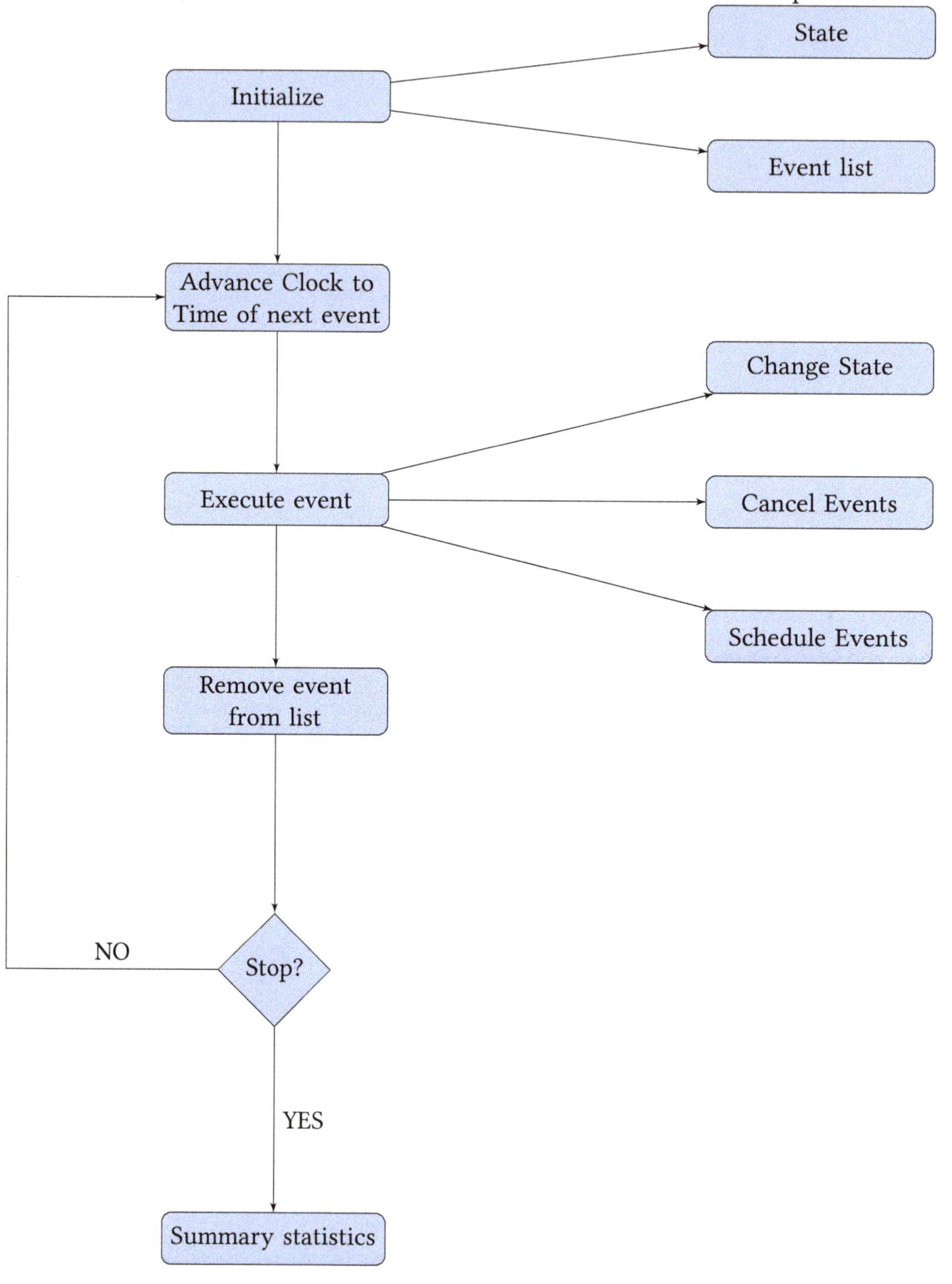

12.3 Building the ERG for two variations of queues

Queue with limited capacity Suppose that for our queue the line is not allowed to extend indefinitely. Rather, when it reaches a value B, then any customer arriving at the queue decides to go elsewhere for service. This can be implemented by the following ERG.

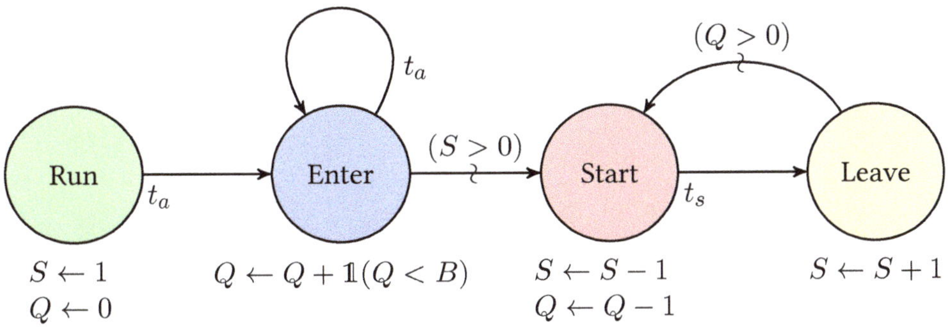

When $Q = B$, then $\mathbb{1}(Q < B) = 0$, and so the Enter event no longer increases the number of customers in line by 1.

A common mistake with this type of problem is to put a condition on the arc from Enter that schedules the next Enter. Do *not* want to do this! Adding a condition like this could interrupt the infinite stream of Enter events. If the execution of Enter does not schedule another Enter, it will cut off the stream of arrivals for all time!

Two types of servers in parallel Suppose that the network has two servers in parallel that could be of different types with different rates. Then every time there is an arrival, it goes to Server 1 if that server is free, or Server 2 if Server 1 is busy and Server 2 is free.

The new state will be (Q, S_1, S_2), where Q is the number of jobs in line, S_1 is the number of servers of type 1

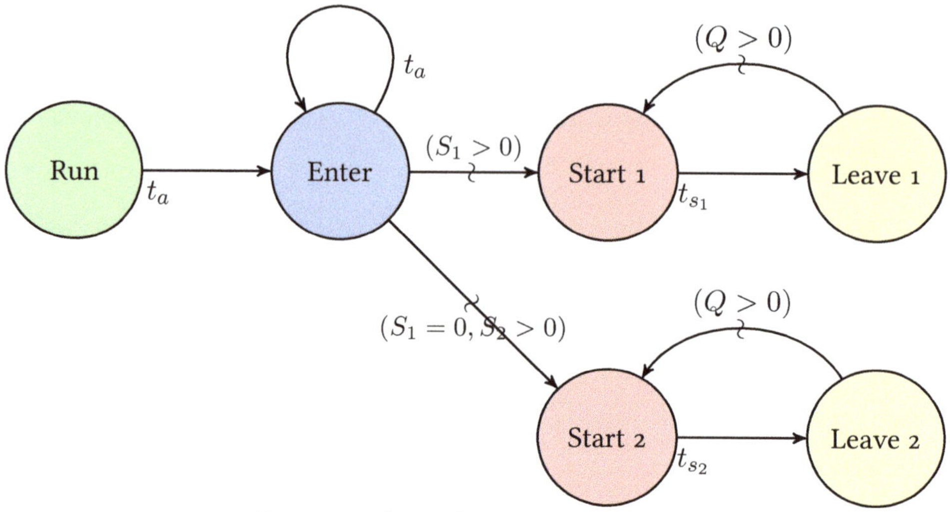

Event	*State changes*
Run	$S_1 \leftarrow 1, S_2 \leftarrow S_2, Q \leftarrow 0$
Enter	$Q \leftarrow Q + 1$
Start 1	$S_1 \leftarrow S_1 - 1, Q \leftarrow Q - 1$
Leave 1	$S_1 \leftarrow S_1 + 1$
Start 2	$S_2 \leftarrow S_2 - 1, Q \leftarrow Q - 1$
Leave 1	$S_2 \leftarrow S_2 + 1$

12.4 *Ties and deadlocks*

Definition 61
A **tie** in a Discrete Event Simulation is when two events are set to execute at the same time.

This can be a problem when two events are using or releasing the same resources.

For example, suppose that a queue with two entry lines uses two states labeled Enter1 and Enter2 that have self-loops to create two streams of arrivals. Further, suppose that at some time both Enter1 and Enter2 events occur simultaneously. Each one wishes to use the last server.

There are two simple ways to resolve ties.

1. Assign each event a priority value and run tied events in order of priority.

2. Assign each time of event a small positive number (such as a uniform from 0 to 10^{-6}) so that the probability that a tie occurs is zero.

Overall, ties might be bad or might be catastrophic. The worst situation is called *deadlock*.

Definition 62
Deadlock occurs when event A would release resources needed by event B, and event B would release resources needed by event A. Then neither order for A and B is acceptable.

The best solution to deadlock is usually *avoidance*, which means constructing systems so that this type of situation does not arise in the first place.

Problems

12.1 When an event executes, it can change the state, cancel existing events, or ______________ new events.

12.2 After an event is executed, what happens to it?

12.3 If event A executes at time 1.4 and rolls that event B is to be scheduled 2.3 time later, when is event B scheduled for?

12.4 If event A executes at time 0.7, and schedules event B for 1.1 time later, and then when event B schedules event C immediately, at what time does event C execute?

12.5 Before the next event is executed, the clock needs to be ______________|.

12.6 When two events occur at the same time, what is it called?

12.7 Deadlock occurs when if either A or B goes first, the other event will not have the ______________ it needs to execute properly.

12.8 The overall plan for coding a DES is called the master ______________.

Chapter 13

Programming in R

Question of the Day

How can R Markdown be used to combine code together with text?

Summary

- **R Markdown** files offer a way to keep your code organized. It offers a simple way to prepare text for publication along with methods for including code.

- A **function** in R is created in the same way as any other variables using the assignment operator <-. A function can have multiple inputs, and a single output given through the **return** command.

13.1 *Using R Markdown*

R Markdown gives a way of organizing the code needed to accomplish tasks in R.

Commands that are entered directly into the console in R are executed immediately. The effects of the command can be felt but the command itself is not recorded anywhere. By using an R Markdown file instead, the commands to be executed can be saved in the same way that a word processor saves text for later use and modification.

In an R Markdown file, the commands executed are saved in what are called *code chunks*. Changes can be made later to this code if a mistake is discovered. They can also be easily expanded upon if a more detailed analysis of the results is needed.

Creating a new R Markdown file To get started, open up RStudio. At the left of the main menu is *File*. Under File is the *New File* option. Hold the mouse over that option brings up a side menu. Selecting *R Markdown* from the side menu will open a new R Markdown file.

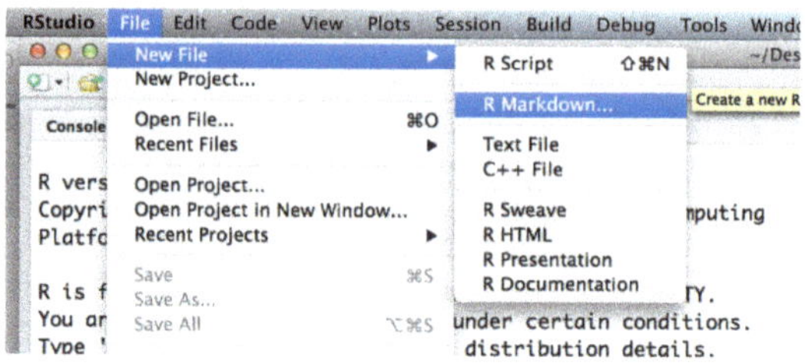

Figure 13.1: *Starting a new R Markdown file on a Mac. The Windows and Linux menu systems are similar.*

At this point a window will pop up that allows you to enter a Title and Author Name. Change the title to *First project*, write in your name under Author, keep the radio box on HTML and select the OK button when you are done.

This will open a new pane in RStudio with a template of an R Markdown file. By default, this is in the upper left of the window. Now press the Knit button in the toolbar right below the main menu.

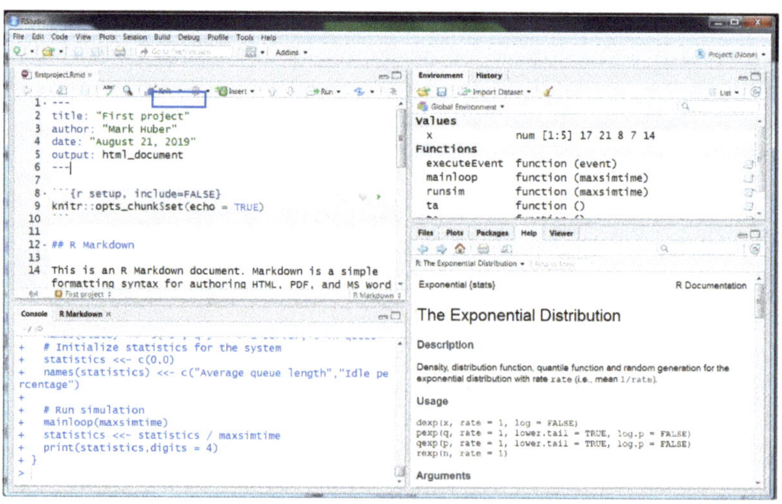

Figure 13.2: *Using the Knit button to turn the code into a document on Windows.*

The first time you press the Knit button, RStudio will ask you to save your R

Markdown file somewhere on your computer's file directory. Go ahead and save the file, without an extension. Then Knit will run, and the result will be an HTML (Hypertext Markup Language, the same format used for webpages) file with your document. A preview will automatically open.

Useful things to know about R Markdown

- When you want to start a new section, start the line with a # symbol. To create a subsection, start with ##, subsubsections with ###, and so on.
- The lines at the beginning of the file between the -- lines form the **YAML header**. The term YAML is a recursive acronym which stands for YAML Ain't Markup Language. Here you can change the title if you change your mind about that, your name if you change your mind about that, and the date as time progresses.
- Mathematics can be inserted into an R Markdown document using LaTeX formatting. The basic idea is that to insert mathematics as part of a sentence put `\(` and `\)` around the mathematics. For instance, `\( a^2 + b^2 = c^2 \)` will put an equation in the middle of a sentence. Using square brackets, such as `\[ a^2 + b^2 = c^2 \]` will put the equation on its own line in the output. A good tutorial to get started can be found at https://www.latex-tutorial.com/tutorials/.

Putting commands for the console in your document A powerful aspect of an R Markdown file is the ability to put commands directly into the R console. These commands are preceded by a line that reads ```` ```{r} ```` and end with a line that reads ```` ``` ````. For instance, if you type the following into your document:

````
```{r}
x <- 4
y <- 5
x + y
```
````

then you will see that portion of your document becomes shaded. This is called a **code chunk**.

Now press the green arrow in the upper right corner of the shaded area. This types these commands into the console, and displays the result right below the shaded area.

In this way, you can add whatever commands you like to a document. If you press the Knit button again, a new HTML document will be created with the code you created and the output of it.

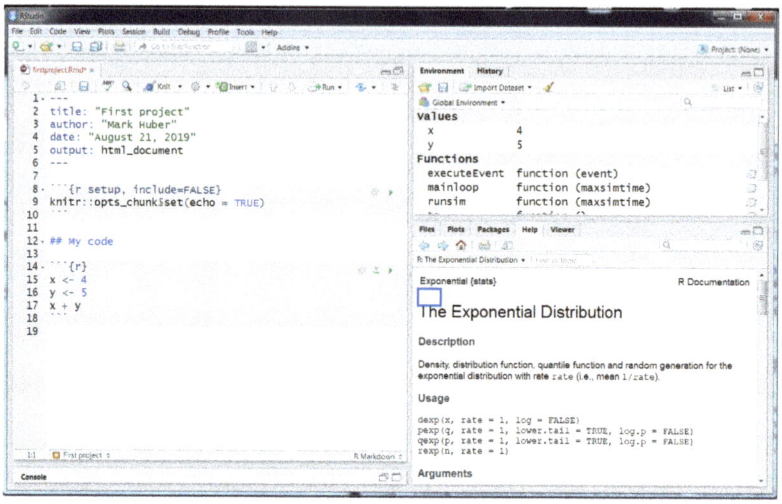

Figure 13.3: *The green arrow can be used to execute a code chunk. (Windows version pictured.)*

13.2 Functions

So far variables have been numbers. For instance, `x <- 4` assigns the value 4 to the variable `x`. The far more complex *function* type can also be assigned to a variable as well.

A function consists of three parts.

- A set of inputs to the function.
- A set of commands to be executed.
- An output to the function.

Try adding the following code chunk to your document.

```
add <- function(x, y) {
  return(x + y)
}
add(3, 4)
```

When you evaluate this code chunk outputs:

```
[1] 7
```

Here the function was placed in the variable named `add`. There are two inputs to this function, `x` and `y`. The function returns the value of `x + y`. This is why `add(3, 4)` returns the value 7.

A function need not have any inputs, and it might not have any outputs either. But be aware that you can always have inputs and an output if you need it.

13.3 Getting help

There are many ways to learn about functions in R. Outside of RStudio, an easy way to learn about something is to Google `<topic> in r`. Inside Rstudio, if you precede the name of a function with a `?`, the help for that function will open up in one of the panes. For instance, `?runif` will take you to the help for the `runif` function, which generates a uniform variate over $[0, 1]$.

13.4 Strings

So far our variables have held numbers and functions. They can also hold a variable type called a *string*. To denote a string in R, surround the characters with either single quotes (') or double quotes (").

```
x <- "Test"
print(x)
```

```
## [1] "Test"
```

```
y <- 'case'
print(y)
```

```
## [1] "case"
```

Whether using single or double quotes, the resulting variable is treated in exactly the same way by R.

Problems

13.1 True or false: strings must always be enclosed in single quotes.

13.2 True or false: preceding a command in R by `?` returns help on the command.

13.3 In R Markdown, mathematics can be included using the ______________ typesetting system.

13.4 For each example, state if the mathematics will appear in the middle of a sentence or on its own line.

a) `\( (x - y)^2 \)`

b) `\[ (x - y)^2 \]`

13.5 True or false: the YAML header of an R Markdown file is at the beginning of the file.

13.6 True or false: the YAML header of an R Markdown file is at the beginning of the file allows the user to set the title and author of the file.

13.7 True or false: functions can be assigned to variables in R.

13.8 Functions take one or more ______________, execute commands and return an output in R.

Chapter 14

Implementing a DES in R

Question of the Day

Consider a $G/G/1$ queue with interarrival times that are uniform over 0 to 2 minutes and service times that are uniform over 0 to 1 minutes. For this queue, use simulation to estimate the average waiting time for a customer.

Summary

R can be used to simulate a DES as follows.

- A **global variable** can be used to keep track of the state of the system.
- One function can handle the selection and execution of the next event. For different event types it calls the appropriate function to handle that event.
- The code follows closely the flowchart created earlier.

Review of Discrete Event Simulation At each step in a DES simulation, the following tasks are performed.

- Pull the earliest scheduled event from the event list to execute.
- Execute the event. This has the following possibilities.
    a. Update the state.
    b. Schedule new events.
- Remove the event from the event list.

This cycle continues until either a stop condition is reached (such as passing a specific time) or there are no events on the event list.

14.1 R Code for the DES

In general, it is not good programming practice to make use of *global variables.*

Definition 63
A **global variable** can be accessed from anywhere in the computing environment, not just in the function in which it was created.

Why are global variables looked down on? The problem is that any one of the programmers working on a project can change the state of a global variable without the rest of the team knowing. This can lead to issues if the variable is not what the other developers thought.

That being said, the use of global variables here enormously simplifies the code for implementing a DES in R. So they will be used here.

The two global variables will be the `sim` variable that contains the event list, and the `state` variable that contains our state. In R a variable is made global by using `<<-`, the global assignment operator.

Our first step in implementing a DES in R is to write a master function that runs these steps. To accomplish this, create a variable `sim` that holds the event list. This variable `sim` will be a *tibble,* which is a type of data variable in R that allows for different types of variables to be combined in a tabular format.

To use a tibble data type, it is necessary to ensure that a *package* (also called a *library*) named `tidyverse` has been loaded into the R environment. This can be done with the `library` function.

Each time R is started, that creates a new *instance* or *environment* in R. It starts with no variables or functions loaded. New functions (and variables) can be created by coding them up. They can also be placed into the environment by *loading* a *library.*

Before a library can be loaded into R it must be added to the installation of R on the computer it is being used. This installation (like the installation of base R) need only be done once. Once installed, a library can be loaded into R each time it is needed without reinstalling it. The command to install the `tidyverse` library into R is

```
install.packages("tidyverse").
```

Again, this needs only be done once per installation of R. Once it is installed, it can be loaded into the environment with

```
library(tidyverse)
```

Unlike the `install.packages` command, the term `tidyverse` does not need to be in quotes for the `library` command. Another library that will be needed is `knitr`. Together, the code for loading these two libraries is

```
library(tidyverse)
library(knitr)
```

Again, note that it might be necessary to use `install.packages` first to install the `tidyverse` and `knitr` libraries before running this code.

The `tidyverse` library allows us to use a data type called a *tibble* which is a table with extra information. The `knitr` library includes commands for displaying tibbles either on the screen or the printed page. Try this out by creating a simple event list as a tibble. Use a tibble to hold the event list. It can be created by calling the function named `tibble`. For instance, the following code creates an initial event list with just one event on it.

```
# Set up the event list as a global variable
sim <<- tibble(
  time = 0,
  type = "Run"
)
```

The first line starts with # to indicate that this is a *comment*. A comment is text that is for anyone reading the code. It is not actually executed. The event list created by the above code can be written as follows.

time	type
0	Run

Next is the main loop. This loop runs the flowchart for the DES, by pulling an event from the event list, removing it from the event list, and executing the event.

```
# main loop of the simulation
mainLoop <- function(maxsimtime, printFlag = TRUE) {
  while((nrow(sim) > 0) & (sim[1, 1] < maxsimtime)) {
    if (printFlag) {
      print(sim)
      cat('\n')
    }
    event <- slice(sim, 1) # take first event (Step 1)
    sim <<- slice(sim, -1) # drop first event (Step 3)
    executeEvent(event) # execute event (Step 2)
  }
}
```

The `mainLoop` function used several new functions. Here is a breakdown of these new commands.

- `slice(sim, 1)` returns the first row of the tibble.
- `slice(sim, -1)` returns the tibble except the first row.
- `nrow(sim)` returns the number of rows in the tibble.
- `sim[1, 1]` returns the element in the first row and column of the tibble. Given the way `sim` is laid out, this is the time of the first event in the event list.
- The `&` symbol means *logical AND* in R. The statement `thing1 & thing2` is true if and only if both `thing1` and `thing2` are true.
- A `while` loop repeats all the instructions surrounded by { and } until the condition in parenthesis that follows the `while` keyword is true. In this case, the loop will run over and over again as long as the event list still has at least one event in it and the time of the next event does run past our limit `maxsimtime`.

The final line in the `while` loop calls `executeEvent`. Until this function has been defined, `mainLoop` cannot be used without throwing an error. So look at that next.

To see how to build such a function, consider our ERG for the $G/G/s$ queue from earlier.

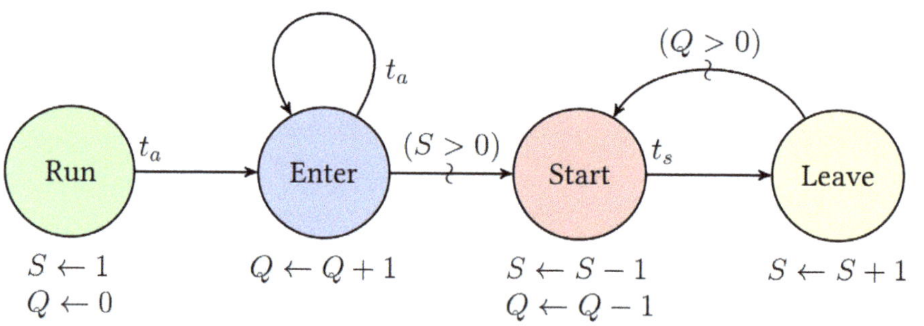

This has four events, `Run` (start the simulation), `Enter` (customer arrival), `Start` (customer begins service), and `Leave` (customer leaves service). Use `if` statements to accomplish this. An `if` statement executes the statement that follows if the logical expression right after the `if` keyword is true. Otherwise, it does nothing. More `if` statements are used to decide what type of event is being executed. They are also used within events to decide if the conditions on ERG arcs are true or not.

```
executeEvent <- function(event) {
  et <- event$time # Time for new clock
  if (event$type == "RUN") {
    sim <<- add_row(sim, time = ta(), type = "ENTER")
  }
  if (event$type == "ENTER") {
    state["q"] <<- state["q"] + 1;
```

```
    sim <<- add_row(sim, time = et + ta(), type = "ENTER")
    if (state["s"] > 0)
      sim <<- add_row(sim, time = et, type = "START")
  }
  if (event$type == "START") {
    state["q"] <<- state["q"] - 1;
    state["s"] <<- state["s"] - 1;
    sim <<- add_row(sim, time = et + ts(), type = "LEAVE")
  }
  if (event$type == "LEAVE") {
    state["s"] <<- state["s"] + 1;
    if (state["q"] > 0)
      sim <<- add_row(sim, time = et, type = "START")
  }
  sim <<- arrange(sim, time) # sort event list by times
}
```

The above used some new functions:

- `add_row` adds a new row to a tibble.
- `arrange` sorts a tibble according to the designated variable.

It also used a new logical operator

- When testing equality in an if statement, use == to test if two things are equal.

These events call the functions `ta` and `ts` to generate interarrival and service times. These functions use the `runif` command that generates draws from a uniform distribution.

```
# Interarrival times Unif([0,2])
ta <- function()
  return(runif(n = 1, min = 0, max = 2))

# Service times Unif([0,1])
ts <- function()
  return(runif(n = 1, min = 0, max = 1))
```

At this point, one more function is needed to initialize the event list, initialize the state, and then start the simulation by calling `mainLoop`. This function is called `runSim`.

```
runSim <- function(maxsimtime, printFlag = TRUE) {
  # Initialize event list
  sim <<- tibble(time = 0.0, type = "RUN")
  # Initialize state of the system
  state <<- c(1, 0)
  names(state) <<- c("s", "q") # 1 server, 0 in queue
  mainLoop(maxsimtime, printFlag)
}
```

The following call runs until time reaches 5.

```
runSim(5)
```

```
## # A tibble: 1 x 2
##    time type
##   <dbl> <chr>
## 1     0 RUN
##
## # A tibble: 1 x 2
##    time type
##   <dbl> <chr>
## 1  1.49 ENTER
##
## # A tibble: 2 x 2
##    time type
##   <dbl> <chr>
## 1  1.49 START
## 2  2.25 ENTER
##
## # A tibble: 2 x 2
##    time type
##   <dbl> <chr>
## 1  2.15 LEAVE
## 2  2.25 ENTER
##
## # A tibble: 1 x 2
##    time type
##   <dbl> <chr>
## 1  2.25 ENTER
##
## # A tibble: 2 x 2
##    time type
```

```
##   <dbl> <chr>
## 1  2.25 START
## 2  2.45 ENTER
##
## # A tibble: 2 x 2
##    time type
##   <dbl> <chr>
## 1  2.45 ENTER
## 2  2.74 LEAVE
##
## # A tibble: 2 x 2
##    time type
##   <dbl> <chr>
## 1  2.74 LEAVE
## 2  3.90 ENTER
##
## # A tibble: 2 x 2
##    time type
##   <dbl> <chr>
## 1  2.74 START
## 2  3.90 ENTER
##
## # A tibble: 2 x 2
##    time type
##   <dbl> <chr>
## 1  3.23 LEAVE
## 2  3.90 ENTER
##
## # A tibble: 1 x 2
##    time type
##   <dbl> <chr>
## 1  3.90 ENTER
##
## # A tibble: 2 x 2
##    time type
##   <dbl> <chr>
## 1  3.90 START
## 2  5.88 ENTER
##
## # A tibble: 2 x 2
##    time type
##   <dbl> <chr>
## 1  4.33 LEAVE
```

```
## 2   5.88 ENTER
```

The code is set up so that if `printFlag` is set to FALSE, then the simulation does not print the event list at every step.

```
runSim(10, printFlag = FALSE)
```

Problems

14.1 A data type that is a table that holds extra information is called what in the tidyverse?

14.2 What is the assignment operator in R that makes a variable global?

14.3 The command `slice(1, A)` returns the ______________ row of the tibble `A`.

14.4 True or false: a tibble is one way to store an event list.

14.5 The function to sort the rows of a tibble with respect to a variable is called ______________.

14.6 The command to draw a uniform random variable from 2 to 4 would be what?

14.7 What function adds a new row to a tibble?

14.8 True or false: the event list for the DES of the $G/G/1$ queue given in the chapter can have at most two events on the list at the end of an iteration.

Chapter 15

Finding statistics for a simulation

Question of the Day

How can the average queue length of a $G/G/1$ queue be estimated from a simulation?

Summary

- **Little's Law** can be used to keep track of statistics that help in estimating the average queue length.
- The use of a **seed** allows us to keep the output of a random simulation constant rather than random.
- **Bar plots** and **boxplots** give an idea of how a random variable is distributed.

15.1 *Adding statistics*

In the Question of the Day, the goal is to both simulate a $G/G/1$ queue and to estimate the average waiting time for the customers involved.

Last time global variables `state` (for the state of the system) and `sim` (for the event list) were introduced. To gather statistics, add a new global variable `statistics`.

There are an infinite number of times in the simulation, but the queue length only changes at a finite number of values. It will be important to be careful about keeping track of the queue length. The idea is to keep track of the area under the graph of the number of customers in the system (much as we did in the proof of Little's law) and use this statistic to find the average waiting time in the end.

The initial mainLoop will need a `statistics` variable with three entries. One entry keeps track cumulatively of the total area under customers in the system.

This will be called `Area`. The second keeps track of the cumulative total of time that the server is idle in an entry named `Idle`. Finally, the third entry keeps track of the total number of arrivals to the queue. This component is named `Arrivals`.

The number of customers in the system consists of those waiting in the queue plus any that are currently being served. In R code, this value is

```
(1 - state["s"]) + state["q"]
```

The above value is multiplied by the length of the time interval where there is no change in the system. The result is added to the total area underneath the customers in the system curve. The length of the time interval can be found by taking the time of the next event minus the current time.

Similarly, the server is idle if `state["s"] > 0`, and multiplying by the time the server is idle adds to the area underneath the idle graph. Finally, keep track of the number of arrivals to the system. This is accomplished by adding one every time the current event type is "ARRIVAL".

```
mainLoopStat <- function(maxsimtime, printFlag = TRUE) {
  time <- 0 # record original time
  while((nrow(sim) > 0) & (sim[1,1] < maxsimtime)) {
    if (printFlag)
      print(sim)
    event <- slice(sim, 1) # take first event (Step 1)
    sim <<- slice(sim, -1) # drop the first event (Step 3)
    executeEvent(event) # execute the event (Step 2)
    # update statistics and clock time
    time <- min(sim[1,1], maxsimtime)
    statistics["Area"] <<-
      statistics["Area"] +
        (time - event$time) * ((1 - state["s"]) +
        state["q"])
    statistics["Idle"] <<-
      statistics["Idle"] +
        (time - event$time) * (state["s"] > 0)
    if (event$type == "ENTER")
      statistics["Arrivals"] <<-
        statistics["Arrivals"] + 1
  }
}
```

These statistics need to be initialized at 0 (and the components named) for this to work properly.

```
runSimStat <- function(maxsimtime, printFlag = FALSE){
  # Initialize event list
  sim <<- tibble(time = 0.0, type = "RUN")
  # Initialize state of the system
  state <<- c(1, 0)
  names(state) <<- c("s","q") # 1 server, 0 in queue
  # Initialize statistics for the system
  statistics <<- c(0, 0, 0)
  names(statistics) <<- c("Area",
    "Idle",
    "Arrivals")
  # Run simulation
  mainLoopStat(maxsimtime, printFlag)
}
```

Once these statistics have been collected, we can use them to find things like the average time a customer spends in the system.

```
reportSimStat <- function(maxsimtime) {
  # Turn totals into averages
  avstat <<- statistics / maxsimtime
  # Use this to estimate waiting time for arrivals
  names(avstat) <<- c("Average system quantity",
    "Idle percentage",
    "Mean interarrival time")
  hatW <- avstat["Average system quantity"] *
    avstat["Mean interarrival time"]
  names(hatW) <- "Estimating waiting time"
  return(hatW)
}
```

Finally, we can do a run for an 8-hour (480 minute) day.

```
endtime <- 480
runSimStat(endtime)
reportSimStat(endtime)
```

```
## Estimating waiting time
##               0.6622592
```

15.2 Pseudo-random numbers

A random stream of numbers is a mathematical idealization of a lack of information. It is possible to come close to this ideal by using complicated algorithms that make the next number in the stream unpredictable. It turns out that this is the same kind of mathematics needed for cryptographic systems. Decades of the Cold War followed by decades of Internet commerce have made our cryptographic schemes (and hence our ability to generate random numbers) very good indeed.

To distinguish an ideal stream of random variables from the kind generated by computers, the computer stream is called a *pseudorandom* stream of random variables.

Definition 64
A stream of numbers generated by a deterministic computer algorithm is called a **pseudo-random** stream of random variates.

Every time a simulation is run, the results will be (with very high probability) different. However, sometimes (for debugging purposes or to compare different codes) it is helpful to have the same pseudo-random variables used each time. The way to accomplish this is to set the *seed* of the generator.

Definition 65
The **seed** of a pseudorandom stream completely determines the values of the stream.

The `set.seed` function can be used to set the seed in R. For instance,

```
set.seed(123)
x <- runif(3)
set.seed(321)
y <- runif(3)
set.seed(321)
z <- runif(3)
kable(tibble(x, y, z))
```

x	y	z
0.2875775	0.9558938	0.9558938
0.7883051	0.9372855	0.9372855
0.4089769	0.2382205	0.2382205

The `x` and `y` variables receive different values, because the seed was set differently before each of these calls. If the seed is set before a simulation is run, then it fixes the random variables generated by the simulation, and so the results will come out the same way each time.

```
set.seed(123454321)
runSimStat(endtime)
reportSimStat(endtime)
```

```
## Estimating waiting time
##                0.534187
```

The above three lines of code will set the seed to 123454321, and will always result in an output of 0.534187 from the simulation no matter how many times it is run.

15.3 Distributions of statistics

Suppose the goal is to know when the length of the queue gets very long, and how often. This information can be estimated with a statistics variable with more rows, and one way to do that is to make the statistics variable into a tibble.

```
statistics <<- tibble(
  time = 0,
  queue_length = 0,
  avail_s = 1
)
```

Now insert this code into `runSimStat`:

```
runSimStat <- function(maxsimtime, printFlag = FALSE) {
  # Initialize event list
  sim <<- tibble(time = 0.0, type = "RUN")
  # Initialize state of the system
  state <<- c(1, 0)
  names(state) <<- c("s","q") # 1 server, 0 in queue
  # Initialize statistics for the system
  statistics <<- tibble(
    time = 0,
    queue_length = 0,
    avail_s = 1
  )
  # Run simulation
  mainLoopStat(maxsimtime, printFlag)
}
```

Next, it is necessary to update our statistics handling in `mainLoop`. Note that the row name of the tibble is one more than the current length of the queue.

```
mainLoopStat <- function(maxsimtime, printFlag = TRUE) {
  time <- 0 # record original time
  while((nrow(sim) > 0) & (sim[1,1] < maxsimtime)) {
    if (printFlag)
      print(sim)
    event <- slice(sim, 1) # take first event (Step 1)
    sim <<- slice(sim, -1) # drop first event (Step 3)
    # update statistics and execute event
    statistics <<- statistics |>
      add_row(time = event$time,
              queue_length = state["q"],
              avail_s = state["s"])
    executeEvent(event) # execute the event (Step 2)
    statistics <<- statistics |>
      add_row(time = event$time,
              queue_length = state["q"],
              avail_s = state["s"])
    time <- min(sim[1, 1], maxsimtime)
    # Update time spent in each state
    #   state["q"] + 1 is the row
    #   1 is the column
   }
}
```

```
runSimStat(100, printFlag = FALSE)
```

With this more detailed data, it is possible to plot the queue length as a function of time. For instance, the following plots the queue length between the times of 25 and 50.

```
statistics |>
  filter(time >= 25 & time <= 50) |>
  ggplot() +
    geom_line(aes(x = time, y = queue_length),
              color = "blue")
```

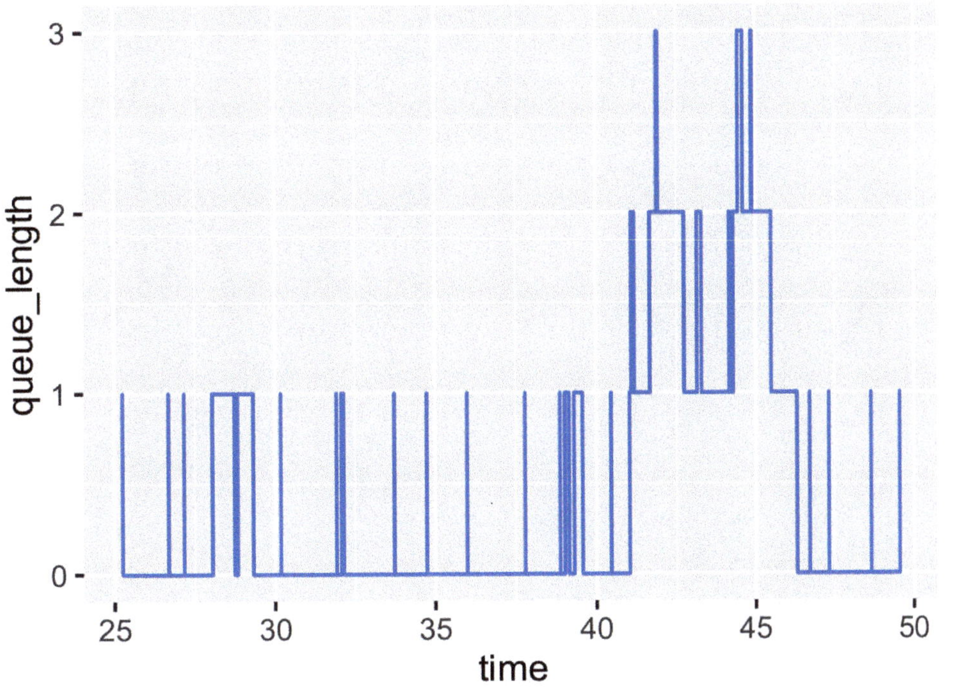

This also gives the server availability over time. For instance, the following is the server availability from times 0 up to 25.

```
statistics |>
  filter(time >= 0 & time <= 25) |>
  ggplot() +
    geom_line(aes(x = time, y = avail_s),
              color = "red")
```

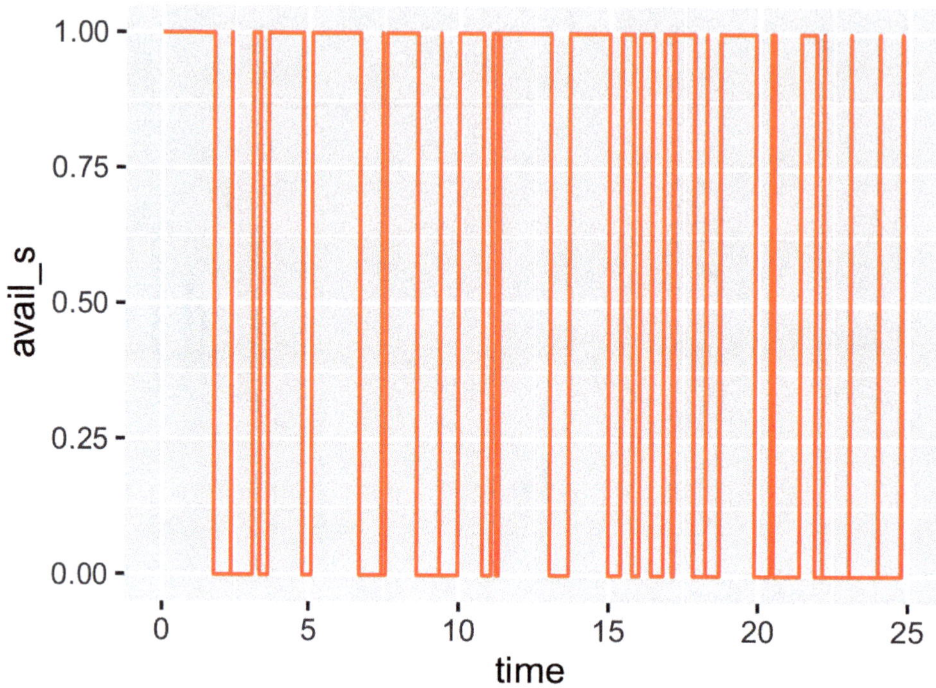

Cumulative statistics of queue length

```
rm(statistics)
statistics <<- tibble(
  queue_length = 0:20,
  time_spent = rep(0, length(queue_length))
)
```

Now insert this code into `runSimStat`:

```
runSimStat <- function(maxsimtime, printFlag = FALSE) {
  # Initialize event list
  sim <<- tibble(time = 0.0, type = "RUN")
  # Initialize state of the system
  state <<- c(1, 0)
  names(state) <<- c("s","q") # 1 server, 0 in queue
  # Initialize statistics for the system
  statistics <<- tibble(
    queue_length = 0:20,
    time_spent = rep(0, length(queue_length))
  )
  # Run simulation
```

```
  mainLoopStat(maxsimtime, printFlag)
}
```

Next, it is necessary to update the statistics handling in `mainLoop`. Note that the row name of the tibble is one more than the current length of the queue.

```
mainLoopStat <- function(maxsimtime, printFlag = TRUE) {
  time <- 0 # record original time
  while((nrow(sim) > 0) & (sim[1,1] < maxsimtime)) {
    if (printFlag)
      print(sim)
    event <- slice(sim, 1) # take first event (Step 1)
    sim <<- slice(sim, -1) # drop first event (Step 3)
    executeEvent(event) # execute event (Step 2)
    # update statistics and clock time
    time <- min(sim[1, 1], maxsimtime)
    # Update time spent in each state
    #   state["q"] + 1 is the row
    #   1 is the column
    statistics[state["q"] + 1, 2] <<-
      statistics[state["q"] + 1, 2] + (time - event$time)
   }
}
```

Consider an $M/M/1$ queue with $\rho = 1/2$.

```
ta <- function() return(rexp(1, rate = 1))
ts <- function() return(rexp(1, rate = 2))
```

```
runSimStat(480, printFlag = FALSE)
```

Now make a bar graph of the results.

```
statistics |>
  ggplot() +
    geom_bar(aes(x = queue_length, y = time_spent),
             stat = "identity", color = "blue",
             fill = "gray") +
    theme_classic()
```

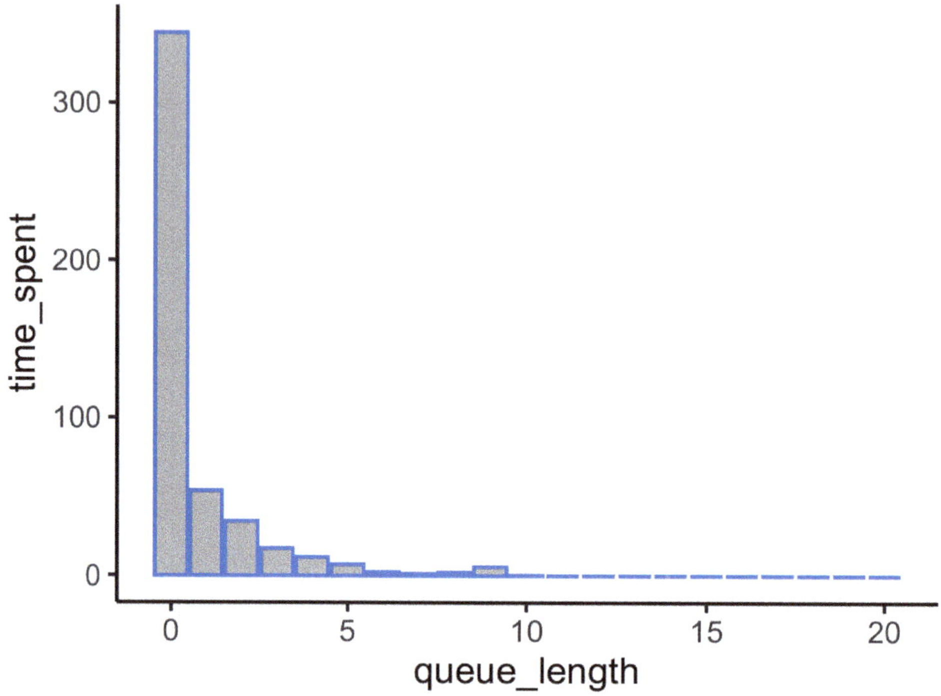

Does this fit with our understanding of continuous time Markov chains? Recall that the analytical solution was that the total number of customers in the system plus one is a geometric random variable with parameter ρ, which is $1/2$ in this example.

Problems

15.1 Consider the following code.

```
ta <- function() return(rexp(1, rate = 4.3))
```

If function `ta` is the distribution of interarrival times, the distribution the service time is a general distribution, and there are 3 servers, what is the notation for this queue?

15.2 Consider the following code.

```
print(mean(rexp(1000000, rate = 4.3))
```

What value will the output be close to?

15.3 True or false: resetting the seed to the same value at start of two simulations will result in the same random choices.

15.4 What will be the output of the following code?

```
set.seed(123)
x <- runif(3)
set.seed(321)
y <- runif(3)
set.seed(321)
z <- runif(3)
print(sum(x == y) + sum(y == z))
```

15.5 Running the following code would get output close to what value?

```
mean(runif(100000))
```

15.6 Running the following code would get output close to what value?

```
mean(runif(100000, min = 2, max = 4))
```

15.7 Suppose the queue length statistics are stored in a tibble `df` with columns named `queue_length` and `time_spent`. Write code to create a bar plot of this data where the bars are filled with blue color and the outline of the bars is black using the classic theme.

15.8 Suppose the queue length statistics are stored in a tibble `df` with columns named `queue_length` and `time_spent`. Write code to create a bar plot of this data where the bars are filled with blue color and the outline of the bars is black.

Chapter 16

Stochastic Petri Nets

Question of the Day

How can a $G/G/3$ queue be modeled using a Stochastic Petri Net?

Summary

- In a **bipartite** graph, nodes are divided into two sets. Edges must contain one node from the first set and one node from the second set.
- A **Petri Net** is a bipartite graph where one set are called **places** and the other set are called **transitions**. Each place is given a nonnegative integer that represents how many tokens are in that place. Each transition **fires** when all incoming places have at least one token. The firing removes one token from each input and adds a token to each output.
- **Stochastic Petri Nets** assign either a number or distribution to each transition: the output tokens do not appear until a time equal to a random variate generated from the distribution.
- **Weighted** arcs entering (leaving) transitions change the number of tokens required to fire (output upon firing).
- **Inhibitor arcs** prevent a transition from firing when the place it comes from is occupied. With inhibitor arcs, Petri Nets are Turing complete.

There are always tradeoffs in the methodology used to build simulations. For instance, DES simulations are incredibly general and able to handle complex situations. Unfortunately, this complexity also makes them difficult to analyze and prove that they are acting as the user desires.

Petri nets are a way to build a simulation that in some cases can be analyzed completely to understand their behavior. They are also simpler for non-computer science experts to understand. They are commonly used as an *agent based simulation* system.

16.1 History

Petri nets were developed by Carl Petri in 1962 with the goal of understanding issues in simulation where multiple events can happen simultaneously.

Formally, they are an example of a *bipartite graph.*

Definition 66
A directed graph with node set V is **bipartite** if there is a partition (V_1, V_2) of V such that any edge (v_1, v_2) has one end in V_1 and the other in V_2.

Definition 67
A **Petri net** is a bipartite graph where nodes are divided into **places** and **transitions**. Each place has a nonnegative integer label that says how many tokens occupy the place.

A Petri Net then works as follows.

- Say at a transition t is *enabled* if every place connected to t by an incoming edge has at least one token.
- Choose any enabled transition to fire. When the transition fires it removes a token from any place with an arc to t, and adds a token to all places connected by an outgoing arc from t.

For example, consider the following state.

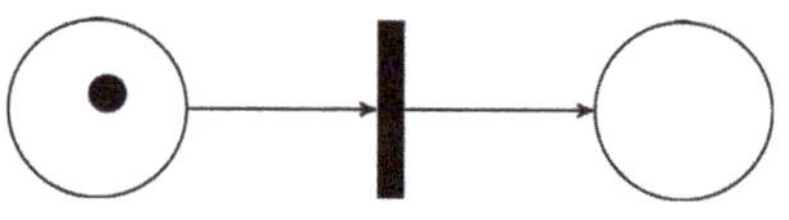

Here the transition is represented by a filled in skinny rectangle, the places are represented by circles, and tokens are represented by small filled in circles.

Because the single place with an arc leading to the transition has a token, the transition is enabled, and because it is the only enabled transition, it fires. This removes the token from the incoming place and adds a token to the outgoing place.

Decisions, decisions

Sometimes there is more than one possible transition that can fire. The point of a Petri Net is that no matter which transition fires first, the Petri Net should be able to handle it. For instance, consider the following simple example.

Here either T_1 or T_2 could fire first. If T_1 fires first the state changes from $(1, 0, 0)$ to $(0, 1, 0)$, while if T_2 fires first the state changes from $(1, 0, 0)$ to $(0, 0, 1)$.

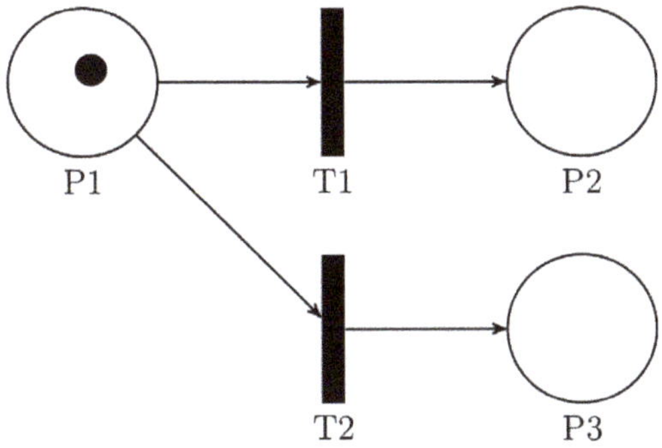

Say that states $(0, 1, 0)$ and $(0, 0, 1)$ are *reachable* from starting state $(1, 0, 0)$. The graph whose nodes are reachable states can be represented using a *reachbility graph.*

Definition 68
A **reachability graph** consists of a node corresponding to a **starting state**, with other nodes corresponding to states reachable via a finite set of (enabled) transition firings. An arc (s_1, s_2) exists if there is an enabled transition that takes the state from s_1 to s_2.

The reachability graph for the above example is

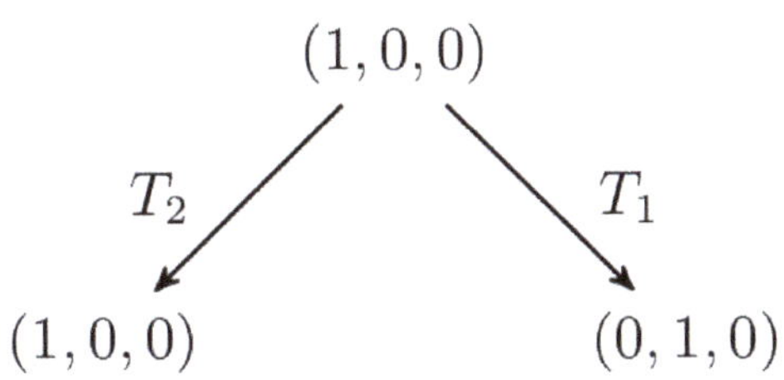

Why Petri nets?

The state at each time step consists of the number of tokens in each place. Because of this, it is often possible to analyze completely the reachable states from a given initial state. That gives the ability to ensure that the simulation stays under control, and nothing unexpected can occur.

Moreover, the idea of a Petri net is that it should be constructed to be robust under firing order. That is, no matter how the choice of which transition to fire is made, the overall behavior of the system should be the same.

Generators

In a DES, a self-loop on an event creates a *generator* that keeps repeating over and over again. This was used to create a set of arrivals for a $G/G/s$ queue.

In Petri nets, a generator is any transition that does not have any incoming nodes. Such a transition is always able to fire.

> **Definition 69**
> A **generator** is a transition with no incoming places.

An example with two generators

Suppose a manufacturing station takes as input an inside piece and a case and puts them together to make a USB drive.
Then for an initial state, the Petri net could look like this.

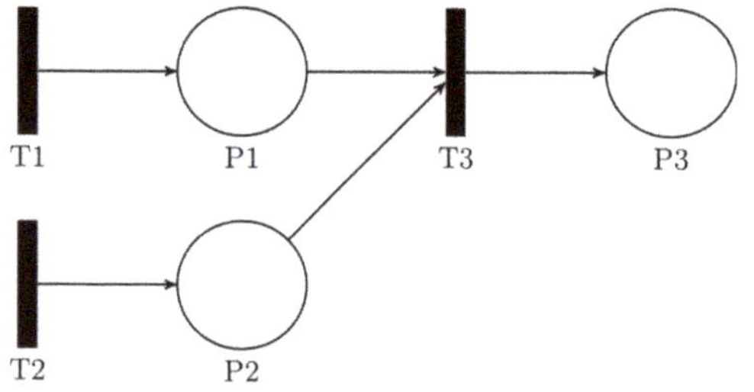

If `T1` fires, the state changes to the following.

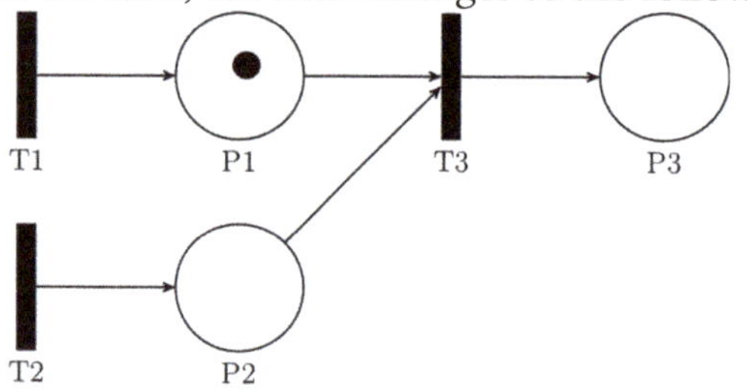

If `T2` then fires, the state changes to the following.

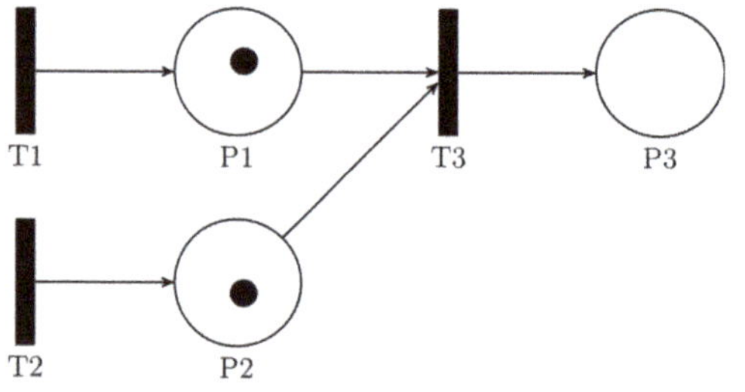

At this point `T1`, `T2`, and `T3` are all enabled. If `T3` fires, the resulting state is:

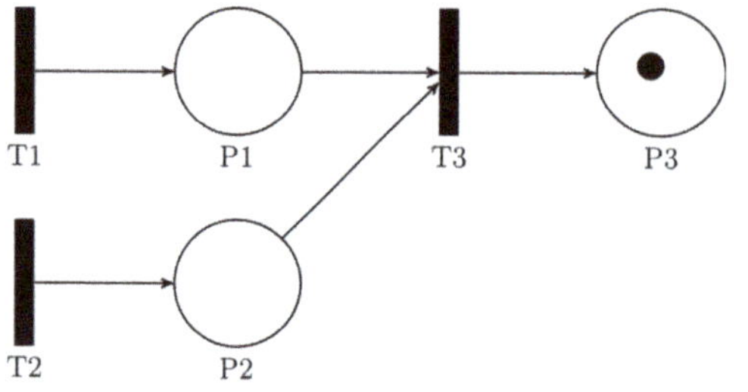

Absorber

The opposite of a generator is an *absorber*, which is a transition with no outgoing edges. This is useful when serviced customers leave the system.

> **Definition 70**
> An **absorber** is a transition with no outgoing places.

16.2 Timed transitions

While the single time step Petri Nets are nice it is a simple extension to add a clock and a time on the transition. In the following net, once the transition on the left fires, the token on the outgoing place does not appear for 2 time steps. This would be a $D/D/1$ queue.

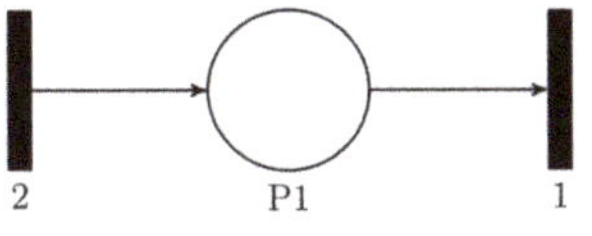

If a random variable is given for the time, then it is independently rolled each time the transition fires.

> **Definition 71**
> A Petri net is **stochastic** if transitions can be labeled with distributions, and an enabled transition fires after an amount of time equal to a draw from that distribution.

With these timed transitions, it is possible to create a $G/G/1$ queue.

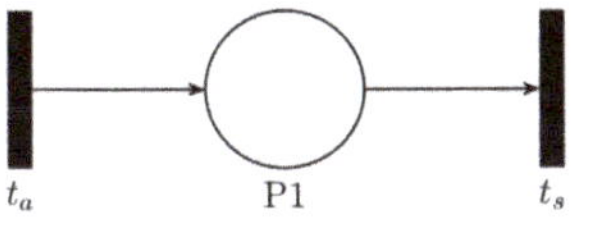

Solving the Question of the Day

However, with more than one server, things become a bit harder. In the Question of the Day, there are three servers.

The idea is to indicate when each server is busy or free with a token. The presence of a token indicates that the server is free. Once it uses its token, it draws in from the queue, and then when the server is finished, it returns the server free token to its place. The final result looks like this.

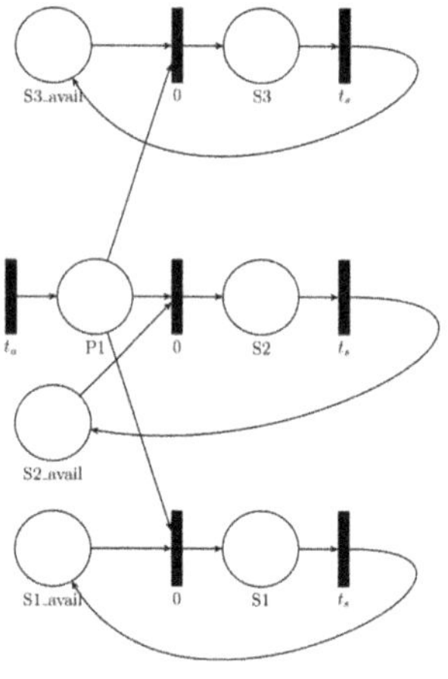

When a token arrives in the queue, any one of the three transitions with time 0 can fire, removing the server free token along with one token in the queue. Then a token is created in the place before one of the three serving transitions. When this transition fires after t_s distributed time, it puts the server free token back into position and is ready to accept another entry from the queue should one be available.

16.3 Weighted transitions

A common extension is to assign a weight to each arc. The weight on an incoming edge to a transition t represents the number of tokens needed to cause t to fire, and this number of tokens is removed during firing. Similarly, the weight on an outgoing edge represents the number of tokens created by t firing.

Consider the following example.

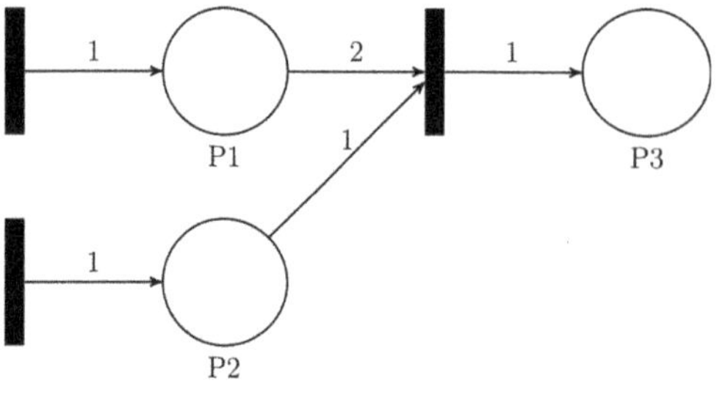

The two transitions on the left are generators, while the one on the right needs 2 tokens from Place 1 and 1 token from Place 2 to produce one token for Place 3.

The states for this net will depend on the order in which the transitions fire. If the generators fire first, followed by the rightmost transition (when enabled), the states will be

$$(0,0,0)$$
$$(1,1,0)$$
$$(0,1,1)$$
$$(1,2,1)$$
$$(0,2,2)$$
$$\vdots$$

No matter what order the transitions fire, Place 1 will be 2 bounded, but Places 2 and 3 are unbounded.

16.4 Inhibitor arcs

An *inhibitor arc* prevents a transition from firing when the place it comes from is occupied. This can be useful in controlling which transition goes first. Moreover, it extends the power of Petri nets greatly: with inhibitor arcs, Petri nets are Turing complete.

Inhibitor arcs are usually denoted using an arc with an empty circle at the end. In the following example, the arc from Place 2 to Transition 3 will prevent Transition 3 from firing as long as Place 2 has one or more tokens.

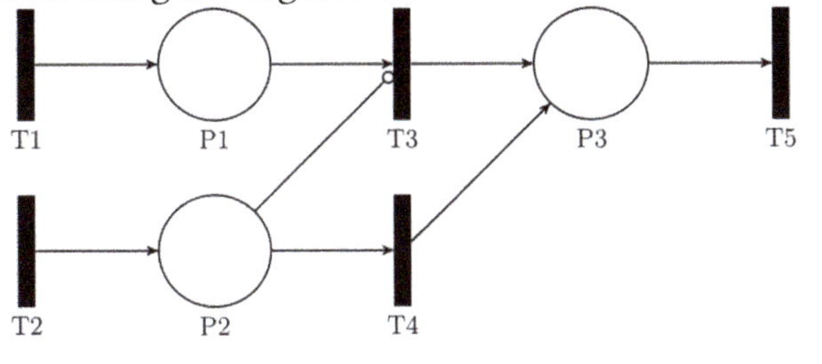

Problems

16.1 A graph where the nodes are partitioned into two sets, and edges must have their head and tail in different sets, is called ______________.

16.2 A Petri Net is a bipartite graph where one type of node is called ______________ and the other type is called ______________.

16.3 The following questions are about unweighted Petri Nets.

a) Transitions fire when there at least _______ token(s) in all input places.

b) True or false: every state is reachable in a Petri Net.

c) True or false: A Petri Net is allowed to fire any enabled transition.

d) True or false: A Petri Net can be represented by a labeled bipartite graph.

16.4 The following questions are about unweighted Petri Nets.

a) Places in Petri Nets are labeled with the number of _______ they contain.

b) True or false: Petri Nets have an order in which they fire their transitions.

c) A transition with no generator is called a ______________.

d) An arrival process for a queue appears as a _______ in a Petri Net.

16.5 An inhibitor arc ______________ a transition from firing when the source place is occupied.

16.6 Suppose a graph is created where the nodes are states of the Petri Net, and an edge connects node i to node j if there is a transition that can fire from node i that leads to node j. This graph is called the ______________ graph of the Petri Net.

16.7 If the transition fires after a random amount of time, the Petri Net is called ______________.

16.8 True or false: in a weighted Petri Net, a certain number of tokens are required to fire a transition indicated by the label on the arc, but only one token is removed per firing from each place at the tail of the arc.

Part IV

Decision Theory

Chapter 17

How to make decisions

Question of the Day

How should decisions be made?

Summary

- **Decision theory** is the study of how to make decisions.
- There are several ways to measure the quality of a decision, they often lead to different decision making.
- The **payoff matrix** of a decision theory problem has a row for each state of nature, a column for each decision, and entries corresponding to utility.
- The **maximin** decision is $\arg\max_{a \in X} \min_{\theta \in \Omega} A(a, \theta)$.
- The **maximax** decision is $\arg\max_{a \in X} \max_{\theta \in \Omega} A(a, \theta)$.
- **Laplace's principle of insufficient reason** chooses $\arg\max_{a \in X} \sum_{\theta \in \Omega} A(a, \theta)$.
- **The Hurwicz principle** for each $\alpha \in (0, 1)$ is

$$\arg\max_{a \in X} \left[\alpha \max_{\theta \in \Omega} A(a, \theta) + (1 - \alpha) \min_{\theta \in \Omega} A(a, \theta) \right]$$

What do decide, herbicide, and homocide have in common? They all end with the Latin prefix -cide. This comes from the Latin caedere, which means *to cut.* When someone de-cides, they are using *de* which is Latin for off. To decide is to cut off the possible actions that might have been taken.

If it is clear what the outcome of a decision will be, then there is no need for decision theory. However, when there are random effects that interact with our decision for the final result, then models can be helpful in deciding which decision is best.

Definition 72
Decision theory is the mathematics of optimal decision making under incomplete knowledge.

17.1 Variables and Payoffs

There are two types of variables in decision theory.

Definition 73
State variables are things that you cannot control.

For instance, the behavior of the U.S. economy over the next five years is out of the control of a decision maker within most corporations. The decision maker must treat this variable as something that is generated independent of their actions. On the other hand, the number of workers to hire for the Christmas season is within most corporation's control. This would be a *decision variable.*

Definition 74
A **decision variable** has a value that you control.

Once you decide on how to set your decision variables, when the state variable values are factored in, the result is a *payoff.*

Definition 75
Given a decision, there will be a **payoff** which is the benefit to you based on the values of the state variables.

Definition 76
If there are a finite number of decisions $a_1, \ldots, a_n$ possible, and only a finite number of possible values for the state variables $s_1, \ldots, s_m$, then the **payoff matrix** is the matrix whose (i, j)th entry is the payoff from employing decision a_i when the true value of the state variable was s_j.

Example 25
The final in the course might be easy or hard. A student can choose to study or not study for the final. The payoff matrix might then be as follows.

	Study	Don't Study
Hard	Satisfaction	Regret
Easy	Wasted Time	Relief

Usually, state variables are random because the decider only has partial information. In the final example, the decider does not know whether the final will be hard or easy, and must make a decision based not on the true answer, but instead upon a probabilistic model of the true answer.

17.2 Utility

The first step in making this a mathematical problem is to assign a numerical value to each outcome. This numerical value is known as the *utility* of the outcome.

Definition 77
A **utility** is a numerical score for each outcome that respects preferences. That is, if the utility of one outcome is less than the utility of the second outcome, the second is preferred over the first.

A note about money.

- Often monetary payoff can be a rough substitute for utility, especially when the numbers are small relative to the decision maker's relative wealth.
- For those with no money, however, utility rarely matches monetary payoff.
- For example, \$10 to someone with no money has a much different value than \$10 to someone with \$1 000 or \$1 000 000.
- This effect is known as *diminishing marginal returns.*
- In terms of Calculus, this means that the derivative of the utility versus money curve is a decreasing function.

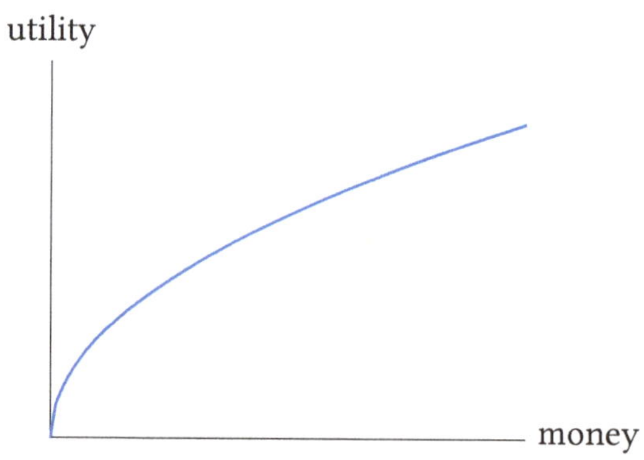

Other terms for a decision are *action* and *strategy*. That is why the formal name for a decision theory problem is a *strategic form*.

Definition 78
The **strategic form** of a decision problem is a triple (X, Ω, A) where

1. X is the nonempty set of strategies for the decider.
2. Ω is the nonempty set of states of nature.
3. $A : (X \times \Omega) \to \mathbb{R}$ is the payoff function.

17.3 Domination

Sometimes decisions are easy to make. If taking one action always results in equal or higher utility than a second action, regardless of the value of the state variables, then it makes sense to always take the first action. Say in this case that the first action *dominates* the second.

Definition 79
For two actions $a_i, a_j \in X$, the action a_i **dominates** a_j if

$$(\forall \theta \in \Omega)(A(a_i, \theta) \geq A(a_j, \theta)).$$

Example 26
Consider payoff matrix with $X = \{a_1, a_2, a_3, a_4\}$ and $\Omega = \{\theta_1, \theta_2, \theta_3\}$.

	a_1	a_2	a_3	a_4
θ_1	5	0	2	1
θ_2	5	3	3	2
θ_2	0	4	2	1

Note that a_3 always beats a_4, no matter what the state of nature is! So in practice, a_4 would never be chosen.

17.4 *Algorithms for making a decision*

Given a set of utilities in a payoff matrix, there are multiple ways that you can use to decide what is the right decision.

Maximin The pessimist fears the worst. The strategy used by such an actor is to choose the action where the worst payoff is the best possible. This is also called the *maximin* choice.

Definition 80
The **maximin strategy** is

$$\arg\max_{a \in X} \min_{\theta \in \Omega} A(a, \theta).$$

Example 27
For our previous example, the worst outcomes from each column are:

a_1	a_2	a_3
0	0	2

Hence pick a_3, since that maximizes the minimum value of the payoff.

Maximax The optimist hopes for the best. The strategy here is to choose the action that has the highest possible payoff over the state variables. That is the *maximax* strategy.

Definition 81
The **maximax strategy** is

$$\arg\max_{a \in X} \max_{\theta \in \Omega} A(a, \theta).$$

Example 28
Continuing our example, the largest payoff in each column is

a_1	a_2	a_3
5	4	3

so the Maximax strategy chooses action a_1.

Laplace's Principle of insufficient reason Laplace considered how to make a decision when you know absolutely nothing about a situation. In this case, it is reasonable to use a uniform distribution. This model makes the state variable θ a random variable where every possible outcome is equally likely. More recently, this principle has become known as using a *Bayesian approach with a noninformative prior.* If every state is equally likely, then it makes sense to pick the strategy that maximizes the *expected utility.*

Example 29
Continuing our example, the expected utility of strategy a_1 in our last example is

$$\mathbb{E}(A(a_1, \theta)) = (1/3)(5) + (1/3)(5) + (1/3)(0) = 10/3.$$

Calculating for all three strategies gives

a_1	a_2	a_3
10/3	7/3	7/3.

So like the optimist, the noninformative prior together with the Bayesian approach yields a choice of a_1.

Of course, dividing each outcome by 3 did not change the relative merits of a_1, a_2, and a_3. Hence the choice made using Laplace's principle is to pick the action with the largest sum of utilities.

Definition 82
Laplace's principle of insufficient reason chooses

$$\arg\max_{a \in X} \sum_{\theta \in \Omega} A(a, \theta).$$

Hurwicz Principle (Degree of optimism) The Hurwicz approach combines the optimistic and pessimistic points of view by taking a linear convex combination of their values.

Definition 83
For $\alpha \in (0,1)$, the **Hurwicz principle** is

$$\arg\max_{a \in X} \left[\alpha \max_{\theta \in \Omega} A(a,\theta) + (1-\alpha) \min_{\theta \in \Omega} A(a,\theta) \right].$$

Some notes:

- When $\alpha = 0$ the result in just maximin strategy.
- When $\alpha = 1$ the result is the maximax strategy.
- When $\alpha \in (0,1)$ the result maximizes a mixture of the minimum and maximum for each column.
- The optimal decision made can be thought of as a function of α.

Example 30
Continuing our example:

$$\begin{array}{ccc} a_1 & a_2 & a_3 \\ 5\alpha & 4\alpha & 3\alpha + 2(1-\alpha) \end{array}$$

Since $5\alpha \geq 4\alpha$ for all $\alpha \in [0,1]$, a_2 can be taken out of the running right now. That leaves the question of when is a_1 better than a_3? To find out solve

$$5\alpha \geq 3\alpha + 2(1-\alpha) = \alpha + 2$$

to get $\alpha \geq 1/2$. Hence the result is

- For $\alpha \in [0,1/2]$, decision a_3.
- For $\alpha \in [1/2,1]$, decision a_1.

Problems

17.1 True or false: higher utility is good.

17.2 True or false: a higher payoff is good.

17.3 True or false.

a) Decision variables are variables that you control.
b) State variables can be either variables that you control or variables that you do not control.

17.4 True or false.

a) There is one right way to make decisions based on a payoff matrix.
b) If the utility is always highest for one action regardless of the state variables, that is the best action.

17.5 Suppose the utility of outcome s_1 is 4, while the utility of outcome s_2 is 4.2. Which outcome is preferred?

17.6 Suppose s_1, s_2, and s_3 have utilities 4.1, 1.2, and 3.7 respectively. Which outcome is preferred?

17.7 Consider the following payoff matrix:

	a_1	a_2	a_3	a_4
Θ_1	4	2	0	6
Θ_2	2	6	0	5
Θ_3	1	3	7	3

a) What decision should you make using the Maximin approach?
b) What decision should you make using the Maximax approach?
c) What decision should you make using the Laplace Principle of Insufficient Reason approach?

17.8 Consider the following payoff matrix:

	a_1	a_2	a_3	a_4
Θ_1	-1	3	4	3
Θ_2	7	6	5	3
Θ_3	2	4	-2	2

a) What decision should you make using the Maximin approach?
b) What decision should you make using the Maximax approach?
c) What decision should you make using the Laplace Principle of Insufficient Reason approach?

17.9 Consider the following payoff matrix:

	a_1	a_2	a_3	a_4
Θ_1	4	2	0	6
Θ_2	2	6	0	5
Θ_3	1	3	7	3

a) What decision should you make using the Hurwicz principle? [For every $\alpha \in [0, 1]$, state what decision is made.]

b) What decision should be made using the Savage minimum regret principle?

17.10 Consider the following payoff matrix:

	a_1	a_2	a_3	a_4
Θ_1	-1	3	4	3
Θ_2	7	6	5	3
Θ_3	2	4	-2	2

a) What decision should you make using the Hurwicz principle? [For every $\alpha \in [0, 1]$, state what decision is made.]

b) What decision should be made using the Savage minimum regret principle?

17.11 Consider the following payoff matrix:

	a_1	a_2	a_3	a_4
Θ_1	4	2	0	6
Θ_2	2	6	0	5
Θ_3	1	3	7	3

Research indicates that Θ_1 and Θ_2 each have a 20% chance of occurring, while Θ_3 has a 60% chance. What decision maximizes expected utility?

17.12 Consider the following payoff matrix

	a_1	a_2	a_3	a_4
Θ_1	-3	2	0	3
Θ_2	2	6	-2	5
Θ_3	1	3	5	3

a) What decision should you make using the Maximin approach?

b) What decision should you make using the Maximax approach?

c) What decision should you make using the Laplace Principle of Insufficient Reason approach?

d) What decision should you make with the Hurwicz Principle for $\alpha \in [0, 1]$?

Chapter 18

The Utility Theorem

Question of the Day

Under what conditions do utilities exist?

Summary

- For a particular action, **regret** is the difference between the best payoff and the payoff you receive.
- The **Savage regret** method tries to minimize the maximum regret you might have over a decision.
- The **Bayesian approach** places a prior distribution over states of nature and makes the decision that maximizes expected utility.
- The von Neumann-Morgenstern Utility Theorem [**vonneumannm1953**] gives sufficient conditions for a utility function to exist.

18.1 Regret

Suppose a decision maker chooses a particular decision a and then later discovers that the true state of nature is θ. Armed with that knowledge, the actor might have chosen differently and made a decision b that resulted in greater utility. The *regret* the decision maker feels is the difference between the best payoff for that state of nature and the payoff that was actually received based upon the initial decision.

Definition 84
The **regret** of decision a and outcome θ is $\max_{b \in X} A(b, \theta) - A(a, \theta)$.

For example, suppose the payoff matrix has the following values.

Payoff Matrix

	a_1	a_2	a_3
θ_1	5	0	2
θ_2	5	3	3
θ_3	0	4	2

For a given decision and outcome, the regret is well-defined. For instance, if the original decision was a_3 and the state ended up being θ_1, the decision maker would regret not picking a_1, since that was higher. To be precise, it was $5 - 2 = 3$ higher, leading to a regret of 3. This can be done for every decision/state pair to form the *regret matrix.*

Regret Matrix

	a_1	a_2	a_3
θ_1	0	5	3
θ_2	0	2	2
θ_3	4	0	2

Therefore, the maximum regret for each decision is

a_1	a_2	a_3
4	5	3

The decision which minimizes the maximum regret for a decision is a_3. This is called the *Savage regret decision.*

Definition 85
The **Savage regret decision** is

$$\arg\min_{a \in A} \max_{\theta \in \Omega} \left[\max_{b \in X} A(b, \theta) - A(a, \theta) \right].$$

18.2 Using partial information

Remember that the way to encode partial information about the state of nature is to use a probability distribution. Consider the following payoff matrix.

	Study	Don't Study
Final is Hard	8	2
Final is Easy	6	10
Sun explodes	0	12

Laplace's principle of insufficient reason would say that $(1/3, 1/3, 1/3)$ is the probability vector for these three states given no information about the three possible states. Someone who knows anything at all about physics just might have a slightly lower than $1/3$ chance for the sun exploding.

The person using Maximin is a pessimist who makes $\mathbb{P}(\text{worst option}) = 1$. But even the worst pessimist would hesitate before putting $\mathbb{P}(\text{sun exploding}) = 1$.

Another problem with Maximin is that it fails to have a property called *row linearity*. The idea of row linearity is that if you add a constant to any particular row, it should not affect the optimal decision.

For instance, the old decision was a_2 (don't study). Say that -3 is added to the first row. The new table becomes:

	Study	Don't Study
Final is Hard	5	-1
Final is Easy	6	10
Sun explodes	0	12

Our new minimum vector is:

S	NS
0	-1

The new decision is a_1 simply by changing the first row.

18.3 Expected Utility Hypothesis

The *expected utility hypothesis* goes back to Daniel Bernoulli in 1738 and is an extension of Laplace's principle. It does satisfy row linearity. The idea is as follows.

1. Assign a probability to each state indicating the partial information an individual has about the truth of the statement (this is called a *prior* distribution or a *statistical model*.)

2. Calculate the expected payoff from each decision.

3. Choose the decision that maximizes expected utility.

Example 31
If there is a 60% chance that the final is hard, $40\% - \epsilon$ that it is easy, and ϵ chance that the Sun explodes

$$\mathbb{E}[\text{payoff}|\text{Study}] = (0.6)(8) + (0.4 - \epsilon)(6) + \epsilon(0) = 7.2 - 6\epsilon.$$

S	NS
$7.2 - 6\epsilon$	$5.2 + 2\epsilon$

So for small ϵ, the action should be to study.

Row linearity To see why this has the row linearity property, suppose that we add a constant C to a particular row. Suppose that row (that state of nature) occurs with probability p_i.

Then the effect of this is to add $p_i C$ to each of the mean payoffs, regardless of the decision made. This does not change the max expected payoff decision, because every decision gets the same constant added to it, so they stay in the same relative order.

Does this work? In 1947, John von Neumann and Oskar Morgenstern considered the condition that were needed to hold before the expected utility hypothesis could be used to obtain the best decision. They came up with 4 rules that if an individual made decisions according to these rules, then there must exist a utility function underlying their decisions. First some definitions.

> **Definition 86**
> A **utility function** is a function that returns a utility value U given the random state of nature $\theta \in \Omega$. That is, $U : \Omega \to \mathbb{R}$.

> **Definition 87**
> A **lottery** is a probability distribution on outcomes, together with a utility function.

For instance, suppose $\Omega = \{a, b, c\}$, and lottery L has

$$\mathbb{P}(\{a\}) = 0.4, \mathbb{P}(\{b\}) = \mathbb{P}(\{c\}) = 0.3$$

with

$$U(a) = 16,\ U(b) = 20,\ U(c) = 5.$$

Then because the state of nature is uncertain, the value of U is a random variable and has an expected value. In this case,

$$\mathbb{E}_L(U) = 0.4 \cdot 16 + 0.3 \cdot 20 + 0.3 \cdot 5 = 13.90.$$

A lottery distribution can be represented by a vector p which has an entry for every state of nature and whose entries add up to 1.

> **Definition 88**
> Let P consist of the set of vectors in $[0, 1]^n$ such that the entries add up to 1. This set is called the **probability simplex**.

Definition 89
For lotteries L, M write

- $L = M$ if the actor is **indifferent** to playing lottery L or M.
- $L \prec M$ if the actor **prefers** lottery M to L.

Note that having $L = M$ does not mean that the probability vector and utility functions are the same, just that given a choice between playing the two lotteries, the actor would be equally happy with either one. Following the usual notation, if $L = M$ or $L \prec M$, then write $L \preceq M$.

Given two lotteries L and M, we can think about flipping a coin that comes up heads with probability p and tails with probability $1 - p$. If the coin comes up heads, then we play lottery L, otherwise we play lottery M. This gives us the *convex linear combination* of the lotteries.

Definition 90
Given two lotteries L and M, suppose $X \sim \text{Bern}(p)$ (where $p \in [0, 1]$) is independent of the state of nature. Let $N = pL + (1 - p)M$ be the lottery where the agent plays L if $X = 1$ and plays M if $X = 0$. Call N the **convex linear combination** of L and M.

(Note often the word *linear* is dropped in practice.)

Definition 91
A set of elements where the convex linear combination of any two elements are in the set is called **convex**.

Because of linearity of expectation, the convex combination of two lotteries has a mean equal to the convex combination of the means.

Fact 33
For lotteries L and M with utility function U, then

$$(\forall p \in [0, 1])(\mathbb{E}_{pL+(1-p)M}(U) = p\mathbb{E}_L(U) + (1 - p)\mathbb{E}_M(U)).$$

Axioms of Utility Theory (vN-M Axioms) Originally, axioms meant things that were self evident. Today, mathematicians use axiom as a synonym for definition. However, while the axioms/definitions created by von Neumann and Morgenstern might not be self-evident, they are also reasonable things to work with. There are four axioms.

Definition 92
The von Neumann-Morgenstern Axioms are:

1. **Completeness** For all lotteries L and M, exactly one of the following is true:
$$L \prec M, L = M, \text{ or } M \prec L.$$
2. **Transitivity** If $L \preceq M, M \preceq N$, then $L \preceq N$.
3. **Continuity** If $L \preceq M \preceq N$, there exists a $p \in [0, 1]$ such that
$$pL + (1-p)N = M.$$
4. **Independence** If $L \prec M$, then for any lottery N and $p \in (0, 1]$,
$$pL + (1-p)N \prec pM + (1-p)N.$$

Theorem 8 (Von Neumann-Morgenstern Utility Theorem)
A complete and transitive preference relation $\preceq$ on a finite set of lotteries satisfies continuity and independence if and only if there is a random variable U such that for all lotteries L and M:
$$L \prec M \Leftrightarrow \mathbb{E}_L[U] < \mathbb{E}_M[U]$$
$$L = M \Leftrightarrow \mathbb{E}_L[U] = \mathbb{E}_M[U].$$

In other words, if the first two axioms hold, then there is a utility function whose value allows us to compare all pairs of lotteries if and only if the last two axioms hold.

18.4 The shape of the utility curve

The Utility Theorem is very powerful, but it tells us very little about the shape of the utility curve as a function of monetary reward. It turns out that three particular shapes are very important.

- Straight line
  - 1st dollar exactly as valuable as the millionth dollar.
  - This is a useful model when the money associated with outcomes is small compared to the actor's net worth.
- Risk Averse (RA)
  - Shape concave (convex down).

  - Avoids big risks.
  - Typical function when outcomes comparable to net worth.

- Risk Seeker (RS)
  - Shape convex (convex up).
  - Millionth dollar worth *more* than 1st dollar.
  - Trying to be first to reach a milestone.
  - Going for the big score.
  - A monopoly will often behave this way.
  - Venture capitalists.
  - "With $100,000, I could open a restaurant!"

In 1979, Kahneman and Tversky designed and ran a series of experiments to see what the utility curve of participants looked like in the real world. It turned out that most people do not use well defined utility curves in making their decisions. In fact, they found that they could alter the curve that was implicitly being used by rephrasing the question in different ways. So while utility maximization is good as a principle, it should not be taken to represent how real people make decisions in practice.

Problems

18.1 True or false: Regret is the negative of utility.

18.2 True or false: The Savage regret method tries to minimize the maximum regret possible.

18.3 For each of the following, say whether or not this vector is part of the probability simplex.

a) $(0.3, 0.5, 0.2)$
b) $(0.3, 1.2, -0.5)$
c) $(0.1, 0.1, 0.2)$
d) $(1 - \epsilon, \epsilon/2, \epsilon/2)$ for $\epsilon \in [0, 0.1)$.

18.4 For each of the following, say whether or not this vector is part of the probability simplex.

a) $(0.3, 0.1, 0.1, 0.2, 0.3)$
b) $(0.5, 0.5)$
c) $(-0.5, 1.5)$

18.5 Suppose that an actor's preferences for lotteries are complete, transitive, continuous, and independent with utility function U.

a) Suppose for lotteries L and M, $U(L) \leq U(M)$. What can be said about the preferences between L and M?

b) Suppose for lotteries L and M, $U(L) < U(M)$. What can be said about the preferences between L and M?

18.6 Suppose that an actor's preferences for lotteries are complete, transitive, continuous, and independent with utility function U.

a) Suppose for lotteries L and M, $U(L) = 17.1$ and $U(M) = 15.2$. What can be said about the preferences between L and M?

b) Suppose for lottery N, $U(N) = 16$. Illustrate the continuous axiom by finding p such that $pL + (1 - p)M = N$.

18.7 If lotteries are transitive, and for lotteries A, B, and C, $A \preceq B$ and $B \preceq C$ what can be said about the preference between A and C?

18.8 Say lotteries are independent, A, B, and C are lotteries with $A \prec B$. What can be said about the lotteries $0.4A + 0.6C$ and $0.4B + 0.6C$?

Chapter 19

Proof of the Utility Theorem

Question of the Day

How is the von Neumann-Morgenstern Utility Theorem proved?

Summary

- Fortunately the axioms are set up so that other mathematical results from analysis can be used to prove the von Neumann-Morgenstern Utility Theorem.

Start by recalling what the Utility Theorem says.

If a set of lotteries is complete and transitive, then they are continuous and independent if and only if there is a utility function that gives preferences.

These first two axioms say the following.

- **Complete** means that for any two lotteries L and M, one of the following is true:
$$L \prec M, L = M, M \prec L.$$
- **Transitive** means that if $L \preceq M$ and $M \preceq N$, then $L \preceq N$.

The last two axioms then are as follows.

- **Continuous** means if $L \preceq M \preceq N$, there is a $p \in [0, 1]$ such that
$$pL + (1 - p)N = M.$$

- **Independence** means that for $L \prec M$, any lottery N, and $p \in (0,1]$,

$$pL + (1-p)N \prec pM + (1-p)N.$$

Begin with the easier direction.

19.1 Proof that Completeness+Transitive+Utility implies Continuity+Independence

Proof. Suppose $L \preceq M \preceq N$. For the case when $L = N$ then any choice of $p \in [0,1]$ will do. Suppose $L \prec N$. Then $\mathbb{E}_N[U] > \mathbb{E}_L[U]$, and $\mathbb{E}_N[U] \geq \mathbb{E}_M[U]$. So let

$$p = \frac{\mathbb{E}_N[U] - \mathbb{E}_M[U]}{\mathbb{E}_N[U] - \mathbb{E}_L[U]}.$$

Recall that a mixture lottery like $pL + (1-p)N$ can be resolved by flipping a Bernoulli B with parameter p. If $B = 1$, then use L, otherwise use N. By the Fundamental Theorem of Probability,

$$\begin{aligned}
\mathbb{E}_{pL+(1-p)N}[U] &= \mathbb{E}_B[\mathbb{E}_{pL+(1-p)N}[U|B]] \\
&= \mathbb{E}_B[\mathbb{1}(B=1)\mathbb{E}_L[U] + \mathbb{1}(B=0)\mathbb{E}_N[U] \\
&= p\mathbb{E}_L[U] + (1-p)\mathbb{E}_N[U]] \\
&= \mathbb{E}_N[U] - p(\mathbb{E}_N[U] - \mathbb{E}_L[U]) \\
&= \mathbb{E}_N[U] - (\mathbb{E}_N[U] - \mathbb{E}_M[U]) \\
&= \mathbb{E}_M[U].
\end{aligned}$$

Since their utilites are equal, the player is indifferent to the lotteries. That means $M = pL + (1-p)N$ and continuity is satisfied.

To show independence, suppose that $L \prec M$, so $\mathbb{E}_L[U] < \mathbb{E}_M[U]$. Then

$$\begin{aligned}
\mathbb{E}_{pL+(1-p)N}[U] &= p\mathbb{E}_L[U] + (1-p)\mathbb{E}_N[U] \\
&< p\mathbb{E}_M[U] + (1-p)\mathbb{E}_N[U] \\
&= \mathbb{E}_{pM+(1-p)N}[U].
\end{aligned}$$

□

19.2 Proof that Completeness+Transitive+Continuity+Independence implies Utility

The other direction is more difficult! Begin by proving a weaker form of the theorem that only works when there is a maximal and minimal lottery.

Fact 34
For any precedence relation on lotteries that is complete, transitive, and continuous, if there exist lotteries L and M such that for all other lotteries N, $L \preceq N \preceq M$, then there is a utility function that respects the precedence relation.

Proof. Set $U(M) = 1$ and $U(L) = 0$. Let N be any lottery. By the continuity axiom there is a $p \in [0, 1]$ such that

$$pL + (1 - p)M = N.$$

Set $U(N) = 1 - p$.

The rest of the proof is to show that this choice of U respects the precedence relation. Let $N_1 \preceq N_2$ be two lotteries. Then $N_1 \preceq N_2 \preceq M$ so by the continuity axiom there is a $p \in [0, 1]$ such that $N_2 = pN_1 + (1 - p)M$.

Say that for $X \sim \text{Bern}(p)$, N_2 plays N_1 if $X = 1$ and M if $X = 0$. Similarly, $N_1 = p_1L + (1 - p_1)M$. So for $Y \sim \text{Bern}(p_1)$ say N_1 plays L if $Y = 1$ and M otherwise. Make X and Y independent.

That means that in order to end up playing L, first $X = 1$ so that N_1 is used, and then $Y = 1$ so L is played. Note $\mathbb{P}(X = 1, Y = 1) = pp_1$. If the lotteries do not end up playing L then they play M.

By continuity, there exists p_2 such that $N_2 = p_2L + (1 - p_2)M$. By the above argument $p_2 = pp_1$. Since $p \in [0, 1]$ that makes $p_1 \geq p_2$ and $1 - p_1 \leq 1 - p_2$. But that makes $U(N_1) \leq U(N_2)$, and the precedence relation is preserved by the utility function. □

Proof for general lotteries If a set of lotteries has no maximal or no minimal lottery, then the problem becomes much deeper. It is necessary to use a result from analysis that for any convex set with a complete, transitive precedence relation, there exists an affine function whose value respects the precedence relation. To begin, consider when a function is *affine*.

Definition 93
A function f is affine if for all vectors x and y and $\lambda \in [0, 1]$,

$$f(\lambda x + (1 - \lambda)y) = \lambda f(x) + (1 - \lambda)f(y).$$

Example: $f(x) = 3x - 2$. Then

$$\begin{aligned} f(\lambda x_1 + (1 - \lambda)x_2) &= 3(\lambda x_1 + (1 - \lambda)x_2) - 2(\lambda + (1 - \lambda)) \\ &= \lambda(3x_1 - 2) + (1 - \lambda)(3x_2 - 2) \\ &= \lambda f(x_1) + (1 - \lambda)(x_2) \end{aligned}$$

Fact 35
Suppose U is a utility function. Then so is $U' = aU + b$ where $a, b \in \mathbb{R}$ and $a > 0$.

Proof. Since $a > 0$, U' is an increasing function of U, so maintains the same ordering. Suppose

$$\mathbb{E}_{pL+(1-p)N}[U] = \mathbb{E}_M[U].$$

Then

$$\begin{aligned}\mathbb{E}_{pL+(1-p)N}[U'] &= \mathbb{E}_{pL+(1-p)N}[aU + b] \\ &= a\mathbb{E}_{pL+(1-p)N}[U] + b \\ &= a\mathbb{E}_M[U] + b = \mathbb{E}_M[aU + b] = \mathbb{E}_M[U']\end{aligned}$$

so continuity is preserved. □

It turns out that for transitive and complete precedence relations, there is always an affine utility function, a result that comes from the mathematical area of analysis.

Fact 36 (Mixture Space Theorem (Weak form), Herstein and Milnor)
Let Π be a convex subspace, so $(\forall x, y \in \Pi)(\forall \lambda \in [0,1])(\lambda x + (1-\lambda)y \in \Pi)$. Let $\preceq$ be a preference relation on Π that is transitive and complete. If the preference relation $\preceq$ on Π is independent and continuous then there exists an affine utility representation $V : \Pi \to \mathbb{R}$ of $\preceq$.

Moreover, if $V : \Pi \to \mathbb{R}$ is an affine representation of $\preceq$, then $V' : X \to \mathbb{R}$ is an affine representation of $\preceq$ iff there exist $a > 0$ and $b \in \mathbb{R}$ such that $V' = aV + b$.

The proof is beyond the scope of this course. Note that this theorem says that there must be an affine representation, not that every utility is affine.

Affine for functions was defined to convex combinations of two vectors, of course by induction that can be extended to any finite number.

Fact 37
Suppose f is affine and $p_1, \ldots, p_n$ add up to 1. Then for $x_1, \ldots, x_n$,

$$f(p_1x_1 + \cdots + p_nx_n) = \sum_{i=1}^{n} p_i f(x_i).$$

Proof. When $n = 2$, this is just the definition of affine! So use induction on n.

Base Case: $n = 1$, this gives a tautology.

Induction hypothesis: assume true for n, consider $n+1$. Let $\lambda = p_1 + \cdots + p_n$ and $y = (p_1 x_1 + \cdots + p_n x_n)/\lambda$. Then

$$\begin{aligned} f(\lambda y + (1-\lambda)x_{n+1} &= \lambda f(y) + (1-\lambda)x_{n+1} \text{ (affine)} \\ &= \lambda \sum_{i=1}^{n} \frac{p_i}{\lambda} x_i + (1-\lambda)x_{n+1} \text{ (induction)} \\ &= \sum_{i=1}^{n+1} p_i x_i, \end{aligned}$$

which completes the induction. □

At this point it is possible to prove that the continuity and independent axioms imply the existence of a utility function.

Proof. The proof basically collects the facts that we have gathered.

- The set of all lotteries Π is an example of a convex set, and so by the Mixture Space Theorem, there is an affine function V that represents the preference relation $\preceq$ over lotteries. The plan is to use V (which is a function of the lottery) to build a random variable U (which is a function of the outcome.)
- For outcome $\omega \in \Omega$, the *Dirac delta lottery* is the lottery $\delta(\omega)$ where $\mathbb{P}(\omega) = 1$. In other words, in the $\delta(\omega)$ lottery, ω is the outcome with probability 1.
- Our random variable is then $U(\omega) = V(\delta(\omega))$.
- Let L be any lottery in Π. It is a mixture of Dirac delta lotteries:

$$L = \sum_{\omega} L(\omega)\delta(\omega).$$

where $\sum_{\omega} L(\omega) = \mathbb{P}_L(\Omega) = 1$.

- Since V is affine,

$$V(L) = U\left(\sum_{\omega} L(\omega)\delta(\omega)\right) = \sum_{\omega} L(\omega)V(\delta(\omega)) = \mathbb{E}_L(U).$$

- Hence U is a utility representation since $V(L) = \mathbb{E}_L(U)$ respects the preference relation.

□

Problems

19.1 If $u(x) = \sqrt{x}$ and the payoff is $X \sim \mathsf{Unif}([0,1])$, what is the average utility?

19.2 If $u(x) = x^2$ and the payoff is is $X \sim \mathsf{Unif}([0,2])$, what is the average utility?

19.3 Suppose $N = 0.4L + 0.6M$, and $X \sim \mathsf{Bern}(0.4)$ is used to determine which of the two lotteries is played in the mixture. If $X = 1$, which lottery is played instead of N?

19.4 Suppose $R = 0.55L + 0.45M$, and $Y \sim \mathsf{Bern}(0.45)$ is used to determine which of the two lotteries is played in the mixture. If $Y = 1$, which lottery is played instead of R?

19.5 True or false: for u a utility function, $3u + 6$ gives the same preferences as u.

19.6 True or false: for u a utility function, $-u + 10$ gives the same preferences as u.

19.7 Suppose f is an affine function with $f((1,1)) = (4,2)$, $f((1,2)) = (5,3)$.

a) Using the usual rules for scaling and adding vectors in $\mathbb{R}^2$, what does $0.4(1,1) + 0.6(1,2)$ equal?

b) Find $f((1,1.6))$.

19.8 Let g be an affine function with

$$g((0,0)) = (3,1)$$
$$g((2,4)) = (-1,2).$$

Find $g((4,8))$.

Chapter 20

Decision Trees

Question of the Day

Archytas Electronics must decide whether to build a new tablet. The product is expected to have a demand that is either high, low, or medium. Since the money involved is small relative to the earnings of the company, the utility is just taken to be the amount of money involved. If the tablet is not built, the company loses nothing. But if it is built, then the expected payoff depends on whether demand is Good, Moderate, or Bad.

	Demand		
	Good	Moderate	Bad
Probability	15%	60%	25%
Payoff	\$1 500 000	\$600 000	-\$700 000

Summary

- A **decision tree** can be a useful tool for making decisions with many branches and outcomes.

Often, decisions involve a series of simpler decisions, one after the other. A *decision tree* can help keep track of the different possibilities.

Definition 94
A **rooted directed tree** is a directed graph where there is a unique node called the **root**, and there is a unique set of nodes connecting the root to any node in the tree. There are four types of nodes.

- The **root node** is where the decision starts.
- Nodes with no outgoing arcs are **leaves**. These are labeled with a utility value.
- Nodes other than the root and leaves are either **decision nodes** or **chance nodes**. Outgoing arcs from decision nodes are labels with actions. Outgoing arcs from chance nodes are labeled with probabilities.

Definition 95
The **optimal value** (often abbreviated to just value) of a tree is the maximum expected value of the tree assuming optimal decision making.

A common way to draw decision trees uses squares to draw decision nodes and circles to draw chance nodes. Since all arcs are oriented away from the root, typically these edges are not drawn with direction.

Example 32 (Question of the Day)
Archytas Electronics must decide whether to build a new tablet. The product is expected to have a demand that is either high, low or medium. Since the money involved is small relative to the earnings of the company, utility is just taken to be money here. The decision tree looks like:

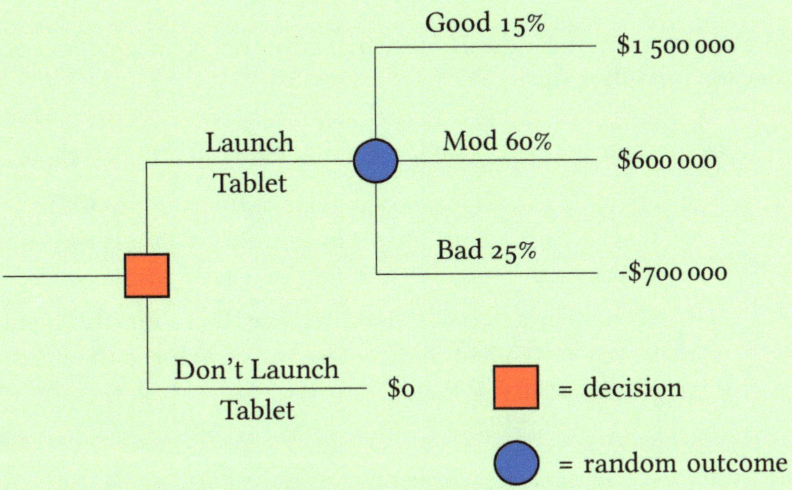

Should the tablet be launched?

Answer There is only one decision to make, right at the beginning. If Archytas launches the product, the expected payoff is:

$$\begin{aligned}(15\%)(1.5\cdot 10^6) + (60\%)(0.6\cdot 10^6) + (25\%)(-0.7\cdot 10^6)\\ = 10^6(.225 + .36 - 0.175)\\ = (0.410)10^6 > 0\end{aligned}$$

So the maximum expected utility decision is to launch the product!

20.1 *Analyzing decision trees*

To solve the Question of the Day, just evaluate the consequences of the first decision. That gives the correct result. If there are multiple decisions and chance nodes, this becomes too complex. Instead, start at the end point (or points) and work backward.

Consider a chance node whose outgoing arcs all lead to leaves with utility outcomes. If that chance node is reached, then the resulting expected utility is just the sum of the probabilities on each branch times the utility value for the leaf it ends up at.

In this approach, replace the chance node with the expected value of the node and the overall tree will retain the same value as before. This operation simplifies the tree while keeping the optimal value the same. This gives the following procedure for analyzing decision trees.

Find the optimal value of a decision tree

- While there are internal nodes (nodes that are either chance nodes or decision nodes) do the following.
    - Pick an internal node whose outgoing edges are all leaves.
        * If this node is a chance node, replace the subtree of the node and its leaves with a leaf node whose utility value is the sum of the outgoing arcs' probability times the leaves' utility value.
        * If this node is a decision node, replace the subtree of the node and its leaves with a leaf node whose utility value is the maximum of its leaves' utility values.

A sample analysis Suppose the decision tree looks like:

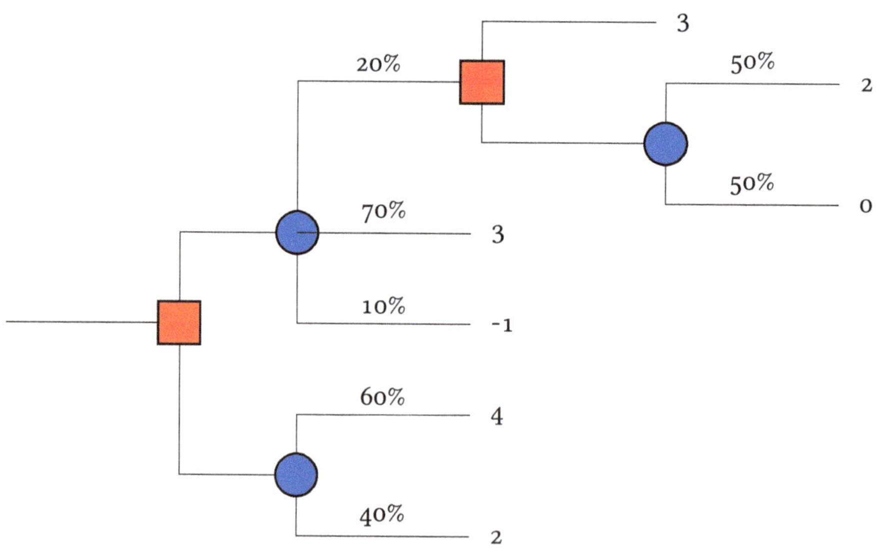

Replace random outcomes in leaves with expectation:

$$(50\%)(2) + (50\%)(0) = 1$$
$$(60\%)(4) + (40\%)(2) = 3.2$$

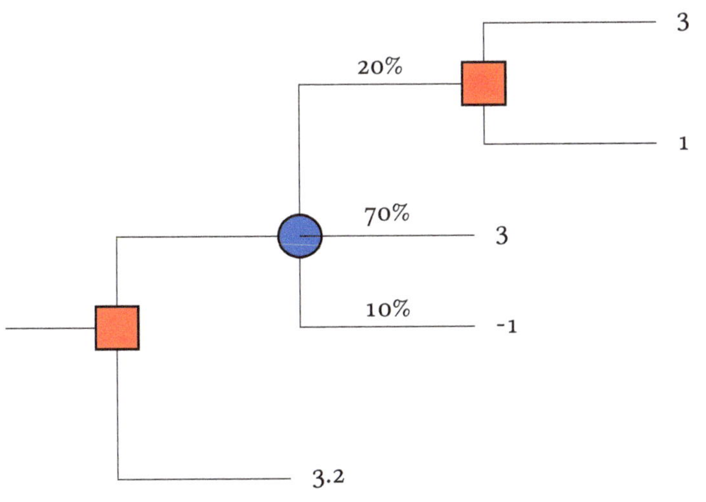

Now consider the decision in the upper right: each outcome of the decision is a number, take the decision that maximizes the value. In this case, take the up branch to gain 3 utility.

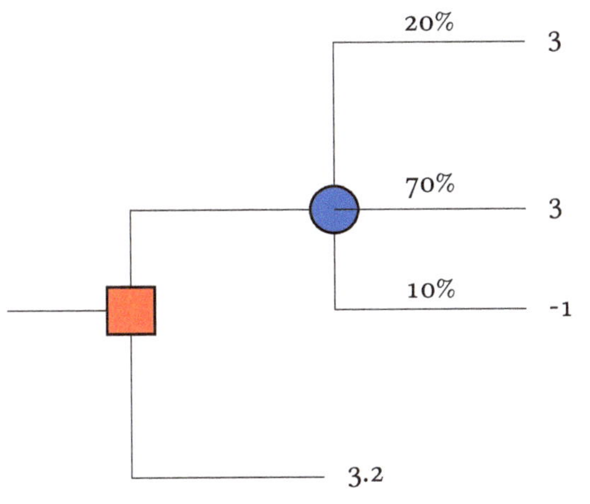

Again trim by finding the expected value:

$$(20\%)(3) + (70\%)(3) + (10\%)(-1) = 2.6$$

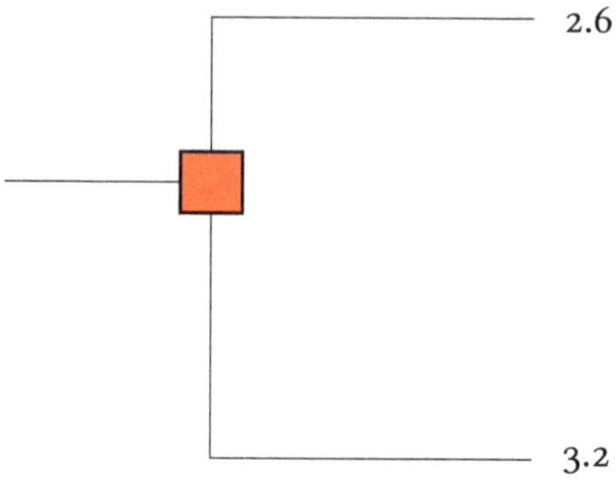

Now there remains only one decision node. Take the down branch to maximize the utility among the leaves.

Note that no matter how large the initial tree is, at each step a chance or decision node is removed. Hence any size tree can be simplified to a root and leaf using this approach!

Problems

20.1 Avatar Pharmaceuticals is thinking about whether or not to pursue a new product. Not pursuing the product costs nothing. If they do pursue the product and it is successful, there is a 30% chance that it will make 1.2 million dollars, but if it is a failure it will cost the company 0.3 million dollars. If money is treated as utility, what should Avatar do to maximize their utility?

20.2 Faramir Electronics is developing new solar cell technologies. The market for their product is believed to have a 40% chance of earning 15 million dollars, and a 60% chance of earning 2 million dollars. If the product costs 3 million dollars to develop and their market cap means that they can treat dollars as utility, what decision should Faramir make?

20.3 A business is testing out a new wind turbine design. It would take \$10 000 000 to develop the design fully. If demand for green energy is good (20%) the business stands to make 30 million dollars, but if it is medium (50%) they will only make 12 million, and if it is bad (30%), they will only make 2 million.

a) Draw the decision tree for this problem.

b) What decision should the business make?

20.4 A government agency is deciding whether to begin an estuary project. The project will cost about three hundred thousand dollars to complete. If severe flooding occurs (which will happen with probability 20%), this will save about one million dollars, but otherwise, it will do nothing.

a) Draw the decision tree for this process.

b) Should the agency undertake the project?

20.5 After working with a consultant, Bender Incorporated has built the following decision tree. What decisions at D_1 and D_2 would maximize expected utility? (Write *up* or *down* for each of the two decisions.)

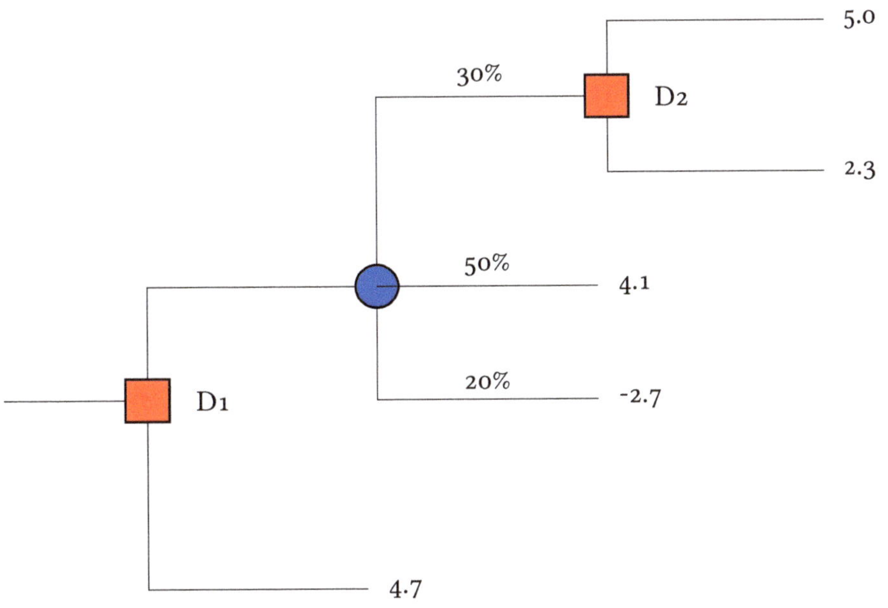

20.6 Canal Incorporated are trying to make several decisions. If their decision tree looks as follows, what is there optimal decision for D_1 and D_2?

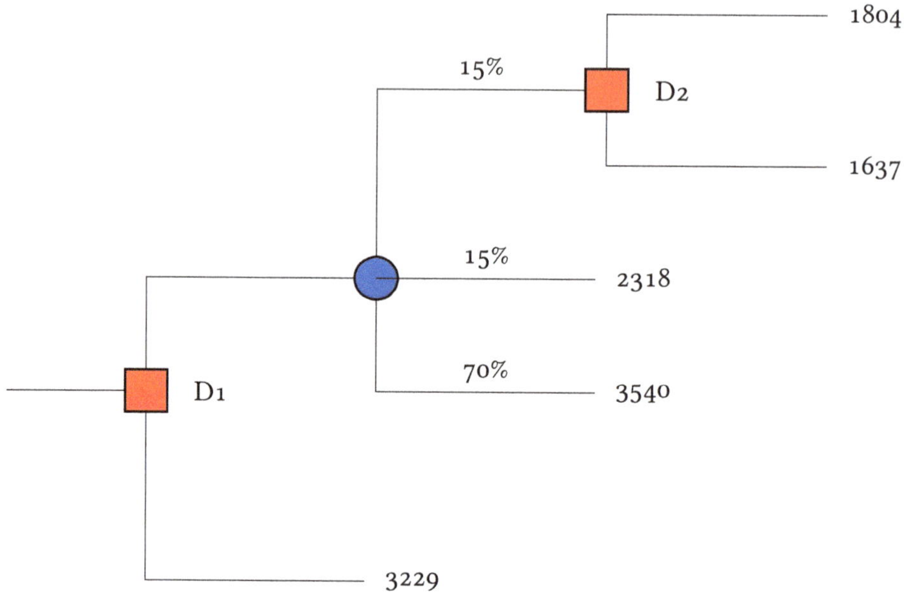

20.7 Suppose that a venture capital (VC) firm has an opportunity to either buy into an IPO for an SSD maker or wait and see how the product performs. If they wait, the SSD maker might sell out its shares, and the VC firm will not be able to invest. The result will be making nothing, and this happens with probability 50%.

If shares remain, then there is a further 35% chance that the shares will be reduced in price, leading to a 23 million dollar windfall. But with 65%, the VC firm will make nothing.

On the other hand, if the VC makes its decision right away, then it must immediately make the next decision whether to buy or not to buy. If it decides to not buy, then again it makes nothing. If it decides to buy, there is an expected 60% chance that it still makes the 23 million dollar windfall, but now with 40% the VC firm loses 5 million dollars.

Draw a decision tree with $D1$ being the first decision to buy or not buy and $D2$ being the second decision to buy in or not buy in.

20.8 Finish the previous problem and determine the optimal decision.

Chapter 21

Psychology of decision making

Question of the Day

What are the common decision making mistakes?

Summary

There are many ways people fail to be rational in decision making. Some of the most common problems are:

- Loss aversion (the Zero illusion)
- Allais Paradox
- Gambler's Fallacy
- Anchoring
- Sunk cost Fallacy

Mathematical models can aid in decision making but they do not tell the whole story. Experiments have shown that people are not always rational when it comes to making choices.

For instance, consider the following scenario. You plan to see a play that costs $40 to attend and find yourself in one of two situations.

- You bought the ticket to the play ahead of time, but when you get to the theater, you find that you have lost the ticket. You still have enough money in your wallet to buy a ticket.

- You did not buy the ticket ahead of time, planning to get it when you arrived at the theater. However, when you open your wallet, you find $40 is missing. You still have enough money in your wallet to buy a ticket.

The question is: in each of these scenarios, do you buy the ticket? It turns out [**kahnemant1982**] that people in scenario 1 where the ticket was lost are much less likely than people in scenario 2 where the money was lost to buy a ticket.

But according to utility theory, that should not happen! In either scenario, you find yourself at the theater without a ticket and down $40. It should not matter *how* you lost the $40, whether directly, or by buying a ticket and then losing the ticket. Still, it does seem to matter to people in making decisions.

This chapter explores the psychological pitfalls that lead to people deviating from expected utility maximization when making choices.

21.1 *Defaults*

Making a decision is hard work, and so anything that helps us avoid the work of making a decision will be justified by our own brains.

Johnson and Goldstein [**johnsong2003**] looked at data about participation in organ donation programs, as recorded on driver's licenses. They found the following participation rates among European countries, presented in Figure 21.1.

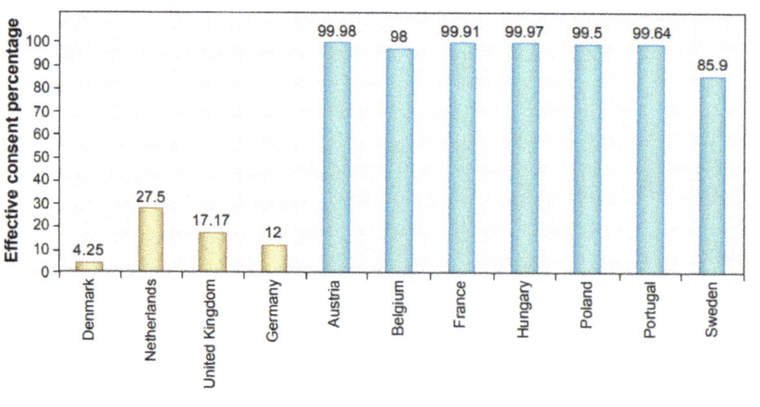

Figure 21.1: *Drawn from [**johnsong2003**].*

There is a sharp gap between the four countries on the left and the seven on the right. But there seems to be no pattern, either socially or geographically that could explain the difference.

The difference was that in the countries on the left, people had to check a box to opt in to organ donation. In the countries on the right, people had to check a box to opt out of organ donation. The default decision was overwhelmingly the reason for the difference.

Why might that be? One theory is that this is a big decision, and big decisions are hard. Much easier is to simply use the *default* position. When evaluating possibilities, it is important to be careful to understand whether the status quo is actually the right decision, or if the goal is just to avoid the difficulty of making a decision.

21.2 Loss Aversion (Zero Illusion)

Loss aversion is the idea that decision makers tend to avoid losses more than enjoy gains. For instance, if I offer two outcomes, a gain of $10 or a loss of $10, the loss is felt as being worse than the gain. The utility curve looks like this.

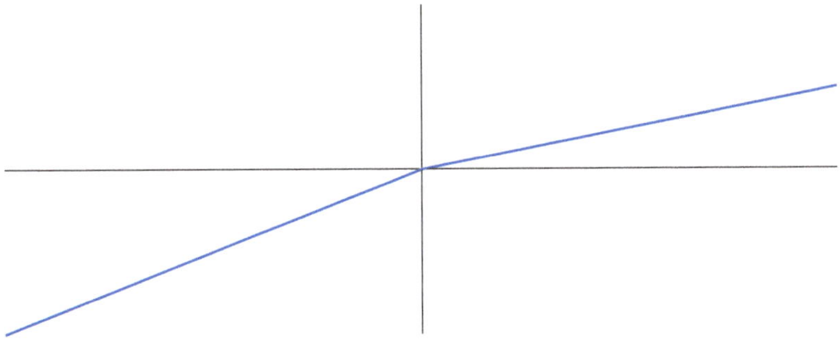

There is a sharp change in the slope of the utility curve at zero (formally a discontinuity in the derivative.) Therefore this phenomenon is also sometimes called the *zero illusion*.

This manifests itself in several ways.

- When dealing with risk, a loss averse investor has a goal of at least breaking even.
- Debt is unduly viewed as bad, and something to be avoided.

21.3 Allais paradox

Maurice Allais [**allais1953**] constructed experiments designed to test if expected utility maximization is the way people make decisions, and ran into a bigger problem than loss aversion. In his findings, there was no utility function at all that would explain the results!

In his study, Allais asked participants to consider two lotteries.

Lottery 1A	100% win $1 million
Lottery 1B	89% win $1 million, 1% win nothing, 10% win $5 million

Given the choice, most people prefer Lottery 1A. Now change the lotteries.

Lottery 2A	89% win nothing, 11% win $1 million
Lottery 2B	90% win nothing, 10% win $5 million

In the same study, they found that participants prefer Lottery 2B. The problem is that this is inconsistent with utility maximization!

Why is this inconsistent?

- Consider a function U.
- Then $1B \prec 1A$ implies $\mathbb{E}_{1B}[U] < \mathbb{E}_{1A}[U]$.

$$\mathbb{E}_{1A}[U] = U(1) > 0.89U(1) + 0.01U(0) + 0.1U(5) = \mathbb{E}_{1B}[U].$$

- Now let's play with $\mathbb{E}_{2A} < \mathbb{E}_{2B}[U]$:

$$\mathbb{E}_{2A}[U] = 0.89U(0) + 0.11U(1) < 0.9U(0) + 0.1U(5) = \mathbb{E}_{2B}[U]$$

- Add $0.89U(1) - 0.89U(0)$ to both sides:

$$U(1) < 0.89U(1) + 0.01U(0) + 0.1U(5)$$

21.4 *Gambler's fallacy*

Suppose a fair coin is flipped 40 times. If it comes up heads 40 times in a row, then the *Gambler's fallacy* is to believe that the next flip is more likely to be a tail. In other words, those falling for this fallacy will think that the probability of a tail coming next will be greater than 50%.

If fact, the situation is even worse than this. Suppose that before the coin is flipped the actor starts with a uniform prior on the probability of heads. After seeing heads come up 40 times in a row, the posterior probability found using Bayes' Rule will have moved most of the probability of heads to be close to 1. So seeing this should cause the user not to believe that a tail is due, but rather the assumption that the coin was fair was false.

21.5 *Anchoring*

The idea of *anchoring* is that hearing numbers that are unrelated to the problem at hand can influence people towards that number. This problem also formed the basis of experiments by Tversky and Kahneman.

Tvesky & Kahneman 1982 Experiment In their experiment, they asked participants what their best guess was for the percentage of African countries that are members of the United Nations. However, before they asked the question, they rolled a random number X uniform from 1 up to 100, and told this number to the participants.

The participants knew that the number was random, and yet they still gave guesses that were closer to the number they were given. This random number X served as an *anchor* for their predictions.

21.6 Sunk Cost Fallacy

In a pure utility decision making framework, people make decisions based on the future effects of a project. However, it is not uncommon for decisions to be made based on past information as well.

For instance, suppose that a company starts a project by investing X dollars. After learning of cost overruns, currently the project needs Y dollars to finish. Should the project be finished?

If the decision makers are trying to maximize expected utility, they should only consider Y and the utility of the outcomes in their decision. The value of X should have no bearing whatsoever on the result.

However, in practice, the amount of money already spent on a project can sharply influence the chance of continuing. Examples where this is often seen include

- Military conflicts,
- large scale real estate projects, and
- choice of undergraduate major.

21.7 What can be done to avoid these fallacies?

The most important thing is to be aware of the various fallacies that prevent rational decision making.

- Try to be explicit about your assumptions in decision making. What are your prior beliefs about probabilities? What are your beliefs about the utility of outcomes?
- At this point you can decide whether you need more information to make an informed decision!

You should also be aware that very smart people have succumbed to these fallacies. Being intelligent does not bring immunity! Some examples.

- Newton lost his fortune in the South Sea Tulip Bubble.
- D'Alembert (who studied in detail the wave equation for the first time) believed the Gambler's fallacy to be true.
- Leibniz (one of the inventors of Calculus and highly regarded philosopher) thought 12 and 11 were equally likely on the sum of two dice.

Everyone has blind spots. Being aware of these problems in our cognition is the first step towards avoiding them.

Problems

21.1 A survey question reads

> *Over 80% of U.K. members surveyed favored greater government expansion. What percentage of U.K. voters do you believe also favored expansion?*

This question is an example of what type of problem in psychological decision making?

21.2 A company is trying to decide to continue their EV project, or abandon it. A board member raises the point that the company has already spent four billion dollars in research on the project. This is an example of what fallacy?

21.3 A company has seen market data that has a good outcome four quarters in a row. They assume that a bad quarter must be coming. This is an example of what fallacy?

21.4 A survey begins with a description that informs participants that 54% of teenagers use their product. The first question of the survey then asks what the person thinks is the percentage of adults that use their product. This is an example of what fallacy?

21.5 Consider lottery N where everyone participating wins 100 dollars, and lottery M where 81% win 100 dollars, 2% win nothing, and the remaining 17% win 250 dollars. Among those surveyed, there is a clear preference for lottery N over lottery M.

In lottery R, 81% win nothing, but 19% win 100 dollars. In lottery S, 83% win nothing, but 17% win 250 dollars. Among those surveyed, there is a clear preference for lottery S with lottery R.

Prove that these choices are not compatible with any utility function.

21.6 Suppose there are lotteries L_1, L_2, L_3, L_4. Lottery L_1 has outcome 34 with probability 85%, 0 with probability 1% and 70 with probability 14%. L_2 always has outcome 34. Those surveyed prefer lottery L_2 with guaranteed winnings to L_1.

Lottery L_3 has outcome 0 with probabiity 85%, and 34 with probabiity 15%. Lottery L_4 has outcome 0 with probability 86%, and 70 with probability 14%. Those surveyed prefer lottery L_4 to L_3.

Show that these preferences are incompatible with the use of expected utility maximization.

21.7 Consider a lottery A with outcomes of 25 dollars and 5 dollars with probabilities 60% and 40$ respectively. Similarly, lottery B is always worth 10 dollars. If an actor prefers to play B to A, show that this is incompatible with any affine utility function, that is, one of the form $U(m) = am + b$ for any positive constant a and m the monetary amount.

21.8 Consider a lottery L_1 that returns \$10 with probability 1/2, and costs \$10 otherwise. A second lottery L_2 is always worth \$0. If the person prefers to play L_2 to L_1, show that this is inconsistent with a utility function of the form $U(m) = am + b$ where m is the monetary payoff and $a > 0$.

Chapter 22

Expected value of perfect information

Question of the Day

Suppose that the economy is expected to be hot, neutral, or cold over the next year. An investor is considering investing either in one of two stocks, or the money market. The payoff matrix is:

	Stock 1	Stock 2	MM
hot	2000	900	600
neutral	200	300	600
cold	-600	-200	600

Given a prob vector for the market of $(40\%, 30\%, 30\%)$, what is the expected value of perfect information to see the future?

Summary

- The **Expected value of perfect information** is the difference between the optimal value of a decision tree where a chance node is replaced with its true value and the optimal value of the decision tree.

Suppose that I can pay \$2 to play a game where I roll a fair single sided die, and receive a number of dollars equal to the roll on the die. Assuming utility equals payoff, then since the game pays \$3.50 on average, the average utility from deciding to play the game is $3.5 - 2 = 1.5$.

Now suppose the person running the game is willing to show me the die before I have to decide whether or not to pay my \$2. How much should the game runner charge for that information? Well, if the die roll is greater than 2, then I would still make the decision to pay the money and play the game. If the die roll is 1 or 2, then I would make the decision not to play and save my money. In this case, I earn \$0. Therefore, on average, each game is worth:

$$(1/6)(0)+(1/6)(0)+(1/6)(1)+(1/6)(2)+(1/6)(3)+(1/6)(4) = 10/6 = \$1.666\ldots.$$

So without the information I earn on average \$1.5, with the information I earn on average \$1.6666..., a slightly higher amount. Therefore the value of the information is (on average)

$$10/6 - 3/2 = 1/6 = 0.1666\ldots.$$

Call this amount the *expected value of perfect information*, or *EVPI* for short.

More generally, call the mean amount of money that can be made given a certain piece of information minus the mean amount of money that can be made without the information the *expected value of perfect information.*

Definition 96
Let $W(I)$ be the utility gained by making an optimal decision given the presence of random outcomes encoded in I. Then the **expected value of perfect information** is the difference between the expected optimal value given the information, and the optimal value without. That is,

$$EVPI = \mathbb{E}\left[\max_{L(I)} \mathbb{E}_{L(I)}(W(I) \mid I)\right] - \max_{M} \mathbb{E}_M(W(I)).$$

To find EVPI

1. Find mean utility of the best decision with no information.
2. Find mean utility of the best decision given the information.
3. Subtract 1 from 2

Question of the day First, it is necessary to find the mean utility without knowledge of the future. There are three investments, each of which have a different expected utility.

$$\mathbb{E}[U_1] = 2000(0.4) + 200(0.3) - 600(0.3) = 680$$
$$\mathbb{E}[U_2] = 900(0.4) + 300(0.3) - 200(0.3) = 390$$
$$\mathbb{E}[U_3] = 600.$$

Therefore, with no information, stock 1 is the decision to make that maximizes expected utility.

On the other hand, let $I \in \{\text{hot,neutral,cold}\}$ tell us the exact state of the market. There are several options.

- If $I = \text{hot}$, choose stock 1 to gain 2000. That means
$$W(I|I = \text{hot}) = 2000.$$
- Similarly,
$$W(I|I = \text{neutral}) = 600$$
because when the market is neutral our best choice is to invest in the money market.
- Last,
$$W(I|I = \text{cold}) = 600,$$
because our best option under these market conditions is also to pick the money market.

Given the probabilities for each of these three outcomes,

$$\mathbb{E}[W(I)] = \mathbb{E}[\mathbb{E}[W(I)|I]] = (0.4)(2000) + (0.3)(600) + (0.3)(600) = 1160.$$

That makes the information worth

$$\text{EVPI} = \mathbb{E}[W(I)] - \mathbb{E}[U] = 1160 - 680 = \boxed{480}.$$

What does this mean? EVPI measures the expected value of reducing uncertainty. In this problem, if a fortune teller could tell you what the market was going to do, you should be willing to pay up to 480 to learn the answer. The EVPI depends on what the information is, and gives a way of measuring the importance of various pieces of information.

22.1 *EVPI for continuous information*

In the question of the day, the information was discrete, but the same idea works just as well for information contained in a continuous setting.

Example Archytas Electronics models demand for their new USB converter in the following way. First, the average consumer demand μ is taken to have distribution Gamma$(10, 0.01)$. Once μ is chosen, actual consumer demand is modeled as Pois(μ). So if D is consumer demand:

$$\mu \sim \text{Gamma}(10, 0.01)$$
$$[D|\mu] \sim \text{Pois}(\mu).$$

Now it costs around \$1800 to change the setting on the factory floor to make the new model. Once the change has been made, the factory will make \$2 per unit sold. So if the decision is to make the new product, the utility will be $2D - 1800$.

1. Given the uncertainly about μ, should we make the product?

2. What is the EVPI to know the value of μ?

This type of model where one parameter is chosen randomly and then another is chosen based on the first is called a *hierarchical model.*

So how did the parameters of 10 and 0.01 introduced in the first place? Presumably, these came from talking to experts and getting information from products introduced earlier.

To solve this problem, it is necessary to understand how conditioning and expected values interact. The most important thing to know is the Fundamental Theorem of Probability.

Theorem 9 (Fundamental Theorem of Probability)
For random variables A and B where A, B and $[A|B]$ all have finite mean,

$$\mathbb{E}[\mathbb{E}[A|B]] = \mathbb{E}[A].$$

Consider using this to find $\mathbb{E}[D]$. The distribution of D is very complicated to determine exactly. Fortunately, it is not necessary to know the distribution of D in order to find its expected value! Recall that $\mathbb{E}[D|\mu] = \mu$ because the mean of a Poisson distributed random variable equals its parameter.

The FTP says to take the expected value again to get rid of any conditioning. This means

$$\mathbb{E}[D] = \mathbb{E}[\mathbb{E}[D|\mu]] = \mathbb{E}[\mu] = 1000.$$

Using this to find the expected utility without information gives:

$$\begin{aligned}\mathbb{E}[2D - 1800] &= \mathbb{E}[\mathbb{E}[2D|\mu]] - 1800 \\ &= \mathbb{E}[2\mu] - 1800 = 2 \cdot 1000 - 1800 = 200.\end{aligned}$$

So without any information, the decision that maximizes expected utility is to make the product!

Now consider how much information about μ is worth. If μ was known exactly, then it is possible to decide more effectively whether or not to make the product. The expected utility conditioned on μ is

$$\mathbb{E}[2D - 1800|\mu] = 2\mu - 1800.$$

If this value is nonnegative, the decision is to make the product, otherwise do not make the product. Hence

$$W(D) = (2D - 1800)\mathbb{1}(2D - 1800 \geq 0) = (2D - 1800)\mathbb{1}(D \geq 900).$$

The easiest way to estimate $\mathbb{E}[W(D)]$ is to use *Monte Carlo simulation* The idea is to generate various values of D and then take the mean to get an estimate.

This can be done in R with the `rgamma` command to generate a random gamma distributed random variable, and the `rpois` command to generate a random Poisson distribution random variable.

```
w <- function(n = 1) {
  mu <- rgamma(n, shape = 10, rate = 0.01)
  d <- rpois(n, mu)
return((2 * d - 1800) * (d > 900))
}
```

Next generate several values and report.

```
set.seed(123456)
n <- 10^8
res <- w(n)
mean(res)
```

```
## [1] 355.7944
```

```
sd(res) / sqrt(n)
```

```
## [1] 0.0479123
```

Notice that the estimate of the standard deviation of our result is the standard deviation estimate divided by the square root of the number of trials we made. To see why, recall that when independent random variables are added together, their standard deviations are added *in quadrature*. This means

$$\mathrm{SD}(X_1 + \cdots + X_n) = \sqrt{\mathrm{SD}(X_1)^2 + \cdots + \mathrm{SD}(X_n)}.$$

Now, the sample average estimate looks like

$$\hat{\mu} = \frac{X_1 + \cdots + X_n}{n}.$$

Then

$$\mathrm{SD}(\hat{\mu}) = \frac{1}{n}\,\mathrm{SD}(X_1 + \cdots + X_n) = \frac{\sqrt{n\,\mathrm{SD}(X_1)^2}}{n} = \frac{\mathrm{SD}(X_1)}{\sqrt{n}}.$$

Therefore, the EVPI for knowing μ is approximately

$$355.7944\ldots - 200 = \boxed{155.8\ldots}.$$

22.2 Eliciting priors in hierarchical models

So how was the prior distribution $\mu \sim \mathsf{Gamma}(10, 0.01)$ chosen earlier? In our case it was given by the problem, but in practice these types of priors from expert knowledge. Once the family of the prior (Gamma) has been determined, experts are asked questions questions like: What are average sales going to be for this product?

A deeper question is to ask: What is a value k such that 50% of time sales are within k of average?

This second question is asking about quantiles of the random variable. That is because it is typically easier for most people to understand quantiles rather than the relatively abstract notion of standard deviation.

Suppose our expert answered 1000 and $k = 215$. One reason to use a Gamma distribution is to ensure that demand is always positive. Next, the goal is to find parameters (α, β) such that these constraints are met. The expected value of such a random variable is α/β, so $\beta = \alpha/1000$.

The next step is to find α values such that the probability that $X \sim \mathsf{Gamma}(\alpha, \alpha/1000)$ satisfies $\mathbb{P}(X \in [785, 1215]) = 0.5$. In R, the command to find this probability is

```
pgamma(1215, alpha, alpha / 1000) - pgamma(785, alpha,
    alpha / 1000)
```

If `alpha <- 20` the result is 0.6674633. The value `alpha <- 5` gives 0.368343. Using the bisection method allows us to narrow in to get $\alpha = 9.75019$ as the best answer.

Of course, since everything is approximate here, using $\alpha = 10$ will not give results much different.

Problems

22.1 Suppose that $\mathbb{E}[X] = 4.3$ and $\mathbb{E}[Y|X] = 2X$. What is $\mathbb{E}[Y]$?

22.2 Say $\mathbb{E}[A] = 1.2$, $\mathbb{E}[B|A] = A - 3$, and $\mathbb{E}[C|B, A] = B - A$. What is $\mathbb{E}[C]$?

22.3 Suppose $T \sim \mathsf{Exp}(\lambda)$, where $\lambda \sim \mathsf{Unif}([1, 5])$.

a) What is $\mathbb{E}[T|\lambda]$?

b) What is $\mathbb{E}[T]$?

22.4 Suppose demand is modeled as $D \sim \mathsf{Pois}(\mu)$ where μ is uniform over $[1, 2]$ million units. What is $\mathbb{E}[D]$?

22.5 An investor believes there is a 30% chance of tariffs being enacted on aluminum soon. If the tariffs are put in place, then purchasing stock in an aluminum mining company will result in a \$2 000 000 profit. if the tariffs are not put in place, then the investor will lose \$500 000.

a) Draw the decision tree for this problem.

b) Should the investor invest?

c) What is the EVPI for $I = \mathbb{1}(\text{tariffs are enacted})$?

22.6 An NGO is trying to decide if it should expend resources to apply for a grant from one program (call this strategy G1), another program (G2), or both (G12). The results will depend on the availability of funding, which can be described as low or high.

The payoff matrix looks as follows:

	G1	G2	G12
high	3	5	6
low	3	0	1

The NGO believes the chance of low funding is 60%, while that of high funding is 40%.

a) Draw a decision tree for this problem.

b) What is the optimal decision assuming the expected utility hypothesis?

c) What is the expected value of perfect information for the information about the state of funding?

22.7 In mathematical finance a *call option* with strike price K returns $S - K$ if a stock ends a time period with value S that is greater than or equal to K, or nothing otherwise. That is, the payoff of the call as a function of K is

$$P = \max(S - K, 0)$$

a) For a stock modeled as $S \sim \text{Unif}([75, 150])$ and a strike price of $K = 110$, what is $\mathbb{E}[P]$?

b) If the call costs \$50 to purchase, should the call be bought? (Use expected utility maximization with utility equal to monetary value.)

22.8 Continuing the last problem, what is the expected value of perfect information on the future value S in respect to the decision of whether or not to buy the call option?

Chapter 23

Framing and a two-envelope problem

Question of the Day

Suppose two envelopes contain two different positive amounts of money. You are allowed to look inside one envelope, then either keep it or switch to the other. Is there a way to choose the envelope with more money more than half of the time?

Summary

- **Framing** phrases a decision either as a gain or loss to change the preferred outcomes.
- **Two envelope** problems deal with random variables with only two values. They are used to illustrate various paradoxes in probability.

23.1 *Framing*

Framing extends the problem of loss aversion by phrasing a decision either in terms of gain or terms of loss. Unfortunately, this can bend in either direction.

- People tend to avoid risk when the outcomes are good.
  - "A bird in the hand is worth two in the bush"
- People embrace risk when outcomes bad
  - "He who hesitates is lost"
  - "In for a penny, in for a pound"

The same question can often be presented in two different ways that elicit different answers. A choice that emphasizes a positive result can lead to risk avoiding behavior but becomes risk seeking when the negative frame is presented.

Tvesky & Kahneman 1981 Experiment In this experiment the researchers asked two versions of the same question. Each person surveyed was asked to choose between Treatment A or Treatment B for a disease that a group of 600 people had. The two versions of the question were the positive frame and the negative frame.

1. *Positive frame.* Treatment A: This treatment will save 200 lives for sure. Treatment B: This treatment has a 33% chance of saving all 600 people, but also has a 66% possibility of saving no one."

2. *Negative frame.* Treatment A: This treatment will lead to 400 deaths for sure. Treatment B: This treatment will have a 33% chance that no people die, but a 66% probability that all 600 will die."

In the positive frame, 72% of participants chose Treatment A, while in the negative frame, only 22% did so. Of course, the outcomes are exactly the same, only how they are presented is different.

So how can the issue of framing be dealt with? The simplest approach is to present both the positive and negative frame simultaneously.

- *Simultaneous frame.* Treatment A: This treatment saves 200 lives, but 400 will die. Treatment B: This treatment has a 33% chance that everyone lives and no one dies, but a 66% probability that no one lives and everyone dies.

This effect is well known and used in marketing to try to convince consumers to make certain decisions. For instance, we have the following strategies.

- Two week trial with a money back guarantee.
  - This is a good outcome so the money back guarantee manages the risk for the customer.
- Discount for cash: rarely do policies state they have a surcharge for using credit.

Frames and happiness The way outcomes are phrased can also affect regret (or its opposite, happiness.)

- Movie Theater promotion #1:
  - June wins $100 for being the millionth customer.

- Movie Theater promotion #2:
  - Betty wins $10 000 for being the millionth customer.
  - Mike wins $1 000 for being customer 1 000 001.

So which customer should be happier with the outcome, June or Mike? In practice, it would typically be June, although objectively Mike should be happier with more money.

Other approaches to minimizing irrational behavior Here are some more ways to minimize irrational behavior based on framing.

- In surveys, present the questions in a random order.
- Make the target aware of biases.
- Use feedback from the results of model.
- Redundant questioning: ask the same question using multiple frames.
- Do not let humans decide which they prefer. Instead, elicit probabilities, try to determine utilities, and then use an automated method to find the best decision. (This is why linear regression routinely outperforms experts in decision making.)

23.2 *Two envelope problems*

There are a number of simple problems involving decisions with unknown amounts of money in each of two envelopes, that illustrate some of the difficulties in building a consistent philosophy of decision making.

Switch or no switch? Start with the following problem. Suppose two envelopes contain different amounts of money, x and y. You do not know what x or y is, but you do know that $y > x$.

Here is how the game is played: you are allowed to look in one envelope and see the amount of money that is inside. After looking in the envelope, you are allowed to switch to the other envelope or stay with your existing envelope. What should you do?

Surprisingly, there is a strategy that guarantees (even though you don't know either x or y ahead of time) that you have a better than 50% chance of picking the envelope with the higher amount of money.

Procedure Start with a probability density f that is positive over $[0, \infty)$. For instance, the absolute value of a normal or Cauchy random variable will accomplish this.

1. Look in an envelope chosen uniformly at random, call result A.
2. Draw $X \sim f$.
3. If $X \leq A$, keep the envelope with A, otherwise switch.

What is the chance that the player ends up with the good envelope? Suppose that $X \leq x < y$. Then the strategy means the player does not switch no matter which envelope they received. There is a $1/2$ chance of initially getting the good envelope, so that is their chance of winning.

Similarly, if $x < y < X$, then the algorithm says to switch. This means that when $y < X$, the chance of ending up with the right envelope equals the chance that the player initially received the wrong envelope, so still $1/2$.

The final case is when $x < X \leq y$. In this case, when the player receives the envelope with x they switch. If they receive the envelope with y they don't switch, so the player always wins, no matter what envelope they started with!

Hence

$$\mathbb{P}(\text{win}) = \frac{1}{2}\mathbb{P}(X \in (-\infty, x]) + \mathbb{P}(X \in (x, y]) + \frac{1}{2}\mathbb{P}(X \in (y, \infty))$$

and since

$$\mathbb{P}(X \in (-\infty, x])) + \mathbb{P}(X \in (x, y]) + \mathbb{P}(X \in (y, -\infty)) = 1,$$

this gives

$$\mathbb{P}(\text{win}) = \frac{1}{2} + \frac{1}{2}\mathbb{P}(X \in (x, y]).$$

This last term is positive since X has positive density over $\mathbb{R}$.

Two envelope paradox Now suppose that you know that one envelope contains exactly twice as much as the second envelope. In other words, $y = 2x$, so the envelopes contain x and $2x$ amount of money.

Now consider the following expectation maximization method.

- Say you look inside and see \$1000
- Then you know the other envelope has \$500 or \$2 000
- Since each is equally likely if you pick the other envelope, you expect to change the amount of money you have by

$$\mathbb{E}(\text{switch}) = (1/2)500 + (1/2)2000 = 1500.$$

- So you should always switch.

Wait a minute, though that cannot be correct. That argument works no matter what amount was seen in the envelope! So we can switch without even seeing what's in the envelope!

But earlier we showed that we can get at least a 50% chance of getting the higher amount by using extra randomness.

Solving the paradox Interestingly, there is no one accepted solution to this problem. Philosophers have written books on it!

That being said, here is one way of resolving the paradox. The original amounts of money in the two envelopes are X and $2X$. Here X is a random variable that has an unknown distribution.

If you chose your initial envelope randomly, then the amount of money in the envelope is $[N|X] \sim \textsf{Unif}(\{X, 2X\})$. If you switch, you obtain money M. Because initially you picked the envelope at random, $[M|X] \sim \textsf{Unif}(\{X, 2X\})$ as well, and there is no paradox as

$$\mathbb{E}[N] = \mathbb{E}[M] = \mathbb{E}[\mathbb{E}[N|X]] = (3/2)\mathbb{E}[X]$$

and you are indifferent to switching.

The mistake in the paradox was in saying that given your choice of N, the envelopes were equally likely to contain $\{N/2, N\}$ as $\{N, 2N\}$. But this ignores the fact that whoever set up the envelopes had to put the money in *first*, and so it is $\{X, 2X\}$ no matter which envelope you pick. In other words, your choice of envelope cannot magically change the set of values of the money inside of the envelopes!

A more sophisticated resolution considers that the person who set up the envelopes did not choose between $(500, 1000)$ and $(1000, 2000)$ with equal probability, and that is where the error in reasoning in the paradox lies.

In this approach to the paradox, a model is needed for how the original x was chosen. Once again (as with the maximum expected utility), the notion of a Bayesian prior on the choice of x can be used.

Consider the following example. Suppose that the smaller amount of money was chosen as a geometric random variable with mean 3. That is, say $X \sim \textsf{Geo}(1/3)$ if

$$(\forall i \in \{1, 2, 3, \ldots\})(\mathbb{P}(X = i) = (2/3)^{i-1}(1/3)).$$

Once we look in the first envelope and see N dollars, that is *data*, and we need to update our probabilities for X given N. In other words, we want to know the distribution $[X|N]$, but our statistical model only gives us $[N|X]$ ($\mathbb{P}(N = X|X) = \mathbb{P}(N = 2X|X) = 1/2$).

To use $[X]$ (the prior) and $[N|X]$ (the statistical model) to get $[X|N]$ (the posterior), we use Bayes' Rule.

Theorem 10 (Bayes' Theorem)
Let A and B be events with positive probability. Then

$$\mathbb{P}(A|B) = \frac{\mathbb{P}(A)\mathbb{P}(B|A)}{\mathbb{P}(B)}.$$

- Let N be amount seen, X be amount in smaller envelope
- Suppose that the data is $N = 4$. What is the new distribution of X given this data?

  First, we know that $X = 2$ or $X = 8$, since $N \in \{X, 2X\}$. Next,

$$\begin{aligned}
\mathbb{P}(X = 2|N = 4) &= \frac{\mathbb{P}(N = 4|X = 2)\mathbb{P}(X = 2)}{\mathbb{P}(N = 4)} \\
&= \frac{\mathbb{P}(N = 4|X = 2)\mathbb{P}(X = 2)}{\mathbb{P}(N = 4|X = 2)\mathbb{P}(X = 2) + \mathbb{P}(N = 4|X = 4)\mathbb{P}(X = 4)} \\
&= \frac{(1/2)(2/3)(1/3)}{(1/2)(2/3)(1/3) + (1/2)(2/3)^3(1/3)} \\
&= 1/[1 + (2/3)^2] = 9/13.
\end{aligned}$$

  So the expected benefit of switching is

$$\frac{9}{13} \cdot (-2) + \frac{4}{13}(4) = -4/13 < 0,$$

  so $\boxed{\text{don't switch!}}$

Problems

23.1 A new disease is spreading! Vaccinations are guaranteed to prevent 90% of infections but have a 1% chance of causing nausea. Among those infected, 3% will require hospitalization.

a) Write this using a positive frame for the vaccination.

b) Write this using a negative frame for the vaccination.

23.2 A metropolitan area typically experiences 36 suicides per year. A new ad campaign is expected to reduce that number by 20%.

a) Write the choice of running the ad campaign or not using a positive frame.

b) Write the choice of running the ad campaign or not using a negative frame.

An awareness campaign will prevent 200 suicides in a metropolitan area.

23.3 In 2007, a contest for best pie gave $100 to each of the three top finishers. In 2008, they gave $500 to first place, $300 to second place, and $150 to third place. Would you rather have won third place in 2007 or 2008?

23.4 A supermarket chain is planning to run an ad campaign where they give $100, $200, and $300 to random customers every hour. Does this seem like a good idea? What might you suggest to the client to improve the outcome?

23.5 Suppose that (unknown to the player) there are two envelopes one with $10 and one with $5. The player is allowed to open one envelope, then has the choice to stay or switch to the other.

The player decides to use the following strategy: randomly generate a Cauchy random variable and take the absolute value. This gives a random variable X with density

$$f_X(x) = \frac{4}{\tau(1+x^2)}\mathbb{1}(x \geq 0).$$

The player then plans to open one envelope uniformly at random and see the value x of money inside. The player then generates X. If $X \leq x$, the player keeps the envelope, otherwise they switch. What is the chance that they end up with the $10 envelope?

23.6 Continuing the last problem, if the smaller envelope had no money in it, what is the chance that they end up with the $10 envelope?

23.7 Suppose that $X \sim \mathsf{Unif}(\{1, 2, 3, 4\})$, and two envelopes are presented, one with X dollars, and one with $2X$ dollars. You are allowed to select one envelope, look inside, and then switch if you'd like.

You decide to randomly choose a continuous uniform W over $[0, 10]$. If the amount in the envelope is smaller than W, switch, otherwise keep your envelope. What is the chance that you end with the larger dollar amount?

23.8 Continuing the last problem. Suppose you now know that $X \sim \mathsf{Unif}(\{1, 2, 3, 4\}$. You look inside the envelope and see 4 dollars. To maximize your expected dollars, should you switch?

Chapter 24

Creating utility functions to test beliefs

Question of the Day

Consider the multiple choice question:

What is the capital of Louisiana?

a) New Orleans
b) Bon Temps
c) Baton Rouge
d) Lousiannaville

How can your true beliefs about the correct answer be elicited?

Summary

- There exists a utility function such that the optimal strategy is to write down your true probability beliefs for multiple choice questions.
- Suppose there are n choices and you must give as your answer a probability vector $(p_1, \ldots, p_n)$. You then receive $\ln(p_c)$ as your payoff, where $c \in \{1, \ldots, n\}$ is the correct outcome. Then the choice that maximizes your expected utility is to put down your true beliefs about the probabilities.

So far expected utility and EVPI have been calculated given a prior on the possible outcomes. But how is that prior determined in the first place? One method is to try to elicit beliefs about probabilities from experts in the field.

24.1 Using share prices/betting odds to estimate probabilities

Suppose I offer you a financial instrument with the following properties. If event A occurs (for instance, the Los Angeles Dodgers win the World Series this year), then the stock will be worth \$100. If they don't then the stock is worthless. How much would you be willing to pay for the stock?

If \$100 is small enough that you are risk neutral to this amount, then you would be willing to pay $100p$, where p is your belief about the probabiltiy that event A occurs. If the stock was being sold for value less than $100p$, you would want to buy the stock, and if you could sell the stock for more than $100p$, you would.

This idea is the basis for a *prediction market*, which puts this idea into action by allowing the buying and trading of stocks for amounts between 0 and 100%. By allowing anyone to buy or sell the stock, a prediction market is an example of crowdsourcing probabilities.

The downside to prediction markets is that they are subject to the same irrational behavior as other markets, including bubbles and crashes. If someone invests in A not because they believe the probability warrants it but because the price of stock A is on the rise, that defeats the purpose.

24.2 Weighted answers for multiple choice questions

Now consider how to elicit correct probabilities for multiple choice questions.

Definition 97
An exam question is **multiple choice** if the set of possible answers is a finite set and there is one correct result.

For a given multiple choice test question, let X denote the true answer. For the test taker, X is a random variable that measures how much information is known about each possible answer.

Suppose that instead of just marking one answer correct, students are allowed to write positive numbers that add to 1 when answering a multiple choice question. Call $m(i)$ the weight given to answer i.

Example 33
If a multiple choice question has choices a, b, c, and d, one possible choice of answer is

$$m_1(a) = 0.2, m_1(b) = 0.3, m_1(c) = 0.25, m_1(d) = 0.25.$$

If the test taker is sure that the answer is c, then they might put all of their weight on c:

$$m_2(a) = 0, m_2(b) = 0, m_2(c) = 1, m_2(d) = 0.$$

If they thought the right answer was either c or d and they were not sure, they might write:

$$m_3(a) = 0, m_3(b) = 0, m_3(c) = 0.5, m_3(d) = 0.5.$$

Consider a user with a probability distribution for X given by the vector p. That is,

$$\mathbb{P}(X = i) = p(i).$$

Now think about what the test taker might write down for their answer based on various utility functions.

24.3 The usual grading scheme

The usual grading scheme for a multiple choice test is to give 1 point if the answer is correct, and 0 points otherwise. A reasonable extension of this to the system where someone writes down a vector that adds to 1 is to give the student whatever they put down on the answer that turns out to be true. This can be encoded as:

$$U(m) = m(X).$$

Example 34
Continuing the last example, suppose that $X = 4$. Then

$$U(m_1) = m_1(X) = m_1(4) = 0.25.$$
$$U(m_2) = m_2(X) = m_2(4) = 0.$$
$$U(m_3) = m_3(X) = m_3(4) = 0.5.$$

Of course the true answer is rarely known, instead, the user has a probabilistic model. Given the model, the *expected utility* can be found given a particular choice of m.

Example 35
Continuing our example, suppose $\mathbb{P}(X = i) = p(i)$ is given by

$$p(1) = 0.5,\ p(2) = 0.2,\ p(3) = 0.15,\ p(4) = 0.15.$$

Then

$$\begin{aligned}
\mathbb{E}[U(m_1)] &= \mathbb{E}[m_1(X)] \\
&= (0.5)(0.2) + (0.2)(0.3) + (0.15)(0.25) + (0.15)(0.25) = 0.235, \\
\mathbb{E}[U(m_2)] &= \mathbb{E}[m_2(X)] = (1)(0.15) = 0.15, \\
\mathbb{E}[U(m_3)] &= \mathbb{E}[m_3(X)] = (0.5)(0.15) + (0.5)(0.15) = 0.15.
\end{aligned}$$

So if the choice of m was between these three possibilities, with this probability vector m_1 yields the highest expected utility.

Is m_1 the best choice for this problem? To answer it is necessary to maximize $\mathbb{E}[U(m)]$, and that is done by placing all the weight on the answer with the largest value of $p(2)$. In this case

$$m_4(1) = 0,\ m_4(2) = 2,\ m_4(3) = 0,\ m_4(4) = 0,$$

yields $\mathbb{E}[U(m_4)] = 0.3$, and that is the best possible

$$\begin{aligned}
\mathbb{E}[m(X)] &= \sum_{i=1}^{3} p(i)m(i) \leq \sum_{i=1}^{3} \left[\max_i p(i)\right] m(i) \\
&= \left[\max_i p(i)\right] \sum_{i=1}^{3} p(i) = \left[\max_i p(i)\right].
\end{aligned}$$

Incidentally, the value

$$B = \arg\max_i p(i)$$

is often called the *best guess* or *mode* for a multiple choice question.

Eliciting probabilities Knowing the best guess is useful, but does not tell as much as what you know about the answer to a question as the entire probability distribution p. So consider, is there a choice of utility function U such that

$$\arg\max_m \mathbb{E}[U(m)] = p?$$

It turns out a risk averse utility function will elicit the correct probabilities. Specifically, use

$$U(m) = \ln(m(X))$$

as the utility function.

This utility function is kind of weird. Since $\ln(1) = 0$, and $\ln(m(X)) < 0$ for any $m(X) < 1$, the best value that can be scored for a question is 0, and most scores will be negative!

Example 36
Consider $m_1 = (0.2, 0.5, 0.25, 0.25)$ from earlier, and $p = (0.5, 0.2, 0.15, 0.15)$. Then for $U(m) = \ln(m(X))$,

$$\begin{aligned}\mathbb{E}[U(m)] &= \mathbb{E}[\ln(m(X))] \\ &= (0.5)\ln(0.2) + (0.2)\ln(0.5) + (0.15)\ln(0.25) + (0.15)\ln(0.25) \\ &= -1.359237.\end{aligned}$$

Is it possible to do better? Suppose the true probabilities are written down as the answer. What is the expected utility then? For $m = p$,

$$\begin{aligned}\mathbb{E}[m(X)] &= \ln(0.5)(0.5) + \ln(0.3)(0.3) + \ln(0.15)(0.15) + \ln(0.15)(0.15) \\ &= -1.276901.\end{aligned}$$

which is slightly better than before.

It turns out that it is not possible to do any better than using the correct probabilities.

Fact 38
Let Ω be the set of positive probability vectors, so positive vectors whose components add to 1. Let $p > 0$ be a probability vector on outcomes. For $m \in \Omega$ and random variable X drawn according to p, let $U(m) = \ln(m(X))$. Then

$$\arg\max_m \mathbb{E}[U(m)] = p.$$

Proof. Proving this result means solving the following optimization problem:

$$\begin{array}{ll}\text{maximize} & f(m) = \sum_i p(i)\ln(m(i)) \\ \text{subject to} & g(m) = m_1 + \cdots + m_n = 1 \\ & (\forall i)(m_i > 0).\end{array}$$

This has linear constraints but is not a linear program since the objective function $\sum_i \ln(m(i))p(i)$ is not a linear function of the argument m.

There is a bit of a difficulty here. The set Ω of feasible points is bounded but not closed, since it only allows positive probability vectors. To get around this, for $\epsilon > 0$ let Ω_ϵ be points in Ω such that for all i, $m_i \geq \epsilon$. Then Ω_ϵ is a closed bounded set, and so it is possible to find the optimum value of $f(m)$ subject to $g(m) = 0$ by evaluating the objective function at the critical points and at the boundary. Because the constraint is an equality constraint, the critical points are found using the method of Lagrange multipliers.

First, find the critical points. Both f and g have continuous first order partial derivatives in the interior of Ω_ϵ, so the critical points satisfy:

$$\nabla f = \lambda \nabla g$$

for some nonzero λ. Here

$$\nabla f = \left(\frac{\partial f}{\partial m_1}, \ldots, \frac{\partial f}{\partial m_n}\right) = \left(\frac{p(1)}{m(1)}, \ldots, \frac{p(n)}{m(n)}\right).$$

Similarly,

$$\nabla g = (1, 1, \ldots, 1).$$

So a Lagrange multiplier critical point is any point where

$$\frac{p(1)}{m(1)} = \cdots = \frac{p(n)}{m(n)} = \lambda.$$

These equations have a solution whenever $p(i) = \lambda m(i)$ for all i. Since this is true for all i, adding these equations together gives

$$p(1) + \cdots + p(n) = \lambda[m(1) + \cdots m(n)] \Rightarrow 1 = \lambda.$$

Hence $p = m$ is the only critical point, at which point

$$f(p) = \sum_i p(i) \ln(p(i)).$$

Second, consider the boundary. If m is on the boundary of $m(i)$, there must be an i with $m(i) = \epsilon$. So that contributes $p(i)\ln(\epsilon)$ to the overall sum. Because the natural logarithm of values in $[0, 1]$ are nonpositive, $\sum_{j \neq i} p(j) \ln(m(j)) \leq 0$. So $f(m) \leq p(i)\ln(\epsilon)$, and for ϵ sufficiently small, this is at most $f(p)$.

Hence for ϵ below some threshold, $f(p)$ is the maximum value of the nonlinear program, and p is the unique argument which maximizes the objective function. □

What this shows is that if your reward is based on the numbers you write on the answers to a multiple choice question is the natural logarithm of the number you put on the correct answer, then to maximize your expected score you should put your true beliefs about the correct probability on each answer.

Problems

24.1 Suppose a user has $p = (0.2, 0.2, 0.3, 0.3)$ for a four answer multiple choice test question. Of the four choices, which maximizes the chance that the answer is correct?

24.2 Suppose a test taker has a belief that of three answers, answers 1 and 2 are equally likely, and answer 3 is twice as likely as the others. What is the chance that answer 3 is correct?

24.3 Suppose a user has $p = (0.2, 0.2, 0.25, 0.35)$ for a four answer multiple choice test question. The test taker is allowed to write a probability vector (m_1, m_2, m_3, m_4) as the answer. If the reward for answering correctly is $U(m_X) = m_X$, where X is the correct answer, then what is the choice of probability vector m that maximizes the expected utility?

24.4 A test taker has beliefs of $p = (0.4, 0.3, 0.3)$ for each of three answers to a multiple choice test question. The test taker is allowed to write a probability vector (m_1, m_2, m_3, m_4) as the answer. If the reward for answering correctly is $U(m_X) = m_X$, where X is the correct answer, then what is the choice of probability vector m that maximizes the expected utility?

24.5 Suppose a user has $p = (0.2, 0.2, 0.25, 0.35)$ for a four answer multiple choice test question. The test taker is allowed to write a probability vector (m_1, m_2, m_3, m_4) as the answer. If the reward for answering correctly is $U(m_X) = \ln(m_X)$, where X is the correct answer, then what is the choice of probability vector m that maximizes the expected utility?

24.6 A test take has beliefs of $p = (0.4, 0.3, 0.3)$ for each of three answers to a multiple choice test question. The test taker is allowed to write a probability vector (m_1, m_2, m_3, m_4) as the answer. If the reward for answering correctly is $U(m_X) = \ln(m_X)$, where X is the correct answer, then what is the choice of probability vector m that maximizes the expected utility?

24.7 Suppose the economy either does well, medium, or poorly next quarter. An expert believes the chance of each outcome is 40%, 30%, and 30% respectively. Let X be the true answer. Find the value of $m \in [0, 1]^3$ that maximizes $\mathbb{E}[U_i(m)]$, where

a) the utility function is

$$U_1(m) = m(X),$$

b) or the utility function is

$$U_2(m) = \ln(m(X)).$$

24.8 A surgeon believes a patient will either recover completely with probability 15%, get to 80% function with probability 70%, and experience worse function with probability 5%. If the goal of a decision maker is to elicit the true probabilities from the surgeon, what should the reward be for predicting the correct outcome?

24.9 The set of points (x, y) such that $x^2 + y^2 = 1$ forms a closed, bounded set. Find the maximum value of $x + y$ subject to $x^2 + y^2 = 1$ using Lagrange multipliers.

24.10 The set of points (x, y) such that $2x^2 + y^2 = 1$ forms a closed, bounded set. Find the maximum value of $x + 2y$ subject to $2x^2 + y^2 = 1$ using Lagrange multipliers.

Chapter 25

Shannon Entropy

Question of the Day

How much can randomly generated data be compressed?

Summary

- **Shannon entropy** is a numerical score of how much randomness (uncertainty) there is in a discrete random variable X. The value of the Shannon entropy is
$$H(X) = -\mathbb{E}[\log_2(p(X))].$$

In chemistry *entropy* refers to the lack of information about particles in a gas or other system. In mathematics, the entropy is the lack of information in a system.

For instance, say $X \in \{1, 2, 3, 4\}$ has probability vector $(0, 1, 0, 0)$. Then $\mathbb{P}(X = 2) = 1$ and $\mathbb{P}(X \neq 2) = 0$. This is the maximum information a probability vector can deliver, and the lowest amount of entropy.

Now suppose that my probability vector is $(0.5, 0.2, 0.15, 0.15)$. Last time it was shown that if the reward given to value X is

$$U(m) = \ln(m(X)),$$

then an optimal choice of m is just exactly p. Of course, multiplying by a constant $c > 0$ so

$$U(m) = c \ln(m(X))$$

also forces the player to behave optimally. Recall that logarithms of different bases only introduce a multiplicative constant into the function. For instance,

$$U(m) = \log_2(m(X)) = \ln(m(X))/\ln(2).$$

Because $m(X) \in [0,1]$, $\log_2(m(X)) \leq 0$. Given that a player plays optimally, say that the negative of the average reward obtained is the *entropy* of the random variable X.

Definition 98
The **entropy** (aka **Shannon entropy** aka **information entropy**) of X with probability vector p is

$$H(X) = -\mathbb{E}[\log_2(p(X))].$$

Example 37
Let $Y \sim \mathsf{Bern}(1/2)$. Then $\mathbb{P}(Y = 0) = \mathbb{P}(Y = 1) = 1/2$, and

$$\begin{aligned} H(X) &= -[(1/2)\log_2(1/2) + (1/2)\log_2(1/2)] \\ &= -[(1/2)(-1) + (1/2)(-1)] = 1. \end{aligned}$$

Example 38
For $X \sim p = (0.5, 0.2, 0.15, 0.15)$, the average reward (playing optimally) is about -1.276901 and there is no way to do better. Therefore the entropy of X is about 1.276901.

Since 1.276901 is slightly higher than 1, X has more randomness in it than a single fair coin flip. Say that X has roughly as much randomness as 1.276901 iid fair coin flips.

For $(0, 1, 0, 0)$ the average reward is 0, which is the best possible: since $p(i) \in [0, 1]$ for all i, $\mathbb{E}[V] \leq 0$.

For a discrete random variable, $p(i)$ is the density of the random variable with respect to counting measure. The definition of entropy can be generalized to include arbitrary density functions.

Fact 39
For $X \in \{x_1, x_2, x_3, \ldots, x_n\}$.

$$H(X) = -\sum_{i=1}^{n} p(x_i)\log_2(p(x_i)).$$

More generally, if $X \in \Omega$ has density f_X with respect to measure μ,

$$H(X) = -\int_{\Omega} \log_2(f_X(s)) f_X(s)\, d\mu.$$

Notation: What looks like a capital "H" letter is actually the capital of the Greek letter eta, standing for entropy.

Earlier, the entropy of a $\text{Bern}(1/2)$ random variable was found to be 1. It turns out that $p = 1/2$ in $\text{Bern}(p)$ maximizes the entropy.

Fact 40
Let $H(B_p)$ be the entropy of $B_p \sim \text{Bern}(p)$. Then $\arg\max H(B_p) = 1/2$ and $\max H(B_p) = 1$.

Proof. Using the product rule

$$[H(B_p)]' = -\ln(p) - p/p + \ln(1-p) + (1-p)/(1-p) = \ln((1-p)/p).$$

So $H(B_p)$ is increasing for $(1-p)/p \leq 1$ and decreasing for $(1-p)/p \geq 1$ which gives a unique maximum at $p = 1/2$. □

In other words, for a single bit, entropy is maximized when the distribution on the bit is uniform.

25.1 Claude Shannon

Shannon is one of the more amazing mathematicians of the 20th century. He is considered to have founded information theory with the 1948 paper "A Mathematical Theory of Communication" which appeared in the *Bell System Technical Journal*.

He was also one of the founders of what is now called Theoretical Computer Science, when he proved that digital circuits could solve all the problems that could solved using Boolean algebra (logic) for his Master's thesis in 1937. At this point computers were either analog (where states varied continuously) or digital (taking on discrete states) and this was a major step forward in understanding the capabilities of digital computers.

During WWII, he worked for Bell Labs on fire-control systems and cryptography. That is when he became interested in understanding how to transmit information when there is randomness laid on top of it.

A side-note: he also worked with Edward Thorp (who was noted for counting cards at blackjack) to build a wearable computer capable of winning at roulette by analyzing the wheel. Unfortunately, the wires from the computer to the speaker in his ear kept breaking, so they never considered it a success. Today most casinos ban the use of computers when gambling because of their efforts.

25.2 Compressing data

The Shannon entropy also limits how much data can be compressed. To understand this, first consider an example. Digital computers work with *bits* (binary digits), numbers that are either 0 or 1. Suppose the goal is to compress the set of bits `01110111`. One way to do that is with a map. For instance, consider the map:

$$\texttt{01} \mapsto \texttt{0},\ \texttt{11} \mapsto \texttt{1}.$$

Then the bit string 01110111 is mapped to 0101. Because the mapped string is half the length of the original string, say this code compressed the data by a factor of 2.

The reason the code was effective is that out of the possible two-bit outcomes $\{00, 01, 10, 11\}$, only the two $\{01, 11\}$ appeared in our string. Unfortunately, most real messages would contain all four possible two bit strings. To handle this situation, a more complicated code is needed. The map should be *invertible.* This means that given any coded message there is a unique original message that would have been mapped to that coded message.

For instance, consider the following code:

```
11 →  1
01 →  01
10 →  001
00 →  0001.
```

This map can be *uniquely decoded.* That means that given a coded sequence 100101001 there is a unique original sequence that would give that code. That is because for each 1 in the coded message, there are either 0, 1, 2, or 3 zeros before the previous 1 appears. And that number tells us if the decoded message bits should be 11, 01, 10, or 00.

Is this a good code? Well, that depends on the message to be encoded. If the original message contains lots of 11 subsequences, then it is a good code because these only take 1 bit to encode. If the original contains lots of 00 subsequences, then the code will be inefficient, as these subsequences require twice as many bits to encode as the original string.

Let p be a probability vector over the outcomes (11, 01, 10, 00). The expected number of bits used by our code is

$$(1)p(1) + 2p(2) + 3p(3) + 4p(4).$$

So for vector $(0.5, 0.2, 0.15, 0.15)$, our code uses on average $0.5+0.4+0.45+0.6 = 1.95$ bits to encode 2 bits of information.

A natural question then arises. Given a sequence of bits X what is the best on average that a code can do? Shannon answered this question in his 1948 paper.

As Shannon did, begin by setting up the idea of an *alphabet* and *words* formed from the alphabet. For a set of letters A, use A^* to denote the set of words formed from those letters.

Definition 99
Let A be a finite set called an **alphabet**. The elements of the alphabet are called **letters**. Then a **word** is a vector of any length whose components are all in A. That is,

$$A^* = \emptyset \cup A \cup A^2 \cup A^3 \cup \cdots .$$

For a word $w \in A^*$, the **length** of the word is the value i such that $w \in A^i$.

For example if our alphabet is $\{a, b, c\}$, then a, $bcabb$, and $\emptyset$ are all words but $aaaaa \cdots$ is not since it contains an infinite number of letters from our alphabet.

Given a code f that transforms the alphabet of A_1 into a word in A_2 (so $f : A_1 \to A_2^*$), a natural question to ask is if f can be extended to a code on A_1^* to A_2^*. To do that, introduce the idea of *concatenation.*

Definition 100
Given words $w = (w_1, \ldots, w_n)$ and $v = (v_1, \ldots, v_m)$, the **concatenation** of the vectors, denoted $w||v$ or $\text{con}(w, v)$, is the single word $(w_1, \ldots, w_n, v_1, \ldots, v_m)$. This definition can be extended naturally to the concatenation of a finite number of words.

Next comes the notion of a one-to-one (also called a 1-1) function.

Definition 101
Say that $f : A \to B$ is a **one-to-one function** if for every $b \in B$ there exists an $a \in A$ such that $f(a) = b$, and if $f(a_1) = f(a_2)$ then $a_1 = a_2$.

If using a code on letters to create a code on words results in a one-to-one function, then the code is *uniquely decodable.*

Definition 102
For finite alphabets A_1 and A_2, and given code $f : A_1 \to A_2^*$, and word $(a_1, \ldots, a_n) \in A_1^*$, define

$$g(a_1, \ldots, a_n) = \text{con}(f(a_1), f(a_2), \ldots, f(a_n)).$$

Say that f is **uniquely decodable** if $g : A_1^* \to A_2^*$ is a one-to-one function.

For example, suppose $A_1 = \{a, b, c, d\}$, $f(a) = 1$, $f(b) = 01$, $f(c) = 10$ and $f(d) = 11$. Then $g(aa) = 11$ and $g(d) = 11$, so g is not a one to one function.

Theorem 11 (Shannon source coding Theorem)
Let A_1, A_2 be two finite alphabets. Suppose that X is a r.v. taking values in A_1, and f is any uniquely decodable code from A_1^* to A_2^*. Let S_f be the length of the word $f(X)$. Then

$$\frac{H(X)}{\log_2(\#A_2)} \leq \mathbb{E}[S_f].$$

Moreover, there exists a code f^* such that

$$\mathbb{E}(S_{f^*}) < \frac{H(X)}{\log_2(\#A_2)} + 1.$$

For our example, the output words are $\{1\}, \{01\}, \{001\}, \{0001\}$. These are elements of A_2^*, where $A_2 = \{0, 1\}$ are the letters that these words are formed from. The probability distribution of the output is

$$p = (0.5, 0.3, 0.15, 0.15).$$

This gives

$$-\sum_{i=1}^{n} p_i \log_2(p_i) = 1.842179$$

Because $\#(A_2) = 2$ it holds that $\log_2(\#(A_2)) = 1$. So *any* code for the two-bits problem must use at least 1.842179 bits on average. So our code that uses 1.95 bits on average is not bad!

25.3 Combining messages

Now suppose that X is a random message and Y is a random message. How much information/entropy is in the combined message (X, Y)?

Unsurprisingly, the information in two or more messages X and Y that are independent random variables is the sum of the information stored in each message.

Fact 41
Suppose $X_1, X_2, \ldots, X_n$ are independent random variables. Then

$$H(X_1, X_2, \ldots, X_n) = H(X_1) + H(X_2) + H(X_3) + \cdots + H(X_n).$$

Proof. Recall that for independent random variables $X_1, \ldots, X_n$, the joint density is the product of the individual densities. That is,

$$f_{X_1,\ldots,X_n}(s_1, \ldots, s_n) = \prod_{i=1}^{n} f_{X_i}(s_i).$$

Taking the log base 2 of both sides gives

$$\log_2(f_{X_1,\ldots,X_n}(s_1,\ldots,s_n)) = \sum_{i=1}^{n} \log_2(f_{X_i}(s_i)).$$

Setting s_i to X_i and taking the negative expectation gives:

$$-\mathbb{E}[\log_2(f_{X_1,\ldots,X_n}(X_1,\ldots,X_n))] = -\mathbb{E}\left[\sum_{i=1}^{n} \log_2(f_{X_i}(X_i))\right].$$

Using linearity of expected value complete the proof. □

So what does that mean for the highest entropy state? Well, for a single bit the highest entropy state is uniform. Therefore, for an iid stream of random bits, the highest entropy state will also be uniform.

Fact 42
For a finite set A, the highest entropy distribution on A is the uniform distribution.

Proof. Let X be a random variable over A. Suppose $\mathbb{P}(X = a) \neq \mathbb{P}(X = b)$. Then $-x\ln(x)$ is a strictly concave function in $(0, 1]$. So creating a new random variable with the same probabilities as X but with $\mathbb{P}(X' = a) = \mathbb{P}(X' = b) = (\mathbb{P}(X = a) + \mathbb{P}(X = b))/2$ has a strictly greater entropy than X. That means that if X has maximum entropy, then all the probabilities must be equal. □

Problems

25.1 What is $\log_2(1/8)$?

25.2 What is $-\log_2(1/64)$?

25.3 True or false: The Shannon entropy is always nonnegative.

25.4 Prove that $X \sim \text{Bern}(p)$ and $Y \sim \text{Bern}(1-p)$ have the same Shannon entropy.

25.5 What is the Shannon entropy of $X \sim \text{Unif}(\{0, 1\})$?

25.6 What is the Shannon entropy of $X \sim \text{Unif}(\{0, 1, 2, 3\})$?

25.7 Consider the code from $\{a, b, c\}$ to $\{0, 01, 10\}$ defined as

$$f(a) = 0,\ f(b) = 01,\ f(c) = 10.$$

Is f uniquely encodable?

25.8 Show that the code generated by

```
11 → 1
01 → 01
10 → 001
00 → 011.
```

is not uniquely encodable.

25.9 Suppose $X_1, \ldots, X_n$ are iid $\mathsf{Bern}(0.7)$. For a given code/compression scheme, what is the minimum number of bits on average needed to encode a length n sequence?

25.10 Suppose $Y_1, \ldots, Y_n$ are iid $\mathsf{Bern}(0.3)$. For a given coding, what is the minimum number of bits on average needed to encode a length n sequence?

Part V

GAME THEORY

Chapter 26

Introduction to Game Theory

Question of the Day

Suppose you are randomly paired with another student in the class. Each of you secretly writes down either α or β. The payoffs are as follows:

- If you put α, other β, you get an A, other gets a C.
- If both put α, both get $B-$.
- If you put β, other α, you get C, other gets a A.
- If both put β, both get $B+$.

What should a rational person do?

Summary

- **Game Theory** involves decision making when games are not being played against nature, but rather against another opponent who is also trying to make decisions to maximize their utility.

Decision theory presents various ways of making optimal decisions given partial information. Decision theory can be viewed as a contest between the player and the state of nature. This state of nature is random (not totally known) but is not inherently antagonistic towards the player.

In *game theory*, there are two or more players that are each trying to maximize their own utility by individually making decisions. Players do not know the decisions that other players are making. Often, this gives the players a chance to *cooperate* with each other and each achieve higher rewards, or *compete* against the other player and cost utility for all.

As with decision theory, often there is a function that reveals the payoff to each player based on the decision each player makes. For n players, this function takes n inputs (the actions for each player) and returns n outputs (the payoff for each player).

When $n = 2$, this can be written in the form of a payoff matrix where the entries are 2-tuples. For the question of the day, this payoff is as follows.

		other	
		α	β
me	α	$(B-, B-)$	(A, C)
	β	(C, A)	$(B+, B+)$

Another way of describing the actions is that the two players can either work together, or each can try to undercut the other player.

Competition Suppose everyone is out for themselves, and always tries to undercut their opponent. Assuming that the grades are ranked $A > B+ > B- > C$, the utility assigned to the grades might be

$$u(A) = 3,\ u(B+) = 1,\ u(B-) = 0,\ u(C) = -1.$$

This would make the payoff matrix

		other	
		α	β
me	α	$(0, 0)$	$(3, -1)$
	β	$(-1, 3)$	$(1, 1)$

What should I choose if I am out for myself? Consider the options

- If the other player chooses α and I choose α then I get 0. If I swap on my own to β I get -1 and do worse.
- If the other player chooses β and I choose α get 3. If I swap on my own to β I get 1 and do worse.
- In either case, choosing α gives a better payoff for me than β!

This makes choosing α a dominating strategy. No matter what the other player does, if I choose α I will do better.

That means that everyone pursuing a policy of local rationality chooses α, and suffers for it. Here (β, β) would be better for both players, but the players will not get there without effort. The economics term for this is that the payoff matrix is *Pareto inefficient*.

This payoff matrix is fairly famous and has been given a name. It is known as the *Prisoner's dilemma* (Flood & Dresher at RAND in 1950)

In the original, story, two criminals are taken prisoner. Each can talk or stay silent. If both stay silent then each serves 1 year. If one talks and the other keeps silent, then the talker is freed, and the other serves 3 years. If both talk, then both serve 2 years. In this setup, the dominant strategy for each is for both to talk.

Cooperation The alternative of cooperation makes more sense. But does it happen?

Well, psychologists have run this test, and it turns out that people will cooperate much more often than might be predicted by self-interest. One theory for why this happens is the notion of *empathy*.

Suppose that each player not only cares about their own grade but also they want their fellow players to do well. This effectively changes the payoff matrix.

Suppose that if a player gets A while other gets C, guilt changes their overall reward to -1. The payoff matrix becomes:

		other	
		α	β
me	α	$(0,0)$	$(-1,-1)$
	β	$(-1,-1)$	$(1,1)$

Unlike earlier, now there is no dominating strategy. If other picks α, best choice α. If other picks β, best choice β.

That is not enough to guarantee that they pick the global optimum, but it is a good start.

Selflessness The notion of *selflessness* goes a bit further than empathy. With selflessness, a player will be happy for the other player when they receive a desirable result. The payoffs for such players could be as follows.

		other	
		α	β
me	α	$(0,0)$	$(-1,3)$
	β	$(3,-1)$	$(1,1)$

Now β is a dominating strategy: it's better no matter what the other player chooses. If everyone thinks this way, leads to taking the best solution! In experiments, about 30% of participants choose β.

So empathy and selflessness are not just about being good people, these traits actually can help society as a whole make decisions that are better overall!

Problems

26.1 True or false: Decision theory can be used to analyze two-person games.

26.2 True or false: Game theory can be used to analyze two-person games.

26.3 True or false: In the Prisoner's Dilemma, cooperation can be undermined by self-interest.

26.4 True or false: In the Prisoner's Dilemma, cooperation can be enhanced by selflessness.

26.5 Suppose that 3 players are making decisions that affect the payoff. The payoff function has how many inputs?

26.6 Fill in the blank. Suppose that 3 players are making decisions that affect the payoff. The payoff will then be a ____-tuple?

26.7 Consider the following payoff matrix, where each of two players is deciding between strategies a_1 and a_2.

		Player 1	
		a_1	a_2
Player 2	a_1	$(0, -1)$	$(4, -2)$
	a_2	$(-3, 4)$	$(3, 2)$

a) If Player 1 is self-interested, what decision will they make?

b) If Player 2 is self-interested, what decision will they make?

26.8 Consider the following payoff matrix, where each of two players is deciding between strategies a_1 and a_2.

		Player 1	
		a_1	a_2
Player 2	a_1	$(2, 0)$	$(2, -2)$
	a_2	$(1, 3)$	$(0, 1)$

a) If Player 1 is self-interested, what decision will they make?

b) If Player 2 is self-interested, what decision will they make?

Chapter 27

Two person zero sum games

Question of the Day

In the game of Rock, Paper, Scissors, two players each shake their hands then *throw* either Rock, Paper, or Scissors. The winner is then determined using Rock beats Scissors, Paper beats Rock, and Scissors beats Paper.

The outcomes of this game can be represented by a payoff matrix. The entry in row i and column j has payoff (a, b). This means that if Player I makes decision i and Player II makes decision j then Player I wins a and Player II wins b.

		Player II		
		r	p	s
	r	$(0,0)$	$(-1,1)$	$(1,-1)$
Player I	p	$(1,-1)$	$(0,0)$	$(-1,1)$
	s	$(-1,1)$	$(1,-1)$	$(0,0)$

What is the best strategy for players to use?

Summary

- In a **zero sum game**, the outcomes (a, b) all satisfy $a + b = 0$. So in a two person zero sum game, it is like Player II is giving a dollars to Player I.
- The **Minimax Theorem** states that every finite two person zero sum game has a value V. There is a mixed strategy for Player I such that they earn on average at V payoff regardless of what Player II does, and a mixed strategy for Player II such that II loses on average V payoff regardless of what Player I does.

27.1 Zero sum games

A particular type of game is when the payoffs earned by the players must sum to zero. For one player to receive a positive payoff, another player must receive a negative payoff.

Definition 103
In a **zero sum game** with n players, the outcome $(a_1, a_2, \ldots, a_n)$ all satisfy $a_1 + \cdots + a_n = 0$.

Example 39
Consider the Odd-Even game where two participants play. The first player chooses an integer, and so does the other player. If the sum of the numbers picked is even, the first player pays the second one dollar, otherwise, the second player pays the first one dollar.

The payoff matrix can be written as

		Player II	
		odd	even
Player I	odd	$(-1, 1)$	$(1, -1)$
	even	$(1, -1)$	$(-1, 1)$

If I play this game a lot of times in a row, and I always pick odd, then after a while my opponent will figure out my strategy and I will always lose. Using a random (mixed) strategy can help!

Note that if I pick even or odd as my strategy, each with 50% probability, then no matter what strategy my opponent uses, the average payoff for myself will be 0. Also, the average payoff for my opponent will be 0. Say that the *value* of the game is 0.

On the other hand, the opponent could do the same thing, in which case no matter what strategy I employ, the expected return will be 0.

This is not a coincidence! In general, for these types of games there is always a random strategy for Player I that no matter what Player II does, the expected return has at least value V. Similarly, there is a random strategy for Player II such that no matter what Player I does the expected return is at most the same value V. This value V is called the *value* of the game.

Other common games similar to this are Rock, Paper, Scissors, and the more complicated game of Rock, Paper, Scissors, Lizard, Spock invented by Sam Kass and Karen Bryla.

Note that for two person zero sum games, it is not necessary to specify the payoff in the form (a_1, a_2), because it is always the case that $a_2 = -a_1$.

Definition 104
A two person zero sum game is said to be in **strategic form** (aka **normal form**) if it is a triple (X, Y, A) where

1. X is the nonempty set of strategies for Player I.
2. Y is the nonempty set of strategies for Player II.
3. $A : (X \times Y) \to \mathbb{R}$ is the payoff function.

The game then proceeds as follows.

- Player I and Player II both choose their action simultaneously. Say Player I chooses $x \in X$ and Player II chooses $y \in Y$.
- Player II then pays $A(x, y)$ utility to Player I.

How to optimize mixed strategies Consider a game where each player holds either 1 or 2 fingers behind their back, and then brings out their arm at the same time. Then

$$X = \{1, 2\}$$
$$Y = \{1, 2\}.$$

The payoff matrix is

		Player II	
		1	2
Player I	1	−2	4
	2	3	−5

Optimizing Player I's strategy The question to answer is: Does one side have an advantage in this game? First, consider the expected payoff if Player I plays strategy 1 with probability $3/5$. This expected payoff depends on the strategy used by Player II. That is,

$$\text{II plays 1} : (3/5)(-2) + (2/5)(3) = 0$$
$$\text{II plays 2} : (3/5)(4) + (2/5)(-5) = 2/5$$

This is a strategy where Player I never loses utility to Player II (on average), but can Player I do better?

Player I's mixed strategy can be fully described by a single parameter p equal to the probability that Player I plays strategy 1. If this occurs, then the expected payoff depends on the strategy played by Player II:

$$\text{II plays 1} : p(-2) + (1-p)(3) = 3 - 5p$$
$$\text{II plays 2} : p(4) + (1-p)(-5) = 9p - 5$$

So if II plays 1, then Player I wants to make p small, but if II plays 2, then Player I wants to make p large.

There is a unique value p in $[0, 1]$ where these two lines cross. That is, there is a unique value p such that no matter what strategy Player II uses, the average amount given from Player II to Player I is the same.

$$3 - 5p = 9p - 5 \Rightarrow p = 8/14.$$

Therefore, the optimal strategy for Player I is to use action 1 with probability $8/14$, and otherwise use strategy 2. This returns an expected value of

$$3 - 5\left(\frac{8}{14}\right) = 9\left(\frac{8}{14}\right) - 5 = 2/14 = 0.1428\ldots.$$

So on average, Player I wins $1/7$ utility from Player II.

Optimizing Player II's strategy The same technique can be applied to optimize Player II's strategy. Let q be the probability that Player II plays strategy 1.

$$\text{I plays 1} : q(-2) + (1-q)(4) = 4 - 6q$$
$$\text{I plays 2} : q(3) + (1-q)(-5) = 8q - 5$$

Setting these two the same gives

$$4 - 6q = 8q - 5 \Rightarrow q = 9/14,$$

and leads to an expected payoff of

$$-2(9/14) + 4(5/14) = 3(9/14) - 5(5/14) = 2/14 = 1/7.$$

If Player II uses their optimal strategy, then they can *limit* how much they transfer to Player I to $1/7$ on average. This seems a remarkable coincidence! By playing as best they can, both players can get a payoff from Player II to Player I of $1/7$, regardless of what the other player does!

It turns out this is not a coincidence! There will always be a random choice of action for Player I and a random choice of action for Player II such that the expected payoff is the same regardless of the other player's strategy! This common payoff is called the *value* of the game.

Terminology To make this a bit more precise, refer to elements of X or Y as *actions*, or *pure strategies*. Mixing these pure strategies together gives a *mixed strategy*.

Definition 105
A random variable over a set of strategies X is called a **mixed strategy**.

The *Minimax Theorem* states that the best mixed strategy for Player I has the same expected rewards as the best mixed strategy for Player II.

Theorem 12 (The Minimax Theorem [**vonneumann1928**])
For every finite two person zero sum game

1. There is a number V called the **value** of the game.
2. There is a mixed strategy for Player I such that Player I wins on average V regardless of what Player II does.
3. There is a mixed strategy for Player II such that II loses average V regardless of what Player I does.

Example 40
In the Question of the Day, the strategy $\boxed{(1/3, 1/3, 1/3)}$ for both Player I and II leads to a value of 0. Hence these are the best strategies to use.

The value V tells us whether Player I is on average winning, Player II is on average winning, or if the game is fair.

Definition 106
Consider a two person zero sum game with value V.

- If $V = 0$, then the game is **fair**.
- If $V > 0$, then the game **favors Player I**.
- If $V < 0$, then the game **favors Player II**.

Example 41
Change the Odd-Even payoff matrix again so that $A(1,2) = 2$ (call the odd strategy 1, and the even strategy 2):

		Player II	
		1	2
Player I	1	−2	2
	2	3	−4

What is the value of this game?

Answer

- Can analyze from either Player I or Player II perspective.
- Say Player I plays strategy 1 with probability p_I and strategy 2 with probability p_{II}.
- Player I:

$$\text{II plays 1} : p_I(-2) + (1 - p_I)(3) = 3 - 5p_I$$
$$\text{II plays 2} : p_I(2) + (1 - p_I)(-4) = 6p_I - 4$$

- Setting them equal gives: $3 - 5p_I = 6p_I - 4 \Rightarrow p = 7/11$
- This makes the value $V = 3 - 5(7/11) = \boxed{-2/11}$

This value could also have been found from Player II's perspective.

- From Player II's point of view:

$$\text{I plays 1} : p_{II}(-2) + (1 - p_{II})(2) = 2 - 4p_{II}$$
$$\text{I plays 2} : p_{II}(3) + (1 - p_{II})(-4) = 7p_{II} - 4$$

- So $2 - 4p_{II} = 7p_{II} - 4 \Rightarrow p = 6/11$
- So the value is $V = 7(6/11) - 4 = -2/11$
- Same value as above! (As guaranteed by the Minimax Theorem)

Relation to linear programming

It turns out that the minimax theorem is a special case of a much bigger theorem called *linear programming duality*. Here the examples were for games in which each player has only two decisions to keep things simple. The same result applies when Player I has n decisions, and Player II has m decisions for any positive integers n and m.

In this case, to find the optimal value of the game, the method of linear programming can be used.

Problems

27.1 Fill in the blank: If the outcomes of a game all satisfy for entry

$$(a_1, a_2, \ldots, a_n)$$

that

$$a_1 + a_2 + \cdots + a_n = 0,$$

call it a(n) ____________ game.

27.2 Fill in the blank: if a player chooses which strategy to use according to a probability distribution, this is a(n) ____________ strategy.

27.3 Consider a zero-sum game with payoff matrix:

		Player II	
		a	b
Player I	a	-6	2
	b	4	-3

Answer the following questions about the strategic form of this two person zero sum game.

a) What is X?

b) What is Y?

c) What is the payoff function A?

27.4 Consider the zero-sum game with entries

		Player II	
		1	2
Player I	1	-5	5
	2	5	-5

Answer the following questions about the strategic form of this two person zero sum game.

a) What is X?

b) What is Y?

c) What is the payoff function A?

27.5 Consider the zero-sum game with entries

		Player II	
		1	2
Player I	1	-5	5
	2	5	-5

If Player I plays strategy 1 with probability 40% and strategy 2 with probability 60%, then what strategy should Player II use to maximize expected utility for Player II?

27.6 Consider the zero-sum game with entries

		Player II	
		a	b
Player I	a	-6	2
	b	4	-3

If Player II flips a fair coin to decide which strategy to play, what strategy should Player I play to maximize expected utility?

27.7 Consider the game with entries

		Player II	
		1	2
Player I	1	-5	5
	2	5	-5

What is the value of this game?

27.8 Consider the game with entries

		Player II	
		1	2
Player I	1	−10	10
	2	10	−10

What is the value of this game?

Chapter 28

Nash Equilibria

Question of the Day

Is there an optimal mixed strategy when dealing with 3 or more players? How about for non zero sum games?

Summary

- For games that are not zero sum or zero sum games with 3 or more players, there is no guarantee that a single strategy is the right option.
- There will exist, however, at least one **Nash equilibrium**, which is a strategy for each player that is locally stable, which means that none of the players can change their strategy unilaterally without reducing their expected payoff.

When dealing with a two person, zero sum game, there will be a unique value of the game V. Player I will have an optimal strategy such that when played, the expected payoff to Player I is V regardless of the strategy employed by Player II.

Similarly, there is an optimal strategy for Player II such that when played, the expected payoff to Player I is V regardless of the strategy used by Player I. However, if the game is not zero sum, or if there are three or more players, there is no such value for the game. Instead, the best that can be done is a weaker result.

To begin, consider the strategic form when there are three or more players.

Definition 107
The **strategic form** (aka **normal form**) for an n-player game is $G = (S_1, \ldots, S_n, u_1, \ldots, u_n)$ where S_i is the set of strategies for player i, and $u_i : (S_1 \times \cdots S_n) \to \mathbb{R}$ tells the payoff for player i given the choice of strategies from all the players.

As usual, assume each player is trying to maximize their expected utility. Consider the following game:

		Player 2	
		a	b
Player 1	a	$(1,2)$	$(0,0)$
	b	$(0,0)$	$(2,1)$

For this payoff table, no pure strategy for either Player 1 or 2 is dominant. On the other hand, there are strategies where once used, neither player can switch strategies without lowering their payoff.

- For strategy (a, a), neither can switch without lowering their payoff.
- For strategy (b, b), neither can switch without lowering their payoff.
- Call strategies (a, a) and (b, b) that have this property *Nash equilibria.*

Now look at the following game

		Player 2	
		a	b
Player 1	a	$(1,2)$	$(4,0)$
	b	$(3,0)$	$(2,1)$

From any pure strategy, some player wants to switch. This means that no pure strategies are Nash equilibria. To achieve a Nash equilibrium one or both of the players will have to randomly decide which strategy to play.

Recall that a probability distribution over a set of strategies is called a *mixed strategy.*

Notation

- Let σ_i be the mixed strategy played by player i.
- Let $\sigma_{-i} = (\sigma_1, \ldots, \sigma_{i-1}, \sigma_{i+1}, \ldots, \sigma_n)$ be the mixed strategies played by every player other than i.
- Let $u_i(\sigma_1, \ldots, \sigma_n)$ be the expected payoff for Player i when each player uses mixed strategy σ_i.

Definition 108
A strategy σ is a **Nash equilibrium** if for all i

$$u_i(\sigma) = \max_{\sigma_i'} u_i(\sigma_i', \sigma_{-i}).$$

In other words, a set of mixed strategies is a Nash equilibrium if changing one player's mixed strategy leads to a lower expected payoff for that person.

Theorem 13 (Nash 1951 [**nash1951**])
Any finite game has at least one Nash equilibrium.

The proof uses Kakutani's fixed point theorem from analysis, and is beyond the scope of this course.

Another way to say it is that at the Nash equilibrium, every player is insensitive to changes in strategy. This is illustrated in the following example.

Example 42
Consider again the payoff matrix:

		Player 2	
		a	b
Player 1	a	$(1,2)$	$(4,0)$
	b	$(3,0)$	$(2,1)$

Show that no pure strategy by the players is a Nash equilibrium.

Answer There are four pure strategies.

- From (a,a) (so Player 1 plays a and Player 2 plays a), Player 1 would do better by moving to strategy b.
- From (a,b), Player 2 does better to move to strategy a.
- From (b,a), Player 2 does better to move to strategy b.
- From (b,b), Player 1 does better to move to strategy a.

So none of the four pure strategies can be a Nash equilibrium.

Despite no pure strategies being a Nash equilibrium, there are mixed strategies that use randomness that form a Nash equilibrium.

Example 43
Consider the payoff matrix from the last example. Find the Nash equilibrium.

Answer Say Player 1 uses a mixed strategy where a is played with probability p. Then the expected payoff for Player 2 depends on whether or not Player 2 plays a or b:

$$\mathbb{E}[\text{Payoff for Player 2}|\text{Player 2 plays } a] = 2p + 0(1-p)$$
$$\mathbb{E}[\text{Payoff for Player 2}|\text{Player 2 plays } b] = 0p + 1(1-p)$$

The first expression is increasing in p, and the second is decreasing in p. Suppose Player 1 chooses p in order to make these expected returns equal.

$$2p = 1 - p \Rightarrow 3p = 1 \Rightarrow p = 1/3.$$

When Player 1 plays a with probability $1/3$, then no matter what strategy Player 2 uses (random or deterministic), Player 2 has the same expected return. But two can play at that game (so to speak)!

Suppose Player 2 plays a with probability q and b with probability $1 - q$.

$$\mathbb{E}[\text{Payoff for Player 1}|\text{Player 1 plays } a] = 1q + 4(1-q)$$
$$\mathbb{E}[\text{Payoff for Player 1}|\text{Player 1 plays } b] = 3q + 2(1-q)$$

Choosing q to make these expected returns equal:

$$1q + 4 - 4q = 3q + 2 - 2q \Rightarrow 2 = 4q \Rightarrow q = 1/2.$$

So a Nash equilibium is:

$$\boxed{((1/3, 2/3), (1/2, 1/2))}$$

Problems

28.1 If a Player has a 50% chance of playing a, and a 50% chance of playing b, this is what type of strategy?

28.2 If a Player always chooses option c, this is what type of strategy?

28.3 Consider the following payoff matrix.

		Player 2		
		a	b	c
Player 1	a	$(-3,-4)$	$(-1,2)$	$(2,-3)$
	b	$(-1,2)$	$(3,-2)$	$(0,0)$

Show that this is not a zero sum game.

28.4 Consider the following playoff matrix.

		Player 2	
		a	b
	a	$(6,4)$	$(5,5)$
Player 1	b	$(3,4)$	$(7,1)$
	c	$(8,2)$	$(3,4)$

Show that this is not a zero sum game.

28.5 Consider the following payoff matrix.

		Player 2		
		a	b	c
Player 1	a	$(-3,-4)$	$(-1,2)$	$(2,-3)$
	b	$(-1,2)$	$(3,-2)$	$(0,0)$

Show that no pure strategies for the players form a Nash equilibrium.

28.6 Consider the following playoff matrix.

		Player 2	
		a	b
	a	$(6,4)$	$(5,5)$
Player 1	b	$(3,4)$	$(7,1)$
	c	$(8,2)$	$(3,4)$

Show that no pure strategy for the players is also a Nash equilibrium.

28.7 Consider the following payoff matrix.

		Player 2	
		a	b
Player 1	a	$(-2,-3)$	$(2,2)$
	b	$(1,1)$	$(0,0)$

Find three Nash equilibria.

28.8 Consider the following playoff matrix.

		Player 2	
		a	b
Player 1	a	$(6, 4)$	$(5, 5)$
	b	$(3, 4)$	$(7, 1)$

Find the Nash equilibrium (or equilibria).

Part VI

Randomized Algorithms

Chapter 29

Randomized Algorithms

Question of the Day

Suppose that at least one element of an array of n elements has value a. What is the fastest way to find such an element?

Summary

- **Randomized algorithms** are allowed to make random choices of which step to take next.
- One type of randomized algorithm is a **Monte Carlo algorithm**, where the output is itself a random variable.
- Another type of randomized algorithm is a **Las Vegas algorithm**, where the number of steps taken by the algorithm is a random variable.
- **Big-O**, **Big-Omegea**, **Big-Theta**, and **little-o** notation give an idea of how a function grows as the size of its input grows.

In decision theory, the user strategizes as though they are playing against an adversary. Usually, the best approach in this situation is to make random decisions. This enabled the expected return to be optimized. It turns out that even when our "adversary" is not another person, but a fixed set of data, it also helps to apply random choices!

When randomness is intentionally introduced into an algorithm, it is (unsurprisingly) called a *randomized algorithm*.

Definition 109
A **randomized algorithm** is an algorithm that can take steps based on the value of one or more random variables.

In general, the assignment of values to a random variable in a randomized algorithm is taken to be independent during each run of the algorithm. That means that two runs of the same algorithm might generate different values. Another way of saying this is that the output of the algorithm is itself a random variable!

Definition 110
A **Monte Carlo** algorithm has output that is a nontrivial random variable.

An early user of Monte Carlo algorithms was Stanislaw Ulam, who advocated for their use during the Manhattan Project, the United States effort to build an atomic bomb. His friend Nicholas Metropolis knew that Stanislaw liked to gamble: and so he jokingly called them Monte Carlo algorithms after the famous casino in Monte Carlo, Monaco.

In the question of the day, the goal is not to have a random result. Instead, the goal is the correct result, but it is possible to use a random number of steps to get it. An algorithm like this is named after another famous location for gambling.

Definition 111
A randomized algorithm whose result is always a deterministic function of the input is a **Las Vegas algorithm**.

For the question of the day, a Las Vegas type of algorithm is what is needed. The next chapter will explore more general Monte Carlo algorithms and what they are capable of.

29.1 Deterministic and random search

Consider the question of the day. The input is an *array* of n elements. That means any number from 1 to n can be passed to the computer and the computer will return the value of the array at that position. The goal is to search for a value known to appear somewhere in the array.

One simple approach is just to query each of the values of the array in order until the value is found. Pseudocode for this approach might use a *for* loop.

Deterministic_search *Input:* Array x, Value a

1) For i from 1 to n
2) If $x(i) = a$ then return i

In order to analyze the running time of such an algorithm, computer scientists use two common approaches, the *average time* and the *worse-case time*. The worst-case time assumes that the data is chosen as badly as possible to make the number of steps used by the algorithm as many as possible. For this algorithm, the worst thing that can happen is to make $x(n) = a$ and $x(i) \neq a$ for all $i < n$. Then the algorithm has to check n different values of the array in order to find one with value a.

Now suppose that instead of starting at 1, start with a random number drawn uniformly from 1 to n. Then search the array in order as before. After reaching the final element of the array, wrap around and start searching from the beginning again.

Random_search *Input:* Array x, Value a

1) Draw X uniformly from 1 to n
2) For i from X to n
3) If $x(i) = a$ then return i
4) For i from 1 to $X - 1$
5) If $x(i) = a$ then return i

On average, this approach uses half as many elements as a deterministic search.

Lemma 1
Let T denote the number of elements of x accessed by Random_search. Then $\mathbb{E}[T] = (n+1)/2$.

Proof. Suppose $x(j) = a$. Then if $X \leq j$, then the number of elements searched is $j - X + 1$. If $X > j$, then the number of elements searched is $n - X + 1 + j$.

$$\begin{aligned}
\mathbb{E}[T] &= \mathbb{E}[(j - X + 1)\mathbb{1}(X \leq j) + (n - X + 1 + j)\mathbb{1}(X > j)] \\
&= \mathbb{E}[j - X + 1 + n\mathbb{1}(X > j)] \\
&= j - \frac{n+1}{2} + 1 + n\left(1 - \frac{j}{n}\right) \\
&= j - \frac{n+1}{2} + 1 + n - j \\
&= \frac{n+1}{2}.
\end{aligned}$$

□

29.2 Measuring running time

For randomized search, $\mathbb{E}[T] = (n+1)/2$. For this notation to make sense, really T should be dependent on n, so $\mathbb{E}[T(n)] = (n+1)/2$. Usually, the input parameters that T is dependent on are clear from the context of the algorithm, and so are omitted in practice.

In this case, the algorithm only saved a factor of 2 by using randomness, but often it is possible to save more than a constant factor. Sometimes using randomness can save a factor that depends on n itself. In analyzing the running time of algorithms, often the *lower order terms* do not matter.

For example, suppose an algorithm runs in $4n^3 + n^2$ steps. For $n = 100$, $4n^3 = 4,000,000$ and $n^2 = 10,000$. The n^2 is small relative to the $4n^2$. It becomes even smaller in relative terms the larger n is. That makes n^2 a lower order term compared to $4n^3$ in this example.

Order notation is designed to ignore these lower order terms. Technically, order notation defines sets of functions. For a function g, the four most commonly used sets are $O(g(n))$, $\Omega(g(n))$, $\Theta(g(n))$, and $o(g(n))$.

Definition 112
Say that $f(n) \in O(g(n))$ if

$$(\exists C)(\exists N)(\forall n \geq N)(f(n) \leq Cg(n)).$$

Example 44
Show that $n^2 + 10n \in O(n^2)$.

Proof Let $C = 20$ and $N = 1$. Let $n \geq N = 1$. Then

$$20n^2 = 10n^2 + 10n^2 \geq n^2 + 10n.$$

This is often called *Big-O* notation. If $f(n) \in O(g(n))$ this means that as n gets large, $g(n)$ dominates $f(n)$ when constant factors are ignored. Note that we could have also shown that $n^2 + 10 \in O(n^3)$. Making the function inside the Big-O bigger does not change the truth of the statement, it just makes the statement less useful.

Constants do not matter in Big-O notation.

Lemma 2
If $f(n) \in O(g(n))$, then for any $c_1, c_2 \in \mathbb{R}$, $c_1 f(n) \in O(c_2 g(n))$.

There is also a corresponding lower bound notation: Big-Omega.

Definition 113
Say that $f(n) \in \Omega(g(n))$ if

$$(\exists C)(\exists N)(\forall n \geq N)(f(n) \geq Cg(n)).$$

Example 45
Show that $n^2 + 10n \in \Omega(n^2)$.

Proof Using $N = 1$ and $C = 1$, let $n \geq 1$. Then $n^2 + 10n \geq n^2$.

When we have a function that is both Big-O and Big-Omega of a function, then it is Big-Theta.

Definition 114
If $f(n) \in O(g(n)) \cap \Omega(g(n))$, then $f(n) \in \Theta(g(n))$.

There's one more order notation that is used, and that is *little-o*. Little-O (like Big-O) is an upper bound, but it is an upper bound that is known to be too weak. In other words, the function is growing more slowly than the function inside the little o.

Definition 115
Say that $f(n) \in o(g(n))$ if

$$(\forall C > 0)(\exists N)(\forall n \leq N)(f(n) \leq Cg(n)).$$

Note the difference between Little-o and Big-O: in Little-o the rest of the statement works for any constant bigger than 0, for Big-O there only needs to be some constant. Hence $O(g(n)) \subseteq o(g(n))$.

Often it is easier to determine function order using limits.

Lemma 3
Suppose $f(n)$ and $g(n)$ are functions such that

$$\lim_{n\to\infty} \frac{f(n)}{g(n)} = L.$$

1. If $L < \infty$ then $f(n) \in O(g(n))$.
2. If $L = 0$ then $f(n) \in o(g(n))$.
3. If $L > 0$ then $f(n) \in \Omega(g(n))$.
4. If $L \in (0, \infty)$ then $f(n) \in \Theta(g(n))$.

Notation 5
When using order notation the equals sign $=$ is often substituted for set inclusion, $\in$.

Example 46
We write things like $n^3 = n^2 + O(n^3)$ and $n^2 + 10n = \Omega(n^2)$.

For the question of the day, both the deterministic and random search use $\Theta(n)$ steps. The next chapter examines an algorithm where randomness does not just improve the constant but changes the order of the number of steps needed.

Problems

29.1 An algorithm with a random output is a ____________ algorithm.

29.2 An algorithm with a random running time is a ____________ algorithm.

29.3 Show that $n^3 + n^2 \in O(n^3)$ by explicitly finding C and n that satisfies the definition.

29.4 Show that $n^3 + n^2 \in \Omega(n^3)$ by explicitly finding C and n that satisfies the definition.

29.5 Given that $n^3 + n^2 \in O(n^3)$ and $n^3 + n^2 \in \Omega(n^3)$, what else can be said about the order of $n^3 + n^2$?

29.6 If you prove that $n\ln(n) + n \in O(n\ln(n))$ and $n\ln(n) + n \in \Omega(n\ln(n))$, what else can you say about $n\ln(n)$?

29.7 Show that $5n \in o(n\ln(n))$ by explicity finding an N value such that for all $C > 0$ and $n \geq N$, $5n \leq n\ln(n)$.

29.8 Show that $n \in o(n^2)$.

29.9 Suppose there is an array with n elements which contains value a in exactly one position.

A randomized algorithm for finding where this value is located does the following: choose uniformly at random a position from 1 up to n. Search that position. If found, quit. Otherwise, start over and independently choose again until the value is found.

What is the expected number of steps needed to find the value?

29.10 Continuing the last problem, consider an array with $n = 100$.

a) What is the chance that the algorithm examines at most 50 positions in the array?

b) What is the chance that the algorithm examines at least 150 positions in the array?

Chapter 30

QuickSort and QuickSelect

Question of the Day

What is the fastest way to find the median of an array of values?

Summary

Assume that you have a set of n real values.

- The **order statistics** is an n-tuple of the values in sorted order.
- The **sample median** is the middle value of the order statistics (or the average of the two middle values if there are an even number of values.)
- **QuickSort** is a randomized algorithm for sorting values that is widely used in practice because it uses about $2n \ln(n)$ comparisons to sort.
- **QuickSelect** is a randomized algorithm for finding a single order statistic (or the sample median) that uses at most $4n$ comparisons.

30.1 *Using QuickSelect to find the median*

An important Las Vegas algorithm is QuickSelect, which is used to find the *sample median* of a set of numerical data in an array. Roughly speaking, this is the middle value of the array. Recall that $\lfloor a \rfloor$ is the *floor* of a, which rounds a down to the closest integer value, and $\lceil a \rceil$ is the *ceiling* of a which rounds a up to the closest integer value.

Given an array of values, the *order statistics* are a permutation of indices that place the values in order. Parentheses around subscripts indicate order statistics. That is, write $x_{(k)}$ for the kth order statistic. Then for an array of n items, $x_{(1)}$ is the smallest value, and $x_{(n)}$ is the largest. Formally, this can be expressed as follows.

Definition 116
For an array $x = (x(1), x(2), \ldots, x(n))$ of values, say that

$$x_{(1)} \leq x_{(2)} \leq \cdots \leq x_{(n)}$$

are the **order statistics** of x if there exists a permutation σ such that for all $i \in \{1, \ldots, n\}$,

$$x_{(i)} = x(\sigma(i)).$$

For an odd sized array, the order statistic in the middle of the array values is the *sample median.* For an even sized array, the arithmetic average of the two order statistics closest to the middle is the sample median. This can be codified in the following way.

Definition 117
For an array x with order statistics $x_{(1)}, \ldots, x_{(n)}$, the **sample median** is

$$m = \frac{x_{(\lfloor (n+1)/2 \rfloor)} + x_{(\lceil (n+1)/2 \rceil)}}{2}.$$

The sample median is also sometimes just called the *median* of the array.

One approach to finding the median is to first find the permutation σ that puts the data in order, and then directly use the definition. Finding σ is known as *sorting* the data, and in general takes $\Theta(n \ln(n))$ comparisons between objects. That $\ln(n)$ factor is slowly growing, but for $n = 10^6$ it is almost 14. This makes it a significant factor in the running time. Is there a way to avoid it?

For convenience in this section assume that all the values in the array are distinct. If they are not, simply assign them a preference based on their original ordering. So for example, if the original array was $(1.1, 1.7, 1.7, 1.4)$, say that the value 1.7 in position 2 beats the value 1.7 in position 3 when it comes to sorting. (This is also known as a *stability* criterion.)

30.2 QuickSort

One randomized algorithm for sorting is called QuickSort. This is a recursive algorithm: it is allowed to call itself, possibly with different parameters. In the case of QuickSort, it randomly selects a value of the array and sorts the array into two pieces. The left piece consists of those values less than the selected value and the right piece consists of those values greater than or equal to the selected value.

```
QuickSort   Input: Array x

Let n be the number of values in the array X
If n = 1, return x
Else
   Choose I uniformly from 1 to n
   Let ℓ and r be empty arrays
   For i from 1 to n
      If x(i) < x(I) then add x(i) to the end of ℓ
      Else add x(i) to the end of r
   ℓ' ← QuickSort(ℓ)
   r' ← QuickSort(r)
   Return the array (ℓ', x(I), r').
```

The running time of sorting algorithms can be measured by the number of *comparisions* they make. In other words, for i and j, how many times do they check if $x(i) < x(j)$? The number of comparisons turns out to be related to the *harmonic numbers*.

$$H_n = 1 + \frac{1}{2} + \frac{1}{3} + \cdots + \frac{1}{n}.$$

Fact 43
Let $T(n)$ be the number of comparisons used by QuickSort on an array of n elements. Then

$$\mathbb{E}[T] = 2(n+1)H_n - 4n.$$

The proof will use two important ideas. To understand the first idea, suppose an array has order statistics

$$3, 4, 8, 9, 11, 17.$$

Consider 4 and 11. If 8 is selected as a pivot, then 4 and 11 are each compared to 8, but they will never be compared to each other. This is because 4 is assigned to the left hand side ℓ and 11 is assigned to the right hand side r, and they become elements of different recursive calls.

If 17 is chosen as the pivot, then both 4 and 11 are sent to ℓ, and they still have a chance of being compared to each other. Out of the elemnts $4, 8, 9, 11$ if either 4 or 11 is chosen as a pivot, then 4 and 11 will be compared to each other, but if 8 or 9 is chosen they will not. Pivots keep getting chosen until one of 4, 8, 9, or 11 is the pivot, so conditional on this happening, there is a $2/4$ chance that they will be compared.

For the ith order statistic $x_{(i)}$ and jth order statistic $x_{(j)}$, the chance that they are compared is $2/|j-i+1|$ because out of the $|j-i+1|$ elements in the interval bounded by $x_{(i)}$ and $x_{(j)}$, there are exactly two choices of pivot that lead to these values being compared.

Now the stage is set for the proof of the running time of QuickSort.

Proof. Let $B_{i,j}$ be the indicator that values $x_{(i)}$ and $x_{(j)}$ are compared in QuickSort. Then the total number of comparisons is

$$T = \sum_{1 \leq i < j \leq n} B_{i,j},$$

and by linearity of expectation

$$\mathbb{E}[T] = \sum_{1 \leq i < j \leq n} \mathbb{E}[B_{i,j}].$$

The mean of a random variable that is either 0 or 1 is just the probability that it is 1, which is (as shown right before the proof)

$$\frac{2}{j - i + 1}.$$

That is,

$$\mathbb{E}[T] = \sum_{1 \leq i < j \leq n} \frac{2}{j - i + 1}.$$

There are $n - 1$ pairs where $j - i = 1$, $n - 2$ pairs where $j - i = 2$, and so on, making,

$$\begin{aligned}
\mathbb{E}[T] &= \frac{2(n-1)}{2} + \frac{2(n-2)}{3} + \frac{2(n-3)}{4} + \cdots + \frac{2}{n} \\
&= 2\left[\frac{n}{2} - 1 + \frac{1}{2} + \frac{n}{3} - 1 + \frac{1}{3} + \cdots + \frac{n}{n} - 1 + \frac{1}{n}\right] \\
&= 2[n(H_n - 1) - n + H_n] \\
&= 2(n+1)(H_n) - 4n.
\end{aligned}$$

□

The harmonic numbers H_n are close to $\ln(n)$.

Fact 44
The harmonic numbers satisfy

$$\ln(n) + \gamma \leq H_n \leq \ln(n) + 1,$$

where $\gamma = 0.5772156649\ldots$ is called **Euler's constant**.

So the mean number of comparisons for QuickSort is about $2n\ln(n)$.

Sorting can also be thought of as looking through permutations trying to find the one that (when applied to the data) gives the order statistics. There are $n!$ permutations for n objects, and each comparison divides the number of permutations in 2. Therefore, $\log_2(n!) = \lg(n!)$ comparisons are needed in general. Using Stirling's bounds to analyze $\lg(n!)$ gives that any algorithm that sorts by comparisons must use an average of $1.44n\ln(n)$ comparisons on randomly arranged data. So QuickSort is pretty close to the best possible, at least on average.

30.3 QuickSelect

Back to the Question of the Day, is it possible to find the median in time faster than $\Theta(n\ln(n))$? After all, a complete sorting of the data is not the goal, the goal is merely to find the order statistic (or two order statistics for an even size array) closest to the middle.

The answer is yes, it is possible to build an algorithm that finds the sample median in $O(n)$ time! It operates in a fashion somewhat similar to QuickSort. Instead of sorting all the elements, first randomly pick a few elements, then only sort those elements. To do this, the algorithm needs to be broader in scope. The algorithm has two inputs: the array, and a value k. The output is then the kth order statistic of the array.

QuickSelect *Input:* Array x, integer k

```
Let n be the number of elements in x
If n = k = 1 then return x(1)
Else
   Draw I uniformly from 1 to n
   For i from 1 to n
      If x(i) < x(I) then add x(i) to the end of ℓ
      Else add x(i) to the end of r
   Let n_ℓ be the number of elements in ℓ
   If k − 1 = n_ℓ, return x(I)
   If k − 1 < n_ℓ, return(QuickSelect(ℓ, k))
   If k − 1 > n_ℓ, return(QuickSelect(r, k − n_ℓ))
```

Let v be the output of the algorithm. Because of possible ties among the array values, the number of indices with a value less than v might not be exactly $k-1$, but it is possible to say something similar.

Fact 45
QuickSelect(x, k) returns a value v such that $x_{(k)} = v$.

Proof. Use strong induction on n. For the base case where $n = 1$, $x_{(1)} = x(1)$ so the algorithm returns the correct value.

Suppose the result holds for all values $n' \leq n$, now consider an array of size $n+1$. If $k = n_\ell$ from the algorithm, then the output satisfies exactly k elements of the array are at most the value n_ℓ. If $k > n_\ell$, then there must be a sort of the array where the first n_ℓ items are in ℓ. The new goal at this point is to find the kth smallest item in this subarray which has size at most n.

Hence the recursive call in line 10 of the algorithm returns the correct value. Similarly, if $k > n_\ell$, then all the values in ℓ are strictly smaller than $x(I)$, so the new goal is to look for the $k - n_\ell$ smallest value in the rest of the array in r. Since r also has size at most n, our induction hypothesis allows us to use the recursive call in line 11 to finish the job. □

So it works, but how long does it take to work?

Fact 46
Let $T(n)$ denote the number of comparisons used by QuickSelect. Then

$$\mathbb{E}[T(n)] \leq 4n$$

Proof. Proceed by strong induction. When $n = 1$, the number of comparisons is 0, so this case is satisfied.

Suppose now that the inequality holds up to $n-1$, and consider an array with n arguments. The goal is to find the kth smallest item. That means that $k-1$ items are smaller, and $n-k$ items are larger.

$k-1$ values	k	$n-k$ values

Each call chooses I and then compares $x(I)$ to the other elements. If I is chosen such that exactly $k-1$ values are less than $x(I)$, then the total number of comparisons is n because the algorithm terminates in one pass.

If $k < n_\ell$ (which happens with probability $(n-k)/n$), then some elements are eliminated from the array. Note $[n_\ell | n_\ell > k] \sim \mathsf{Unif}(\{k+1, \ldots, n\}$, and the elements up to n_ℓ are kept. So on average

$$\mathbb{E}[n_\ell | n_\ell > k] = (n+k+1)/2$$

elements of the array are left.

Similarly, if $k > n_\ell$ (which happens with probability $(k-1)/n$), eliminate on average

$$\mathbb{E}[n_\ell - 1 | n_\ell < k] = (k - 1 + 1)/2 - 1$$

elements from the array. That leaves (on average) $n + 1 - (k/2)$ elements.

Hence if $\mathbb{E}[T(i)] \leq 4i$ for all $i < n$,

$$\mathbb{E}[T(n)] \leq n + 4\left[\frac{n-k}{n} \cdot \frac{n+k+1}{2} + \frac{k-1}{n} \cdot \frac{2n-k+2}{2}\right].$$

The right hand side is a quadratic equation in k, and so easy to maximize. The largest the righthand side can be occurs at $k = (n+1)/2$, which gives,

$$\mathbb{E}[T(n)] \leq n + 4\left[\frac{(3/2)n^2 - 1}{2n}\right] \leq n(1+3) = 4n,$$

which completes the induction. □

Hence the median of an array of n elements can be found in $\Theta(n)$ average time!

Floyd-Rivest

In QuickSelect only a single pivot was used, which led to our constant of 4. By using more initial random values, it is possible to get an algorithm that to first order only requires $1.5n$ comparisons on average to find the sample median. This was introduced in 1975 by Floyd and Rivest and is now known as the Floyd-Rivest algorithm.

Problems

30.1 Find the sample median of $8, 4, 4, 5, 3$.

30.2 Find the sample median of $8, 4, 4, 5, 3, 10$.

30.3 For $x = (8, 4, 4, 5, 3)$, answer the following.

a) What would `QuickSort(x)` return?

b) What would `QuickSelect(x, 2)` return?

c) What would `QuickSelect(x, 4)` return?

30.4 For $x = (13.5, 4.2, -1.7, 2.4)$, answer the following.

a) What would `QuickSort(x)` return?

b) What would `QuickSelect(x, 2)` return?

c) What would `QuickSelect(x, 4)` return?

30.5 Suppose $\mathbb{E}[T(n)] \leq \mathbb{E}[T(n-1)] + 2$ and $\mathbb{E}[T(0)] = 0$. Prove by induction that $\mathbb{E}[T(n)] \leq 2n$.

30.6 Suppose $\mathbb{E}[T(n)] \leq \mathbb{E}[T(n-1)] + 1/n$ and $\mathbb{E}[T(0)] = 0$.

a) Prove by induction that $\mathbb{E}[T(n)] \leq H_n$.

b) Prove that $\mathbb{E}[T(n)] \leq \ln(n)$.

30.7 A recursive algorithm when presented with input of size $n \geq 2$, makes one call of size $n - 1$ and another of size $n - 2$. If the input is size 0 or 1, then 1 operation is needed. Prove by strong induction that the running time is at most α^n where $\alpha = (1 + \sqrt{5})/2$.

30.8 A recursive algorithm when presented with input of size $n \geq 2$, makes one call of size $n - 1$ and two calls of size $n - 2$. If the input is size 0 or 1, then 1 operation is needed. Prove by strong induction that the running time is at most 2^n.

Chapter 31

Randomized Verification

Question of the Day

Suppose A, B, and C are three n by n matrices with the claim that $A \cdot B = C$. Is it possible to verify the claim without again multiplying the matrices together from scratch?

Summary

- It is generally faster to verify that a solution to a problem is correct than to solve it from scratch.

- An example of this is *matrix multiplication*, which for an n by n matrix has an $O(n^2)$ randomized verification algorithm. To solve from scratch takes time $O(n^{2.3728596...})$ (as of 2024).

- **Freivald's Algorithm** returns true if the answer is correct, and if the answer if false, then it returns false at least 50% of the time. Running the algorithm independently multiple times can bring the failure probability as low as desired.

31.1 Matrix multiplication

If you have learned some linear algebra, you have learned about the *dot product* of two vectors in $\mathbb{R}^n$.

Definition 118
The **dot product** of two vectors $x = (x_1, \ldots, x_n)$ and $y = (y_1, \ldots, y_n)$ where each $y_i \in \mathbb{R}$ and each $x_j \in \mathbb{R}$ is

$$x \cdot y = x_1 y_1 + \cdots x_n y_n = \sum_{i=1}^{n} x_i y_i.$$

Since the definition of the dot product involves n multiplications and n additions, the total number of arithmetic operations to calculate the dot product is $O(n)$. Calculating the dot product requires reading the vector x, and so it is also $\Omega(n)$. Hence the running time is $\Theta(n)$.

An n by n real-valued matrix A is a table of numbers such that A_{ij} refers to the number in the ith row and the jth column. Multiply an n by n matrix times a column vector as follows.

Definition 119
If A is a real-valued n by n matrix, and x is a column vector, then the **matrix-vector product** is

$$Ax = y,$$

where y is also a column vector whose ith entry is the dot product of the ith row of A and x.

To calculate a matrix-vector product, it is necessary to calculate n different dot products. Therefore, finding a matrix-vector product requires $O(n^2)$ arithmetic operations. It also requires reading A which contains n^2 entries, so the time to compute a matrix-vector product for general matrices is $\Theta(n^2)$.

An n by n matrix B can be written as n column vectors.

$$B = \left(\begin{array}{c|c|c|c|c} b_1 & b_2 & b_3 & \cdots & b_n \end{array} \right)$$

Then each column of the *matrix product* AB has columns equal to the product of A times the columns of B.

Definition 120
Let A and B be real-valued n by n matrices. Let b_j denote the jth column of B. Then $C = AB$ is also an n by n real-valued matrix known as the **matrix product** of A and B if the jth column of C is Ab_j for all $j \in \{1, \ldots, n\}$.

Using the definition to calculate matrix multiplication of two n by n real-valued matrices shows that matrix multiplication can be accomplished in $O(n^3)$ time. Unlike the dot product and matrix-vector multiplication, the input size to matrix multiplication is $\Omega(n^2)$. So it is possible that better algorithms for matrix multiplication than the definition will be found. In fact, there is an algorithm that runs in $O(n^{2.372\ldots})$. So if the best possible matrix multiplication requires $\Theta(n^\omega)$ time, the best bounds (as of 2023) that are known are $2 \leq \omega \leq 2.372\ldots$.

31.2 Verification

Solving the matrix multiplication problem is still open, but how about the *verification problem*? In a verification problem, the algorithm is given the solution, and the output is either true or false depending on whether or not the solution is correct or incorrect. This is also known as a *decision problem.*

Definition 121
Let $\mathcal{P}$ be a proposition that takes input $I \in \mathcal{I}$ and returns either T or F. Then the **decision problem** for $\mathcal{P}$ is to create an algorithm $\mathcal{A}$ such that

$$(\forall I \in \mathcal{I})(\mathcal{A}(I) = \mathcal{P}(I)).$$

For example, the input set $\mathcal{I}$ might be the set of positive integers, and the proposition something like "the number that is input is prime."

Another way to say this is given a particular proposition, is there an algorithm that determines for each input if the proposition is true or false? So far the question of what is an *algorithm* has been set aside. Traditionally, this is done via the model of digital computation called a *Turing machine.* However, this level of abstraction will not be needed for what follows.

In the decision problem, the input is given and the goal is to determine if the proposition is true or not. A more difficult problem is to *solve* the proposition by finding the input for which the statement is true.

Definition 122
Let $f : \mathcal{I} \to \mathcal{J}$ be a computable function. Then the **function problem** is to find an algorithm $\mathcal{A}$ such that

$$(\forall I \in \mathcal{I})(f(I) = \mathcal{A}(I)).$$

Given a particular run of a function problem algorithm, the *verification problem* is to show that the output is correct. That is, given an input and a potential output, the verification problem is to show that the output was correct for the given input. Formally, this can be set up as follows.

Definition 123
The **verification problem** associated with a function problem $f : \mathcal{I} \to \mathcal{J}$ is the decision problem $\mathcal{V}$ over input set $\mathcal{I} \times \mathcal{J}$ where

$$(\forall I \in \mathcal{I})(\forall J \in \mathcal{J})(\mathcal{V}(I, J) = (f(I) = J)).$$

It seems that verification should be easier than the solution problem. After all, the algorithm is handed the solution and is just asked whether the solution works or not. So this should be easier than finding the solution in the first place, right? This intuition is correct, often there are faster algorithms for verification problems than what are known for function problems.

Matrix multiplication

An example of this phenomenon is matrix multiplication.

Consider the problem of verifying that the multiplication of two n by n matrices A and B leads to a third matrix C. The input set for the verification problem is then of the form $((A, B), C)$ where A, B, and C are n by n matrices. The proposition of interest is then:

$$\mathcal{V}((A, B), C) = (AB = C).$$

As of June 2024, actually solving for C given A and B (the function problem) can be done using an $O(n^{2.372\ldots})$ algorithm [**williams2024new**] for matrix multiplication. But can the verification problem be done faster? The answer is yes! This is shown using *Freivald's Algorithm.*

31.3 Freivald's Algorithm

Freivald [**freivalds1977**] developed a randomized algorithm to check if $AB = C$ for any three input matrices A, B, and C.

Freivald's_Alg *Input:* A, B, C	
0)	Let n be such that A, B, and C are n by n matrices
1)	Draw x uniformly from $\{0, 1\}^n$
2)	Let $y \leftarrow A(Bx) - Cx$
3)	Return the value of proposition $(y = 0)$

Fact 47
If $AB = C$, then Freivald's_Alg will always return true (T). However, if $AB \neq C$, there is at least a 50% chance that the algorithm will return false (F).

Proof. Let $D = AB - C$. If $AB = C$ then D is the matrix of all 0's, and Dx is the vector of all 0's no matter what choice of x is made. So if $AB = C$, then the algorithm always returns T.

However, if $AB \neq C$, then there must be an i and j such that entry $D_{ij} \neq 0$. Let r_i be the ith row of D, and consider

$$r_i \cdot x = D_{ij}x_j + \sum_{k \neq j} D_{ik}x_k.$$

Then the summation on the right hand side must add to some value. Since x_j was chosen uniformly from $\{0, 1\}$, $D_{ij}x_j$ is either 0 or $D_{ij} \neq 0$ with equal probability. Hence the chance that $r_i \cdot x = 0$ is at most 50%. So the algorithm has at least a 50% chance of detecting that nonzero entry! □

31.4 RP, co-RP, and BPP

There are several classes of randomized algorithms for decision problems. An algorithm belongs to a particular class based on its running time as a function of the input size, on the probability that it gets the answer correct when the output is true, and the probability that it gets the answer correct when the output is false. Start with *randomized polynomial time* or RP for short.

Definition 124
Let $\mathcal{I}$ be an input space and $\forall I \in \mathcal{I}\, \mathcal{P}(I)$ is either true or false. Say that algorithm $\mathcal{A}$ is in the complexity class **randomized polynomial time** (abbreviated **RP**) if the following holds.

- The running time of $\mathcal{A}(I)$ is polynomial in the input size with probability 1.
- For all $I \in \mathcal{I}$, if $\mathcal{P}(I) = \mathsf{T}$ then $\mathbb{P}(\mathcal{A}(I) = \mathsf{T}) \geq 1/2$.
- For all $I \in \mathcal{I}$, if $\mathcal{P}(I) = \mathsf{F}$ then $\mathcal{A}(I) = \mathsf{F}$.

The last two conditions can be expressed more compactly using indicator functions. Recall that $\mathbb{1}(p) = 1$ if p is true and is 0 otherwise. Then the last two conditions to be RP are equivalent to

$$(\forall I \in \mathcal{I})(\mathbb{P}(\mathcal{A}(I) = \mathcal{P}(I)) \geq 1/2 + (1/2)\mathbb{1}(\mathcal{P}(I)).$$

Pictorially, an algorithm in RP obeys the following rules:

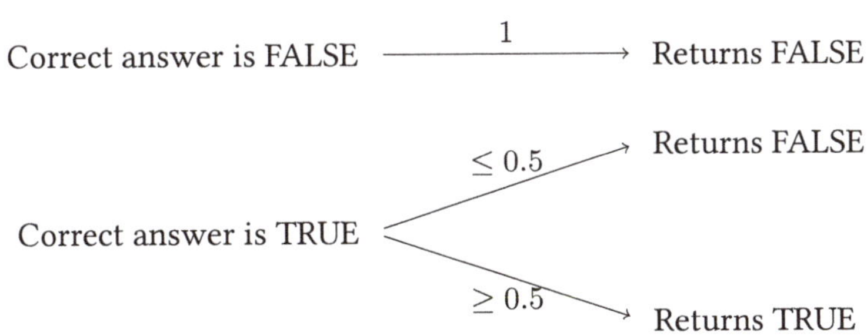

Okay, but this is not actually what Frievald's algorithm does. When the answer is true (so $AB = C$), Frievald's algorithm is guaranteed to generate an output of true, whereas when $AB \neq C$ Freivald's algorithm has a maximum error rate of 50%. This is an example of what is called a *complementary randomized polynomial time* or co-RP algorithm.

Definition 125
Let $\mathcal{I}$ be an input space and $\forall I \in \mathcal{I}\ \mathcal{P}(I)$ is either true or false. Say that algorithm $\mathcal{A}$ is in the complexity class **complementary randomized polynomial time** (abbreviated **co-RP**) if the following holds.

- The running time of $\mathcal{A}(I)$ is polynomial in the input size with probability 1.
- For all $I \in \mathcal{I}$, if $\mathcal{P}(I) = \mathsf{F}$ then $\mathbb{P}(\mathcal{A}(I) = \mathsf{F}) \geq 1/2$.
- For all $I \in \mathcal{I}$, if $\mathcal{P}(I) = \mathsf{T}$ then $\mathcal{A}(I) = \mathsf{T}$.

In both RP and co-RP, there is one output where the randomized algorithm always returns the correct answer. But what if there is a chance of making an error for both true and false outputs? When the running time is polynomial in the input size, these are called *bounded probability polynomial time* randomized algorithms.

Definition 126
Let $\mathcal{I}$ be an input space and $\forall I \in \mathcal{I}\ \mathcal{P}(I)$ is either true or false. Say that algorithm $\mathcal{A}$ is in the complexity class **bounded probability polynomial time** (abbreviated **BPP**) if the following holds.

- The running time of $\mathcal{A}(I)$ is polynomial in the input size with probability 1.
- For all $I \in \mathcal{I}$, if $\mathcal{P}(I) = \mathsf{F}$ then $\mathbb{P}(\mathcal{A}(I) = \mathsf{F}) \geq 2/3$.
- For all $I \in \mathcal{I}$, if $\mathcal{P}(I) = \mathsf{T}$ then $\mathbb{P}(\mathcal{A}(I) = \mathsf{T}) \geq 2/3$.

So for an algorithm in BPP, there is at most a $1/3$ chance of making an error regardless of the correct answer. Why only $1/3$ instead of $1/2$ as in RP and co-RP? Because if an algorithm were just to flip a fair coin and use heads for true and tails for false, this algorithm would already have only a $1/2$ chance of making an error! Limiting the error probability to $1/3$ ensures that the algorithm is actually putting in some work to get the error below that coming from a random guess.

31.5 Amplification

The above complexity classes are defined in terms of a $1/2$ or $1/3$ chance of failure. But what if the goal is to limit the chance of failure to $1/8$? $1/100$? Even smaller?

The technique of *amplification* can be used to accomplish this task.

False positives and negatives

Say that the algorithm has a *false positive* if it returns TRUE when the correct answer is FALSE. Similarly, say that it returns a *false negative* if the algorithm returns FALSE when the correct answer is TRUE.

Then one way to describe an RP algorithm is that it is a polynomial expected time algorithm where the false positive rate is 0 and the false negative rate is bounded above by $1/2$. What if the false positive rate is needed to be smaller?

One approach is to run the RP algorithm multiple times, making independent choices at each run for the random value. Consider running Freivald's Algorithm four times on the same set of matrices. Suppose that output was

T, T, F, T.

If the correct answer was T, then the randomized algorithm would never have given a false answer, so in this case, the correct answer must be F. On the other hand, if the output was

T, T, T, T

then there are two possibilities. Either, the correct answer was T, or the correct answer was F, and the algorithm was wrong four times in a row. The chance of this occurring is at most $(1/2)^4$. The picture looks like this:

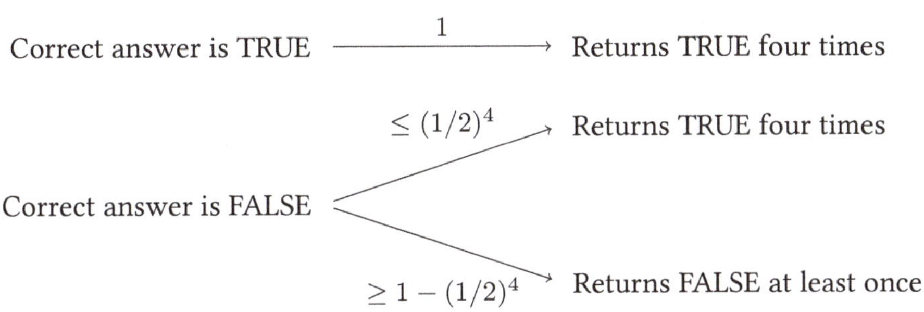

> **Definition 127**
> Running a randomized algorithm independently multiple times to reduce the error rate is called **amplification**.

Amplification_coRP *Input:* I, k

```
For i from 1 to k
    Let A_i ← 𝒜(I)
Return ∧_{i=1}^k A_i
```

Fact 48
Suppose $\mathcal{A}$ is an algorithm in co-RP for the decision problem $(\mathcal{P}, \mathcal{I})$. Then $\mathcal{B}(I, k) =$ Amplification_coRP(k) satisfies

- If $\mathcal{P}(I) = \mathsf{T}$, then $\mathcal{B}(I, k) = \mathsf{T}$ with probability 1.
- If $\mathcal{P}(I) = \mathsf{F}$, then $\mathbb{P}(\mathcal{B}(I, k) = \mathsf{F}) \geq 1 - (1/2)^k$.

Proof. Suppose $\mathcal{P}(I)) = \mathsf{T}$. Then $\mathcal{A}(I)$ returns T with probability 1, no matter how many times the algorithm is run. The logical AND of all three of the outputs will be 1 with probability 1.

Similarly, if $\mathcal{P}(I) = \mathsf{F}$, then the only way $\mathcal{B}(I, k)$ is not false is if every single $A_i = \mathsf{T}$. This happens with probability at most $(1/2)^k$. The complement rule then gives the result. □

Example 47
Suppose the goal is to build a version of Frievald's Algorithm that is right at least $7/8$ of the time. Then run it three times and take the logical AND of the output. By the above result, the chance of giving a wrong answer is at most $(1/2)^3 = 1/8$, so the chance of a correct answer is at least $1 - 1/8 = 7/8$.

A similar result holds for RP. Because these algorithms are always right when the answer is false, when the correct answer is false the output of the RP algorithm will always be false. But if the correct answer is true, there is at least a 50% chance of the output being true. Therefore, a single true output is enough to guarantee that the right answer is true.

That means that the amplification procedure is to run the algorithm independently k times and take the logical OR of the result.

```
Amplification_RP    Input: I, k
For i from 1 to k
    Let A_i ← A(I)
Return ∨_{i=1}^{k} A_i
```

The error bound for amplification for RP is similar to that of co-RP.

Fact 49
Suppose $\mathcal{A}$ is an algorithm in RP for the decision problem $(\mathcal{P}, \mathcal{I})$. Then $\mathcal{B}(I, k) = \text{Amplification\_RP}(k)$ satisfies

- If $\mathcal{P}(I) = \text{F}$, then $\mathcal{B}(I, k) = \text{F}$ with probability 1.
- If $\mathcal{P}(I) = \text{T}$, then $\mathbb{P}(\mathcal{B}(I, k) = \text{T}) \geq 1 - (1/2)^k$.

Amplification is a bit different for BPP algorithms. Because there is a chance of either a false positive or false negative, the logical AND cannot be used to determine the final result. Instead, make k an odd integer, run the algorithm independently k times, and return true or false depending on which appears most often

```
Amplification_BPP   Input: I, k

For i from 1 to k
    Let A_i ← 𝒜(I)
Return 𝟙(∑_i(𝟙(A_i)) > k/2)
```

For instance, if $k = 9$ and for the results $A_1, A_2, \ldots, A_9$, exactly 7 are true and 2 are false, the amplification algorithm returns true. But if at most 4 are true and at least 5 are false, then the amplification algorithm returns false as the final answer.

Finding the error in amplification for BPP involves finding the tail probabilities of binomially distributed random variables.

Example 48
A BPP algorithm is run 3 times and the majority winner is taken. What is the largest chance that it made an error?

Answer Say a trial is R if the answer is right and W if it is wrong. Then the majority winner is wrong if the three trials are WWW, WWR, WRW, RWW, which has probability at most

$$(1/3)(1/3)(1/3) + 3[(1/3)^2(2/3)] = 7/27 \approx 0.2592\ldots.$$

Note the answer is the same as $\mathbb{P}(X \geq 2)$ where $X \sim \text{Bin}(3, 1/3)$.

31.6 *Zero-error probabilistic polynomial time*

Las Vegas algorithms that are correct all the time, are in the problem class *ZPP*.

Definition 128
An algorithm $\mathcal{A}$ is in **zero-error probabilistic polynomial time** or **ZPP** if $\mathcal{A}(I)$ has output to the question of $(\exists I)(\mathcal{P}(I))$ such that

- The running time of the algorithm is a random variable whose expected value is polynomial in the input size with probability 1.
- $(\forall I \in \mathcal{I})(\mathbb{P}(\mathcal{P}(I) = \mathcal{A}(I)) = 1)$.

In terms of false positive and false negative rates, this can be summarized as follows.

Algorithm Type	False Positive Rate	False Negative Rate
RP	0	1/2
co-RP	1/2	0
BPP	1/3	1/3
ZPP	0	0

Problems

31.1 True or false: A BPP algorithm might return the correct answer $1/2$ of the time.

31.2 True or false: An RP algorithm has to be right at least $2/3$ of the time.

31.3 An RP algorithm is run twice and the output is the logical OR of the two runs. What is the largest chance that it made an error?

31.4 A co-RP algorithm is run five times and the output is the logical AND of the runs. What is the largest chance that it made an error?

31.5 A BPP algorithm is run 5 times and the majority winner is taken. What is the largest chance that it made an error?

31.6 A BPP algorithm is run 7 times and the majority winner is taken. What is the largest chance that it made an error?

31.7 How many times must an RP algorithm be run to guarantee that the chance of failure is at most 1%?

31.8 How many times must an RP algorithm be run to guarantee that the chance of failure is at most 10^{-6}?

Chapter 32

Randomized algorithms for Linear and Integer programming

Question of the Day

Consider the following *set cover* problem. Let $\mathcal{U} = \{1, 2, 3, 4, 5, 6, 7\}$ and

$$\begin{aligned} S_1 &= \{1, 6\} \\ S_2 &= \{3, 4\} \\ S_3 &= \{5\} \\ S_4 &= \{1, 2, 3\} \\ S_5 &= \{2, 4, 6, 7\} \\ S_6 &= \{4, 5, 6\} \\ S_7 &= \{7\} \end{aligned}$$

Find the smallest collection of S_i whose union is $\mathcal{U}$.

Summary

This section discusses the following topics.

- The **set cover** problem.
- Integer programming.
- Linear programming.
- Randomized rounding.

Two of the most powerful tools in Operations Research are *linear programming* and *integer programming*.

These are used for optimization. Unlike decision problems, optimization problems try to make a function of the inputs either large or small. This function is called the *objective function*. Write opt to stand in for either max or min.

Definition 129
An optimization problem of the form

$$\operatorname*{opt}_{x \in \Omega} f(x),$$

has **objective function** $f : \Omega \to \mathbb{R}$.

When the objective function f is a linear function of x, and the state space Ω is a subset of $\mathbb{R}^n$ formed using linear constraints, then call the problem a *linear program*.

Definition 130
A **linear program** has the form

$$\operatorname{opt} c \cdot x, \text{ subject to } \{x : Ax \leq b\},$$

for fixed $c, b \in \mathbb{R}^n$.

Here $c \cdot x$ is the dot product between a fixed vector c and the solutions x.

If the values of the variables are also required to be integers (so $\Omega \subseteq \mathbb{Z}^n$), then the problem is an *integer program*,

Definition 131
An **integer program** has the form

$$\operatorname{opt} c \cdot x, \text{ subject to } \{x : Ax \leq b\} \text{ and } x \in \mathbb{Z}^n,$$

for fixed $c, b \in \mathbb{R}^n$.

In 1947, George Dantzig revolutionized Operations Research when he invented the *simplex method*. This is an algorithm for solving linear programs that runs very quickly in practice. Later versions of this method have been developed that provably run in time polynomial in the input size.

Integer programming is far more difficult. In fact, the famous conjecture of whether or not problems whose solutions can be verified in polynomial time can also be solved in polynomial time (also known as the P = NP question) would be solved in the affirmative if there was a polynomial time method for integer programming problems.

32.1 Set cover as an integer programming problem

The question of the day is an example of a *set cover* problem.

> **Definition 132**
> The **set cover** problem consists of a universe set $\mathcal{U}$ and a set of subsets of $\mathcal{U}$ called $S_1, \ldots, S_n$ such that $\cup_{i=1}^{n} S_i = \mathcal{U}$. The goal is to find the smallest value of k such that a subset of $\{S_1, \ldots, S_n\}$ of size k has union $\mathcal{U}$.

The set cover problem serves are a simple model of any situation where placing resources, factories, or service buildings is needed to serve different areas of a community or company. For example, in the question of the day, a company might be building seven cell towers at specific sites to serve seven different regions of an area.

The number of sets k needed to cover all n elements satisfies $k \leq n$, but how much smaller can k be? The problem is in NP because any answer (a subset of $\{1, 2, \ldots, n\}$) can be checked to be correct or incorrect in time polynomial in the input size. It is also NP-complete. Karp showed in 1972 [**karp1972**] that if this problem could be solved in time polynomial in the input, then *any* problem in NP could be solved in polynomial time. That would make P = NP, and so the set cover problem is an example of an NP-complete problem.

The problem can be written as an integer program in the following way.

- Create indicator variables x_i that are 0 if S_i is not in the subset and 1 if S_i is in the subset.

- To ensure that the union of the S_i covers $\mathcal{U}$, it must be true that for each element $u \in \mathcal{U}$, the sum of x_i where $u \in S_i$ must be at least 1. So there is a linear constraint for every element $u \in \mathcal{U}$.

- The objective is to minimize the sum of the x_i (that counts how many of the S_i are in the subset.)

Example 49
In the question of the day, the integer program is

$$\begin{aligned}
\min x_1 + x_2 + x_3 + x_4 + x_5 + x_6 & \\
x_1 + x_4 \geq 1 & \quad \text{cover 1} \\
x_4 + x_5 \geq 1 & \quad \text{cover 2} \\
x_2 + x_4 \geq 1 & \quad \text{cover 3} \\
x_2 + x_5 + x_6 \geq 1 & \quad \text{cover 4} \\
x_3 + x_6 \geq 1 & \quad \text{cover 5} \\
x_1 + x_4 + x_6 \geq 1 & \quad \text{cover 6} \\
x_5 + x_7 \geq 1 & \quad \text{cover 7} \\
(\forall i)(0 \leq x_i \leq 1) & \\
(\forall i)(x_i \in \mathbb{Z}) &
\end{aligned}$$

Note that $x_1 + x_4 \geq 1$ can be written as $-x_1 - x_4 \leq -1$ so this still falls into the integer programming definition that uses $Ax \leq b$.

32.2 Linear relaxation

A general principle is that removing constraints from an optimization problem can only increase the set of valid solutions.

Definition 133
For a problem $\text{opt}_{x \in \Omega} f(x)$, let Ω' be such that $f : \Omega' \to \mathbb{R}$ is defined. Then if $\Omega \subset \Omega'$, call

$$\underset{x \in \Omega'}{\text{opt}} f(x)$$

a **relaxation** of the problem.

Note that because there are more choices for x, the solution of the relaxation will always be better than that of the original problem.

Definition 134
For an integer program with constraint $x \in \mathbb{Z}^n$, removing this constraint gives the **linear relaxation** of the integer program.

The purpose of constructing a linear relaxation is to move from an integer program which is difficult to solve to an LP that is fast to solve. The problem is that the solution to the LP is not usually a solution to the IP, as it might contain fractional values.

32.3 Randomized rounding

To move from a solution $x \in [0,1]^n$ to a solution $y \in \{0,1\}^n$, use the *randomized rounding* approach. In this approach, each number $p \in [0,1]$ is used as the parameter of a Bernoulli random variable. So with probability p the number is rounded up to 1, and probability $1-p$ it is rounded down to 0.

Definition 135
For $x \in [0,1]^n$, let $y_i \sim \text{Bern}(x_i)$ be iid. Call $y = (y_1, \ldots, y_n)$ a **randomly rounded** version of x.

Because y_i is a $\{0,1\}$ random variable, $\mathbb{E}[y_i] = x_i$. By linearity for any linear objective function with $c \in \mathbb{R}^n$,

$$\mathbb{E}[c \cdot y] = c \cdot x.$$

So on average, the objective value is the same as that solution to the LP relaxation. But is the solution feasible for the IP?

Consider the constraint:

$$x_2 + x_5 + x_6 \geq 1.$$

For $y_2 + y_5 + y_6$ to equal 0, it must hold that $y_2 = y_5 = y_6 = 0$. Because the y_i were chosen independently, this occurs with probability

$$(1 - x_2)(1 - x_5)(1 - x_6).$$

It is straightforward to use a technique such as Lagrange multipliers to show that this product is maximized when the x_i are equal, so

$$\mathbb{P}(y_2 + y_5 + y_6 = 0) \leq (1 - 1/3)(1 - 1/3)(1 - 1/3) = (1 - 1/3)^3 \leq \exp(-1).$$

Suppose this rounding is repeated t times independently. Let w_i be the maximum of the y_i values over the t iterations. Then

$$\mathbb{P}(w_2 + w_5 + w_6 = 0) = \mathbb{P}(y_2 + y_5 + y_6 = 0)^t \leq \exp(-t).$$

There are n constraints that could be unsatisfied, and so the union bound tells us that the probability that any of the constraints is unsatisfied is at most $n\exp(-t)$.

Let $X_1, X_2, \ldots$ be the objective function for each trial of the randomized rounding. Then $\mathbb{E}[X_i] \leq t \cdot \text{OPTLP} \leq t \cdot \text{OPT}$, where OPTLP is the optimal objective function for the LP relaxation, and OPT is the optimal objective function for the original IP.

Let T be the total number of steps until a feasible IP solution is found. Since each run is independent, T is a geometric random variable with at least a $1 - n\exp(-t)$ chance of success. So $\mathbb{E}[T] \leq 1/[1 - n\exp(-t)]$. Also

$$\mathbb{E}[X_T] \leq \sum_{i=1}^{T} \mathbb{E}[X_i] \leq \mathbb{E}[T]\mathbb{E}[X_i] \leq \frac{t}{1 - n\exp(-t)} \cdot \text{OPT}$$

by Wald's identity.

In particular, if $t = \ln(n) + \ln(\ln(n))$, then

$$\mathbb{E}[X_T] \leq \frac{\ln(n) + \ln(\ln(n))}{1 - 1/\ln(n)} \cdot \text{OPT}.$$

Other places randomized rounding can be used include:

- Facility location problems.
- Multicommodity flow problems.

Problems

32.1 Consider the following optimization problem.

$$\begin{aligned} \max\ & x_1^2 + x_2^2 \\ \text{subject to } & x_1 + x_2 \leq 4 \\ & x_1 \geq 0 \\ & x_2 \geq 0 \end{aligned}$$

Is this a linear program?

32.2 Consider the following optimization problem.

$$\begin{aligned} \max\ & 3x_1 - x_2 \\ \text{subject to } & x_1 + x_2 \leq 4 \\ & x_1 \geq 0 \\ & x_2 \geq 0 \end{aligned}$$

Is this a linear program?

32.3 Suppose $\mathcal{U} = \{1, 2, 3, 4\}$,

$$\begin{aligned} S_1 &= \{1, 2\} \\ S_2 &= \{3, 4\} \\ S_3 &= \{1, 2, 3, 4\}. \end{aligned}$$

a) Does $\{S_1, S_2\}$ cover $\mathcal{U}$? (That is, does the union of S_1 and S_2 equal $\mathcal{U}$?)

b) Is there a smaller set cover?

32.4 Suppose $\mathcal{U} = \{1, 2, 3, 4, 5\}$,

$$\begin{aligned} S_1 &= \{1, 2\} \\ S_2 &= \{3, 4\} \\ S_3 &= \{2, 3, 4, 5\}. \end{aligned}$$

Find a set cover of size two.

32.5 Suppose $\mathcal{U} = \{1, 2, 3, 4, 5\}$,

$$\begin{aligned} S_1 &= \{1, 2\} \\ S_2 &= \{3, 4\} \\ S_3 &= \{2, 3, 4, 5\}. \end{aligned}$$

a) Write the problem of finding the smallest set cover as an integer program.

b) What is the linear relaxation of this IP?

32.6 Continuing the last problem, find the optimal solution of the LP relaxation, and discuss how that also solves the original IP problem.

32.7 Consider the IP

$$\begin{aligned} \max x_1 + x_2 \\ (1/2)x_1 + x_2 &\leq 1 \\ 3x_1 + x_2 &\leq 2 \\ (x_1, x_2) &\in \{0, 1\}^3. \end{aligned}$$

The linear relaxation would be

$$\begin{aligned} \max x_1 + x_2 \\ (1/2)x_1 + x_2 &\leq 1 \\ 3x_1 + x_2 &\leq 2 \\ (x_1, x_2) &\in [0, 1]^3. \end{aligned}$$

The optimal solution to this is

$$(x_1, x_2) = (2/5, 4/5).$$

a) If randomized rounding was then used to generate a solution from the original IP, what would the expected objective value be?

b) What is the chance that the $(1/2)x_1 + x_2 \leq 1$ constraint is satisfied?

32.8 Consider the IP

$$\begin{aligned} \min x_1 + 2x_2 \\ x_1 + 2x_2 \geq 1 \\ 3x_1 + x_2 \geq 2 \\ (x_1, x_2) \in \{0,1\}^3. \end{aligned}$$

The linear relaxation would be

$$\begin{aligned} \max x_1 + 2x_2 \\ x_1 + 2x_2 \geq 1 \\ 3x_1 + x_2 \geq 2 \\ (x_1, x_2) \in [0,1]^3. \end{aligned}$$

The optimal solution to this is

$$(x_1, x_2) = (3/5, 1/5).$$

a) If randomized rounding was then used to generate a solution from the original IP, what would the expected objective value be?

b) What is the chance that the $(1/2)x_1 + x_2 \leq 1$ constraint is satisfied?

Part VII

Time series

Chapter 33

Forecasting

Question of the Day

Consider the value of the Dow Jones Industrial Average for the 27th of March through the 5th of April, 2017. Call the 27th of March day 0.

Day	DJIA Index
0	20550.98
1	20701.50
2	20659.32
3	20728.49
4	20663.22
5	20650.21
6	20689.24
7	20648.15

Predict the value for day 8.

Summary

- A **time series** is a collection of random variables indexed by time.

- **Forecasting** is the process making an estimate of the value of a time series based on observations at previous times.

33.1 Predicting the future

A set of data values indexed by time is typically called a *time series*. One of the goals of studying time series is to give a best guess prediction for the next data point in the series based on the data up to the current time.

There are two main methods for using data to predict the next data point: Extrapolation and Causal Methods.

- **Extrapolation** includes methods such as moving averages and smoothing.
- **Causal Methods** typically build a statistical model of the data, such as using linear regression.

Here, y_t is used to denote the actual value of the time series at time t. Use $\hat{y}_t$ to denote an estimate of the time series.

33.2 The baseline model

The simplest model of a time series is the *baseline mode*, which assumes that there is a baseline value for the data that is perturbed by a random error independently at each step.

Model 1
The **baseline model** is

$$y_i = b + \epsilon_i.$$

The simplest estimate for this model is an estimate of b using all the previous data.

Estimate 1 (Average estimate)
For y_i using the baseline model, for $k \in \{1, 2, \ldots\}$

$$\hat{y}_{t+k} = \frac{1}{t} \sum_{i=1}^{t} y_i.$$

This model says that no matter how far into the future the prediction goes, always just use the average of the values given up until the current time t.

Example 50
In the question of the day,

$$\hat{y}_8 = \hat{y}_9 = \cdots = 20661.38\ldots,$$

which is $\boxed{20660}$ to four sig figs.

33.3 Moving averages

The problem with the average of all the data is that the base of the baseline model b tends to drift over time. For instance, stock values or a player's batting average might improve with the economy or training, leading to a new value of b.

A *moving average* operates by not averaging all the data, but only the last few entries. Use the parameter n to indicate how many of the last entries are part of our prediction.

Estimate 2 (Moving average)
For parameter n, the **moving average estimate** for $k \in \{1, 2, \ldots\}$ is

$$\hat{y}_{t+k} = \frac{1}{n} \sum_{i=0}^{n-1} y_{t-i}.$$

Example 51
In the question of the day, if the moving average is of the last three periods ($n = 3$), then the prediction for Day 3 given the information in Day 0, 1, and 2 is:

$$\frac{20550.98 + 20701.50 + 20659.32}{3},$$

and the prediction for Day 5 given the information up to Day 4 is

$$\frac{20701.50 + 20728.49 + 20663.22}{3},$$

and so on. That gives us a table:

Day	Index	Prediction	Error
0	20550.98		
1	20701.50		
2	20659.32		
3	20728.49	20637.27	91.22
4	20663.22	20696.44	−33.22
5	20650.21	20683.68	−33.47
6	20689.24	20680.64	8.60
7	20648.15	20667.56	−19.41

The last column of our table is the *forecast error*, the difference between the true value and the predicted value.

Definition 136
The **forecast error** for $\hat{y}_t$ predicting y_t is

$$e_i = y_t - \hat{y}_t.$$

33.4 Standard and mean absolute deviations

Different values of n in the moving average will have different errors in the prediction. The hope is to make the spread in the error of prediction as small as possible.

A common way to measure the spread in a random variable X is to use the standard deviation of X, written $\text{SD}(X)$. This is usually easy to compute, especially when X is the sum of independent random variables. The method *addition in quadrature* will be used to find the standard deviation.

Fact 50
If $x_1, X_2, \ldots, X_n$ are independent random variables, then

$$\text{SD}(X_1 + \cdots + X_n) = \sqrt{\text{SD}(X_1)^2 + \cdots + \text{SD}(X_n)^2}.$$

While addition in quadrature is easy, it is sometimes the case that the expected value of a random variable X can exist, but the standard deviation can be infinite!

Therefore, there is another deviation called the *mean absolute deviation* is often used in assessing predictions.

Definition 137
The **mean absolute deviation** of a random variable X is

$$\text{MAD}(X) = \mathbb{E}[|X - \mathbb{E}(X)|].$$

The advantage of the mean absolute deviation over the absolute deviation is that having finite expectation is enough to give finite mean absolute deviation.

Fact 51
When $\mathbb{E}(X)$ exists and is finite, then $\text{MAD}(X)$ exists and is finite.

For many common distributions, the MAD ends up being a multiple of the SD.

Example 52
For $X \sim \mathsf{Exp}(\lambda)$, find $\mathrm{MAD}(X)$.

Answer The density of X is: $f_X(s) = \lambda e^{-\lambda s}\mathbb{1}(s \geq 0)$. So the mean of the random variable is

$$\mathbb{E}(X) = \int_{-\infty}^{\infty} s f_X(s)\, ds = 1/\lambda.$$

By the Law of the Unconscious Statistician:

$$\begin{aligned}
\mathrm{MAD}(X) &= \mathbb{E}(|X - \mathbb{E}(X)|) \\
&= \int_{-\infty}^{\infty} |s - 1/\lambda| f_X(s)\, ds \\
&= \int_{-\infty}^{\infty} |s - 1/\lambda| \lambda e^{-\lambda s}\mathbb{1}(s \geq 0)\, ds \\
&= \int_{0}^{\infty} |s - 1/\lambda| \lambda e^{-\lambda s}\, ds \\
&= \int_{0}^{1/\lambda} -(s - 1/\lambda)\lambda e^{-\lambda s}\, ds \\
&+ \int_{1/\lambda}^{\infty} (s - 1/\lambda)\lambda e^{-\lambda s}\, ds \\
&= \boxed{\frac{2}{e} \cdot \frac{1}{\lambda}}.
\end{aligned}$$

Some notes about the deviations.

1. $\mathrm{MAD}(X), \mathrm{SD}(X), \mathbb{E}(X)$ all have the same units.
2. Alternate notation: $\mathrm{MD}(X) = \mathrm{MAD}(X)$
3. $\mathrm{MAD}(cX) = |c|\,\mathrm{MAD}(X)$
4. If you do need to calculate $\mathrm{MAD}(X_1 + \cdots X_n)$ for a particular distribution, this can usually be estimated accurately using Monte Carlo.

Some more calculations yield the following.

Dist	$\mathbb{E}(X)$	$\mathrm{SD}(X)$	$\mathrm{MAD}(X)$
$\mathsf{Exp}(\lambda)$	$1/\lambda$	$1/\lambda$	$(2/e)(1/\lambda)$
$\mathsf{Unif}([a,b])$	$(a+b)/2$	$(b-a)/\sqrt{12}$	$(b-a)/4$
$\mathsf{N}(\mu,\sigma)$	μ	σ	$\sigma \cdot 2/\sqrt{\tau}$

33.5 Estimating mean absolute deviation

If $\mathbb{E}[E_i] = 0$, then the mean absolute deviation of the forecast error is just $\mathbb{E}[|E_i|]$. An estimate of MAD can be found by taking a sample average of the absolute errors of the predictions.

$$\widehat{\text{MAD}} = \frac{1}{t}\sum_{i=1}^{t} |e_i|.$$

Example 53
In the question of the day when $n = 3$:

$$\widehat{\text{MAD}} = \frac{|91.22| + |-33.21| + |-33.46| + |8.6| + |-19.41|}{5} \approx 37.18.$$

A simple rule of thumb for choosing n for a large data set is to pick the value of n that minimizes $\widehat{\text{MAD}}$.

- For stock data: $n = 4$ has $\widehat{\text{MAD}}$ of 22.41.
- $n = 2$ has $\widehat{\text{MAD}}$ of 35.702.
- For $n \in \{2, 3, 4\}$, one would probably go with $n = 4$ for that reason.

Problems

33.1 Consider data

time	sales
0	4.3
1	3.7
2	7.2
3	4.5
4	6.1.

Estimate the baseline average.

33.2 Add a new column to this table of the forecast error using the baseline average.

33.3 Continuing the last problem, find the $n = 2$ and $n = 3$ moving averages for this data.

33.4 Continuing the last problem, using the MAD error criterion, would you go with the $n = 2$ or $n = 3$ moving average?

33.5 For $U \sim \text{Unif}([0, 1]$, find $\text{MAD}(u)$.

33.6 For $Z \sim \text{N}(0, 1)$, find $\text{MAD}(Z)$.

33.7 For X an integrable random variable, prove that $\mathrm{MAD}(X) = \mathrm{MAD}(X + a)$ for any constant a.

33.8 For X an integrable random variable, prove that $\mathrm{MAD}(cX) = c\,\mathrm{MAD}(X)$ for any constant c.

Chapter 34

Simple Exponential Smoothing

Question of the Day

How can small fluctuations in time series data be smoothed out?

Summary

- **Simple exponential smoothing** is a model where the effects of prior history on the next forecast are dampened exponentially fast as you move farther back in time.
- The model is

$$\hat{y}_{t+k} = \alpha y_t + (1 - \alpha)\hat{y}_t.$$

The *moving average estimate* is intended to deal with the problem of a drifting value of b in our baseline model. This approach is sharp: either a past element of y_{t-i} is included in the average, or it is discarded.

A smoother estimate includes all of the y_{t-i} in the prediction $\hat{y}_t$ but does it so that the further in the past we look, the less impact the data has on the prediction.

One such model is *simple exponential smoothing*, or SES. This model works by using a convex linear combination of the most recent data value together with the previous prediction. By adjusting the parameter of the combination, one can form a prediction that relies heavily on the previous data, or more strongly on current data.

Model 2 (Simple exponential smoothing (SES))
The SES estimate has one parameter $\alpha \in (0, 1)$. Given an estimate $\hat{y}_t$, the forecast for $k \in \{1, 2, \ldots\}$ is

$$\hat{y}_{t+k} = \alpha y_t + (1 - \alpha)\hat{y}_t.$$

Example 54
Suppose our previous prediction of the next data point was 54. When the actual data point is seen, it turns out to be 58. So if $\alpha = 0.2$, then the prediction for the next point would be

$$\hat{y}_{t+1} = (0.2)(58) + (0.8)(54).$$

Some remarks:

- This style of prediction always uses all of the data, simply because $\hat{y}_{t-1}$ depends on all the data from time 1 up to $t-1$, and then also includes the data value y_t.
- The model does not specify how to start the process. Two common ways of starting are to not make a prediction immediately, but then set $\hat{y}_0 = y_0$. Alternately, use $\hat{y}_1 = 0$.

34.1 Error view of SES

As earlier, let e_t denote the forecast error:

$$e_t = y_t - \hat{y}_t.$$

The SES estimate will be (in terms of error)

$$\begin{aligned}
\hat{y}_{t+k} &= \alpha y_t + (1 - \alpha \hat{y}_t) \\
&= \hat{y}_t + \alpha(y_t - \hat{y}_t) \\
&= \hat{y}_t + \alpha e_t.
\end{aligned}$$

That is, the new prediction is the old prediction plus a fraction of the error from the old prediction.

If the old prediction had a high error, then it was too low, so the new prediction is higher. If the error was negative, that meant the old prediction was too high, and so adding a fraction of the error makes it lower.

Example 55
With $\alpha = 0.75$ for stock data from before:

Day	Index	Prediction	Error
0	20550.98		
1	20701.50	20550.98	150.52
2	20659.32	20663.87	-4.55
3	20728.49	20660.46	68.03
4	20663.22	20711.48	-48.26
5	20650.21	20675.29	-25.08
6	20689.24	20656.48	32.76
7	20648.15	20681.05	-32.90

Here $\hat{\text{MAD}} = 51.72$.

34.2 *How to choose α*

For moving averages, choose the parameter n to minimize the estimate of the mean absolute deviation. Follow the same principle here, choosing α that minimizes the estimate of the mean absolute deviation.

In this case, α is a continuous random variable with possibly several local minima. Rather than tackle this complicated optimization problem, a simple approach is to only try α values that are integer multiples of 0.05 and keep the best. In the question of the day, this is $\alpha = 0.75$.

In practice $\alpha = 0.1, 0.3$, or 0.5 are commonly used. A value of $\alpha > 0.5$ indicates that some other trend such as seasonality is present because past values are discounted so severely.

34.3 *The effect of SES on data*

So why is this called exponential smoothing?

Consider the first few estimates:

$$\begin{aligned}
\hat{y}_{1+k} &= \alpha y_1 + (1-\alpha)\hat{y}_0 \\
&= \alpha y_1 \\
\hat{y}_{2+k} &= \alpha y_2 + (1-\alpha)\hat{y}_1 \\
&= \alpha y_2 + \alpha(1-\alpha) y_1 \\
\hat{y}_{3+k} &= \alpha y_3 + (1-\alpha)\hat{y}_2 \\
&= \alpha y_3 + \alpha(1-\alpha) y_2 + \alpha(1-\alpha)^2 y_3
\end{aligned}$$

The data point i time steps before $t+1$ is given a weight of $\alpha(1-\alpha)^i$. So all of the previous data values are being used. To compare to the weights seen earlier, let $r = 1 - \alpha$. Then the weights are as follows.

	y_t	y_{t-1}	$\cdots$	y_{t-n+1}	y_{t-n}	$\cdots$	y_1
Average	$1/t$	$1/t$	$\cdots$	$1/t$	$1/t$	$\cdots$	$1/t$
Moving average	$1/n$	$1/n$	$\cdots$	$1/n$	0	$\cdots$	0
SES	α	αr	$\cdots$	αr^n	αr^{n+1}	$\cdots$	αr^t.

Note that weights in the first two rows add up to 1. The weights for SES add up to slightly less than 1, but they add up to something very close to 1 as t gets large.

When $\alpha = 2/(n+1)$, then $r = 1 - \alpha = 1 - 2/(n+1)$, and $r^{n+1} \approx \exp(-2)$. So the SES estimate will be similar to the moving average estimate with n periods.

34.4 Holt's method

Now suppose that our time series is not roughly constant, but that the baseline itself has a linear trend.

Model 3
The **linear trend model** model is

$$y_t = b + mt + \epsilon_t.$$

Holt [**holt1957**] developed an extension of SES for the linear trend model which is known as *Holt's method.*

The idea is to create an estimate $\hat{b}_t$ for b, $\hat{\ell}_t$ for y_t (that is the *level* of the series, and then predict using

$$\hat{y}_{t+k} = \hat{\ell}_t + \hat{m}_t k.$$

To be precise, the method is as follows.

Estimate 3 (Holt's Method)
This method has two parameters, α for the level, and β^* for the trend.

First, update the level estimate based on the current data point and our previous prediction.

$$\hat{\ell}_t = \alpha y_t + (1 - \alpha)(\hat{\ell}_{t-1} + \hat{m}_{t-1}).$$

Next, update our trend estimate using the difference between level estimates smoothed with the previous estimate.

$$\hat{m}_t = \beta^*(\hat{\ell}_t - \hat{\ell}_{t-1}) + (1 - \beta^*)\hat{m}_{t-1}.$$

Then our prediction is

$$\hat{y}_{t+k} = \hat{\ell}_t + k\hat{m}_t.$$

Often the initial values $\hat{m}_0$ and $\hat{\ell}_t$ are drawn from previous data.

Example 56
Use Holt's method to predict Blu-ray sales (in thousands of units) with $\alpha = 0.3$, $\beta = 0.1$, $\hat{\ell}_0 = 25.3$ and $\hat{m}_0 = 7.4$

Month	Sales	$\hat{\ell}_t$	$\hat{m}_t$	Prediction	e_t
		25.3	7.4		
1	32	32.49	7.379	32.7	-0.7000
2	40	39.9083	7.38293	39.869	0.1310
3	38	44.503861	7.1041931	47.29123	-9.291
4	56	52.92563787	7.235951477	51.6080541	4.391
5	67	62.21311254	7.441103797	60.16158935	6.838

Dealing with data that grows exponentially

Some data (including economic data) grows exponentially rather than linearly. Note that Holt's method can still be used: it is just that the logarithm is used first to turn it into linear data.

For instance, with the model,

$$x_t = ab^t \nu_t,$$

taking the logarithm gives

$$\ln(x_t) = \ln(a) + t\ln(b) + \ln(\nu_t).$$

Set $y_t = \ln(x_t)$, and proceed as before.

Problems

34.1 Suppose a prediction for y_1 was $\hat{y}_1 = 10$. If $\alpha = 0.4$ with simple exponential smoothing, what would the prediction $\hat{y}_2$ be if y_1 turned out to have value 12.

34.2 Suppose a prediction for y_1 was $\hat{y}_1 = 100$. If $\alpha = 0.1$ and y_1 was observed to be 50, what would the prediction $\hat{y}_2$ be using simple exponential smoothing?

34.3 The California milk per cow from organic herds is summarized in the following table (drawn from https://www.californiadairymagazine.com/read/adtrack/2017/0717/2016cdfamilkreport.pdf accessed 2024-04-15.) It also includes predictions made using simple exponential smoothing with $\alpha = 0.6$ using $\hat{y}_1 = y_0$.

Year	Annual Milk per cow (pounds)	pred
2012	14904	NA
2013	15204	14904.00
2014	15480	15084.00
2015	16284	15321.60
2016	15816	15899.04

Find an estimate of the mean absolute deviation of the error.

34.4 The following table gives deliveries of Boeing 747 planes from 1995 through 2000. (Drawn from https://en.wikipedia.org/wiki/Boeing_747 accessed 2024-04-15.)

Year	Deliveries	Pred
1995	25	NA
1996	26	25
1997	39	
1998	53	
1999	47	
2000	25	

a) Fill out the rest of the table using SES with $\alpha = 0.75$.

b) Estimate the MAD for your predictions.

34.5 Continuing the California cows data from earlier, here are the predictions for $\alpha = 0.6$ and $\alpha = 0.4$. Which would be chosen as the better value of α using MAD to make the decision.

Year	Annual Milk per cow (pounds)	$\alpha = 0.4$	$\alpha = 0.6$
2012	14904	NA	NA
2013	15204	14904.00	14902.00
2014	15480	15084.00	15024.00
2015	16284	15321.60	15206.40
2016	15816	15899.04	15637.44

34.6 Continuing the Boeing data from above, fill out the above table using SES for $\alpha = 0.6$ and $\alpha = 0.25$. Which would you choose (using MAD as the criteria for the decision.)

34.7 Domestic U.S. data for passengers scheduled to fly month by month in 2000 is as follows. (Drawn from transtats.bts.gov/TRAFFIC on 2024-04-15.)

Period	Scheduled
January 2000	41540
February 2000	43714
March 2000	52977
April 2000	50344
May 2000	52309
June 2000	54673
July 2000	55568
August 2000	54474
September 2000	46363
October 2000	50920
November 2000	49632
December 2000	47051

Using $\hat{\ell}_0 = 40000$ and $\hat{m}_0 = 3000$ together with Holt's method with $\beta = 0.1$ and $\alpha = 0.5$, predict the number of passengers for March 2001.

34.8 Repeat the last problem with $\alpha = 0.4$ and $\beta = 0.05$.

Part VIII

DECISION MAKING FOR STOCHASTIC PROCESSES

Chapter 35

Marginal Analysis

Question of the Day

Suppose that a shop can buy a toy for \$4.00 from a wholesaler. The toy sells in the shop for \$6.25. Toys that do not sell can only be sold back to the wholesaler for \$2.75. The shop has developed a simple probabilistic model of sales. Let S be the number of sales.

i	$\mathbb{P}(S = i)$
1000	0.6
2000	0.3
3000	0.1

How many toys should the supplier buy?

Summary

Marginal analysis looks at the expected effect caused by changing a decision by one unit. This allows for quick optimization of complex problems. This can be applied to simple inventory purchase/sell-back models.

35.1 *Convex functions*

Optimization problems are the easiest when dealing with a *convex* objective function.

Example 57
Consider the graph of the absolute function: $f(x) = |x|$, which looks like this:

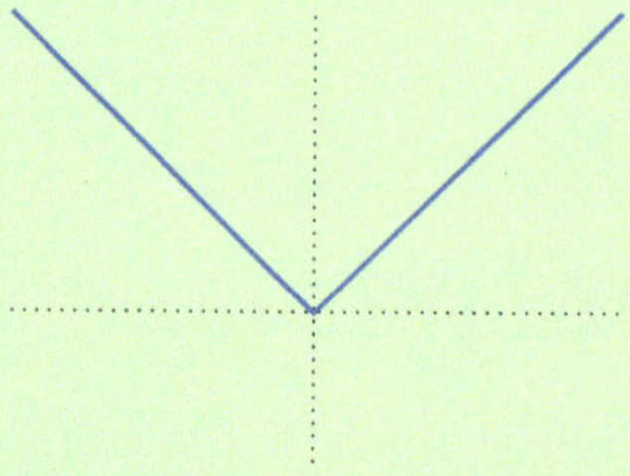

Suppose that I pick any two points on this graph, and consider the line segment that connects those two points. Then it always lies on or above the graph of the original function. Here are three examples:

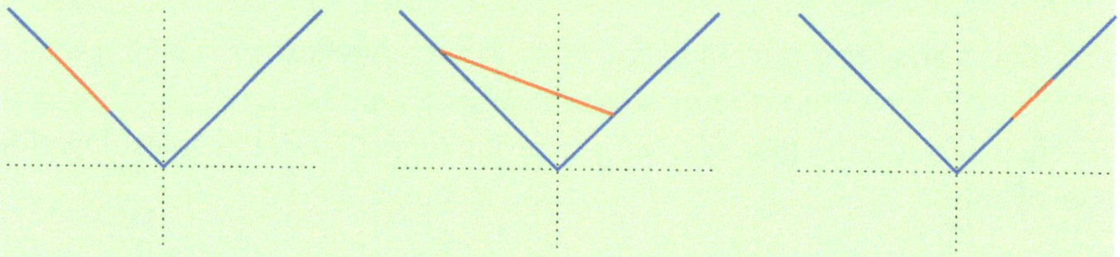

To describe this mathematically, use the idea of a *convex combination* between values.

Definition 138
Given $a < b$, the **convex combination** between a and b is a point $\lambda a + (1 - \lambda)b$ where $\lambda \in [0, 1]$.

Note that when $\lambda = 0$ the convex combination is just b, when $\lambda = 1$, the convex combination is just a, and for $\lambda = 1/2$ it is the point exactly halfway between a and b.

A function f is convex if f applied to a convex combination between a and b is smaller than the convex combination of $f(a)$ and $f(b)$.

Definition 139
A function f is **convex** if

$$(\forall a < b)(\forall \lambda \in [0, 1])(\lambda f(a) + (1 - \lambda)f(b)) \geq f(\lambda a + (1 - \lambda)b)).$$

The nice thing about convex functions is that they are easy to optimize. First, distinguish between a *local* and *global* minimum. A minimum is global if it is the minimum over the whole domain of the function.

Definition 140
For a real valued function f with domain $A \subseteq \mathbb{R}$, say that $(x^*, f(x^*))$ is a **global minimum** if

$$\left(\min_A f(x), \arg\min_A f(x)\right) = (x^*, f(x^*)).$$

To be a local minimum, it only has to be a minimum within a narrow range of the input value.

Definition 141
For a real valued function f with domain $A \subseteq \mathbb{R}$, say that $(x^*, f(x^*))$ is a **local minimum** if there is an $\epsilon > 0$ such that

$$\left(\min_{(x^*-\epsilon, x^*+\epsilon)\cap A} f(x), \arg\min_{(x^*-\epsilon, x^*+\epsilon)\cap A} f(x)\right) = (x^*, f(x^*)).$$

Fact 52
For a convex function f, if $(x^*, f(x^*))$ is a local minimum, then it is also a global minimum.

Sometimes this type of function is called *convex up*, because the function is going up as it moves away from its minimal value.

If the function f happens to have two continuous derivatives (write $f \in C^2$) then there is a simpler way to show that it is convex.

Fact 53
Let f be a function for which f'' is continuous. If $f'' \geq 0$, then f is a convex function.

35.2 Buy-back inventory model

Now consider the simple model of inventory given in the question of the day. A retailer can buy items for a fixed cost per item from a wholesaler. Some, or all, or none of the items are sold by the retailer, but if they are, then because the retailer is selling for a higher price than they bought, the retailer will make a small amount of money on each item sold.

If any items are not sold, then the retailer can sell back the remaining items to the wholesaler at a cost lower than what they paid.

First some notation.

$$\begin{aligned} q &= \text{amount ordered by the retailer (vendor)} \\ d &= \text{actual demand, that is, amount sold} \\ c(d,q) &= \text{cost to the vendor when ordering } q \text{ and selling } d. \end{aligned}$$

The *cost* is the negative of utility.

In an ideal world, the vendor orders an amount equal to the demand. In this case, the cost $c(d,d) = 0$. When $q < d$, then the vendor incurs a cost because the vendor could have ordered more and sold more. When $q > d$, then the vendor incurs a cost because the vendor should have ordered less.

> **Definition 142**
> When $q < d$, the lost income is called **understocking cost**. When $q > d$, the utility lost through buy-back is called **overstocking cost**.

In the question of the day:

- Each overstocked toy costs the vendor $\$4.00 - \$2.75 = \$1.25$.
- Each understocked toy costs the vendor $\$6.25 - \$4.00 = \$2.25$.

A graph of the cost function $c(q,d)$ for various values of d looks something like this.

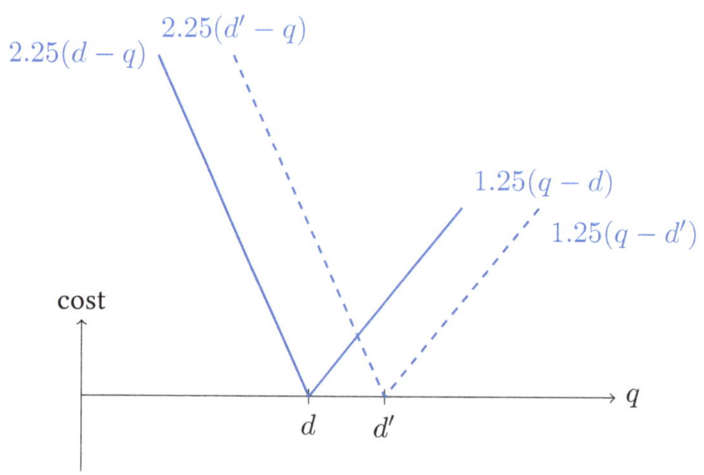

The problem, of course, is that the true demand D is a random variable, so it is not possible to know exactly how much to order. But it is possible to minimize the expected cost.

$$\min_q \mathbb{E}[c(D,q)].$$

Here is a nice fact about the expected value of a convex function that helps us out here.

Fact 54
If $f(x,y)$ is a convex function in y for every value of x, then

$$\mathbb{E}[f(X,y)]$$

is a convex function in y assuming the mean exists.

Proof. To show that it convex, let $y_1 < y_2$ and $\lambda \in [0,1]$. Then

$$\begin{aligned}
\mathbb{E}[\lambda f(X,y_1) + (1-\lambda)f(X,y_2)] &= \int_x \lambda f(x,y_1) + (1-\lambda)f(x,y_2)\,dX \\
&\geq \int_x f(x, \lambda y_1 + (1-\lambda)y_2)\,dX \\
&= \mathbb{E}[f(X, \lambda y_1 + (1-\lambda)y_2)].
\end{aligned}$$

That is exactly what it means for $\mathbb{E}[f(X,y)]$ to be convex in y! □

35.3 Marginal analysis

Now it is possible to define *marginal analysis*, which optimizes a function (with integer inputs) by looking at the change in the objective function when the input is increased by one.

In our case, the goal is to minimize $\mathbb{E}[c(D,q)]$, so consider what happens when q is increased by 1. Linearity of expectation gets us started.

$$\mathbb{E}[c(D,q+1)] - \mathbb{E}[C(D,q)] = \mathbb{E}[c(D,q+1) - c(D,q)].$$

When q is increased by 1, there will be one extra unit of overstocking cost c_o if $D \leq q$. On the other hand, if $q < D$, then increasing q by 1 removes one unit of understocking cost c_u. Hence

$$\begin{aligned}
\mathbb{E}[c(D,q+1)] - \mathbb{E}[C(D,q)] &= c_o\mathbb{P}(D \leq q) - c_u\mathbb{P}(D > q) \\
&= c_o\mathbb{P}(D \leq q) - c_u(1 - \mathbb{P}(D \leq q)) \\
&= -c_u + (c_o + c_u)\mathbb{P}(D \leq q).
\end{aligned}$$

A bit of algebra reveals that this is negative if and only if $\mathbb{P}(D \leq q) < c_u/(c_o + c_u)$, and nonnegative otherwise.

This buyback scheme historically applied to newsvendors, who after a strike were given the right to sell back unsold issues to the publisher at the end of the day. So the result goes by the name of the *newsvendor theorem.*

Theorem 14 (Newsvendor theorem)
Let c_u be the cost of one unit of understock, c_o the cost of one unit of overstock, D the random demand, and q^* the optimal amount of inventory to order. Then

$$q^* = \inf\left\{q : \mathbb{P}(D \leq q) \geq \frac{c_u}{c_u + c_o}\right\} = \arg\min_q \mathbb{E}[c(D,q)].$$

Recall that *inf* here stands for infimum, and means the smallest value such that the inequality on the right hand side is satisfied.

This theorem sometimes appears as *Littlewood's Rule.* Littlewood developed it in the context of deciding how many seats in an airplane to devote for first class versus coach passengers.

Example 58
For the question of the day,

$$\frac{c_u}{c_o + c_u} = \frac{2.25}{2.25 + 1.25} = 0.6428\ldots.$$

Looking at the demand distribution,

$$\mathbb{P}(D \leq q) = \begin{cases} 0.6 & q \in \{1000, \ldots, 1999\} \\ 0.9 & q \in \{2000, \ldots, 2999\} \\ 1 & q \in \{3000, \ldots\} \end{cases}$$

Therefore purchase $\boxed{2000}$ of the item, since this is the smallest amount that makes $\mathbb{P}(D \geq q) \geq 0.6428\ldots$.

Problems

35.1 The cost per unit when demand is higher than inventory is the ______________ cost.

35.2 The cost per unit when inventory is higher than demand is the ______________ cost.

35.3 True or false: the function $f(x) = x^2$ is convex.

35.4 True or false: the function $f(x) = x$ is convex.

35.5 Suppose that a Christmas tree seller can obtain trees for \$13.50 and that they sell in the local market for an average of \$110.00. Any trees left over after Christmas require payment of \$5.15 for disposal. If demand is modeled as a negative binomial distribution with parameters 1000 and 0.42, what is the optimal number of trees for the lot to buy?

35.6 A marketer is trying to decide how many flyers to give away at a conference. Each flyer costs 30 cents to produce, and each person at the conference who receives a flyer buys things that lead to 40 cents of profit. Excess flyers are destroyed at no cost. The number of attendees at the conference is modeled as uniform over $\{900, 1000, 1100, \ldots, 1800\}$. How many flyers should the marketer produce to maximize expected utility?

Chapter 36

Markov Decision Processes

Question of the Day

A printer is either perfectly aligned, almost aligned, somewhat aligned, or badly aligned. At the beginning of each month, it is possible to spend \$1500 to realign the printer back to perfect alignment. In perfect alignment the printer can be expected to earn \$4000 during a month, almost aligned \$3000, somewhat aligned \$2000, and badly aligned \$1000. The probability of moving from one alignment to another is shown in the figure below. What policy should the owner of the printer use?

If no alignment is carried out, the transition probabilities are:

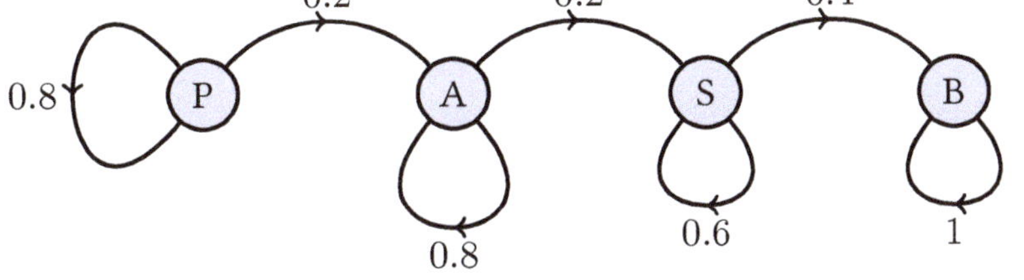

If alignment is carried out, the move always goes back to the perfectly aligned state with probability 1.

Summary

A discrete time process is a **Markov chain** if the distribution of X_t given $X_0, \ldots, X_{t-1}$ only depends on X_{t-1}.

A **Markov decision process** allows someone to make a decision based on the history of the process so that the distribution of the next state depends on the current state and the decision made. Based on the decision and the state, an expected reward is accrued.

A method for making decisions at each step is a **policy**. The value of a policy for an MDP often uses **long-term average reward** or **discounted reward**.

36.1 Discrete time Markov chains

Markov chains are memoryless processes. In the case where the time is discrete (so $t \in \{1, 2, \ldots\}$), this leads to the following definition.

> **Definition 143**
> A discrete time stochastic process $X_0, X_1, X_2, \ldots$ is a **Markov chain** if
> $$(\forall t)([X_t | X_{t-1}, X_{t-2}, \ldots, X_0] \sim [X_t | X_{t-1}]).$$

Intuitively, a Markov chain at time t only depends on the previous value, and knowing the rest of the history of the process does not further change the distribution.

Because the distribution of the state at time t only depends on the value of the chain at time $t - 1$, the model can be written as a discrete time Markov chain using *transition probabilities.*

> **Definition 144**
> For a Markov chain over a finite state space Ω, the **transition probabilities** are
> $$p(j|i) = \mathbb{P}(X_t = j | X_{t-1} = i).$$

36.2 Adding decisions

Now add a further wrinkle: at each time step, suppose that a decision can be made that also affects the distribution at the next time step. This gives us a *Markov decision process.*

Definition 145
A **Markov decision process** (MDP) consists of a

1. State space Ω which is finite.
2. Decision sets. for each $i \in \Omega$, a set of decisions $D(i)$.
3. Transition probabilities $p(j|i,d)$ so that
$$\mathbb{P}(\forall i,j)(\mathbb{P}(X_{t+1} = j|X_t = i, d) = p(j|i,d).$$
4. Expected rewards. If the process is currently in state i and decision d is made, call the expected reward $r_{i,d}$.

For instance, in the question of the day:
$$\Omega = \{P, A, S, B\}$$
$$(\forall i \in \Omega)(D_i = \{R, \neg R\}),$$
where R means realign the printer and $\neg R$ means do not realign the printer. The transition probabilities can then be broken up into two cases based on the decision to align or not align. First, if the printer is not realigned at the beginning of each step:
$$T_{\neq R} = \begin{pmatrix} 0.8 & 0.2 & 0 & 0 \\ 0 & 0.8 & 0.2 & 0 \\ 0 & 0 & 0.6 & 0.4 \\ 0 & 0 & 0 & 1 \end{pmatrix},$$
If the printer is realigned at the beginning of each month, then it immediately moves back to state P. From there, there is a 0.8 chance of staying in P and a 0.2 chance of moving to A. Hence the transition matrix becomes:
$$T_R = \begin{pmatrix} 0.8 & 0.2 & 0 & 0 \\ 0.8 & 0.2 & 0 & 0 \\ 0.8 & 0.2 & 0 & 0 \\ 0.8 & 0.2 & 0 & 0 \end{pmatrix}.$$
So $p(j|i,R) = T_R(i,j)$ and $p(j|i,\neg R) = T_{\neg R}(i,j)$.

If the printer is not realigned, then the reward for starting in state P, A, S, B is $4000, 3000, 2000, 1000$ respectively. If the printer is realigned, then \$1500 is spent. Still, the user gets the reward for being perfectly aligned, which is \$4000. Hence

	R	$\neg R$
P	2500	4000
A	2500	3000
S	2500	2000
B	2500	1000

36.3 Policies

A *policy* is a choice of what decision to make given the evolution of the MDP from time 1 up to the current time.

Definition 146
A **policy** for an MDP is a distribution over decisions for each state i that is a function of the entire history of the process.

In the context of MDP, a *stationary policy* is one that only looks at the current state of the chain when deciding what to do next and not the entire history.

Definition 147
A policy is **stationary** if it only depends on the current state.

(This should not be confused with the stationary distribution of the Markov chain, which is a distribution such that if the current state is a draw from that distribution, and a step in the Markov chain is taken, then the next state also comes from that distribution.)

Evaluating policies

So how to decide which policy is best? There are two main approaches.

1. Maximize the **long-term average reward** over time.

2. Maximize the **discounted reward**.

The average expected reward is the long term average over the rewards gained by following a certain policy.

Definition 148
Given a policy δ, the **long-term average reward** is

$$\mathbb{E}\left(\lim_{t\to\infty}\frac{r_{X_1,d_1}+r_{X_2,d_2}+\cdots+r_{X_t,d_t}}{t}\right).$$

The discounted reward recognizes that a reward now is worth more than a reward that is to be given in the future. This could be the result of inflation, or just the uncertainty of ever receiving the future reward. Given a parameter $\beta \in (0,1)$, the discounted value of a reward r to be given k time steps in the future is only $\beta^k r$. Therefore, rewards given far in the future are less valuable than rewards given today ($k = 0$).

Definition 149
Given a policy δ, the **discounted reward** is

$$V_\delta = \mathbb{E}\left(\sum_{t=1}^{\infty} \beta^{t-1} r_{X_t,d_t}\right).$$

Here the discounted reward will be used as our goal.

Definition 150
For Δ the set of all policies, say that δ^* is an **optimal policy** if

$$(\forall \delta \in \Delta)(V_{\delta^*} \geq V_\delta).$$

No matter which method is used to measure the infinite time horizon reward, this is difficult because decisions have to be made at an infinite number of time steps! Fortunately, the problem can be simplified considerably with an important theorem found by Blackwell in 1962 [**blackwell1962**].

Theorem 15 (Blackwell's optimal stationary policy theorem)
If the values of the rewards are bounded, then there exists an optimal policy that is stationary.

This is huge! It means that it is not necessary to examine the entire history of the process, but only need to consider the current state when making our decision.

Problems

36.1 A strategy that tells the distribution of choices for each state in a Markov Decision Process is called a(n) _______.

36.2 A policy that only depends on the current state is called ______.

36.3 Suppose $\beta = 1/2$ and the reward is $r_{X_t,d_t} = 5$ for every value of X_t and d_t. What is the discounted reward of the policy.

36.4 Suppose for every state and every policy, the reward is uniform over $\{5, 10\}$. For $\beta = 0.3$, what is the discounted reward for the policy.

36.5 Suppose with a particular policy that r_{X_t,d_t} converges to uniform over $\{1, 2, 3, 4\}$ as t goes to infinity. What will the long term average reward be?

36.6 Suppose with a particular policy that r_{X_t,d_t} converges to uniform over $\{1, 2, \ldots, 10\}$ as t goes to infinity. What will the long term average reward be?

Chapter 37

Finding the optimal stationary policy

Question of the Day

A printer is either perfectly aligned, almost aligned, somewhat aligned, or badly aligned. At the beginning of each month, it is possible to spend \$1500 to realign the printer back to perfect alignment. In perfect alignment the printer can be expected to earn \$4000 during a month, almost aligned \$3000, somewhat aligned \$2000, and badly aligned \$1000. The probability of moving from one alignment to another is shown in the figure below. What policy should the owner of the printer use?

If no alignment is carried out, the transition probabilities are:

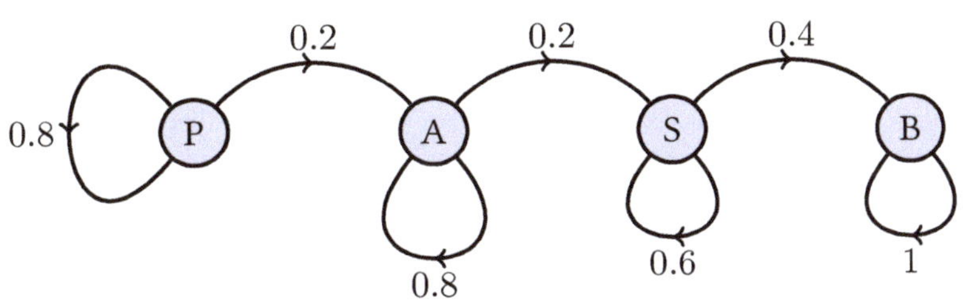

If alignment is carried out, the move always goes back to the perfectly aligned state with probability 1.

What is the stationary policy with the greatest average reward?

Summary

For a Markov Decision Process, we can optimize the average reward through linear programming. We can optimize the discounted utility through value iteration.

37.1 Stationary policies and Markov Decision Processes

Suppose $\{X_1, X_2, \ldots\}$ is an MDP that follows a stationary policy. That means that when the current state is i, we choose our decision independently of the history. So we can say that $q_i(d)$ is the probability that we make decision d given the current state is i.

Recall that $D(i)$ is the set of decisions that we can make when the current state is i. Let D_t be the decision that we actually make at time t. Then with our notation:

$$q_i(d) = \mathbb{P}(D_t = d | X_t = i).$$

Now consider $\mathbb{P}(X_{t+1} = j | X_1, X_2, \ldots, X_t = i)$. To find this, we break it into pieces based on what decision we made. So

$$\begin{aligned}
&\mathbb{P}(X_{t+1} = j | X_1, X_2, \ldots, X_t = i) \\
&\quad = \sum_{d \in D(i)} \mathbb{P}(X_{t+1} = j, D_t = d | X_1, \ldots, X_t = i) \\
&\quad = \sum_{d \in D(i)} \mathbb{P}(D_t = d | X_1, X_2, \ldots, X_t = i) \mathbb{P}(X_{t+1} = j | X_1, \ldots, X_t = i, D_t = d) \\
&\quad = \sum_{d \in D(i)} q_i(d) p(j | i, d).
\end{aligned}$$

Note that this right hand side does not depend on $X_1, \ldots, X_{t-1}$, the history of the chain before X_t does not matter! That means that the process is a Markov chain.

Fact 55
A Markov Decision Process that follows a stationary policy is a Markov chain.

In order to understand the long-run behavior, let π_i be the long-run amount of time that we spend in state i, and π_{id} be the long-run amount of time that we spend in state i when we make decision d. Then because when we are in state i the chance of making decision d is $q_i(d)$, we have

$$\pi_{id} = \pi_i q_i(d).$$

For example, if we spend 5% of our time in state 4, and 20% of the time when in state 4 we make decision 1, then $(0.05)(0.20) = 0.01$ of the time we will be in state 4 and make decision 1 (on average).

From Markov chain theory, we know that the long-run amount of time that we spend in a state must be in *balance*. That means at each step, π_i amount of probability leaves state i, and that probability must be replenished by probability flowing in. That is,

$$\begin{aligned}\pi_i &= \sum_j \mathbb{P}(X_t = j)\mathbb{P}(X_{t+1} = i | X_t = j) \\ &= \sum_j \pi_i \mathbb{P}(X_{t+1} = i | X_t = j)\end{aligned}$$

Note that we must make some decision at each step, so

$$\pi_i = \sum_{d \in D(i)} \pi_{id},$$

and

$$\mathbb{P}(X_{t+1} = i | X_t = j) = \sum_{d \in D(j)} q_i(d) p(j | i, d).$$

Putting this together gives

$$\begin{aligned}\sum_{d \in D(i)} \pi_{id} &= \sum_i \pi_i \sum_{d \in D(i)} q_i(d) p(j | i, d) \\ &= \sum_i \sum_{d \in D(i)} \pi_i q_i(d) p(j | i, d) \\ &= \sum_i \sum_{d \in D(i)} \pi_{id} p(j | i, d)\end{aligned}$$

The final version of the equation only uses π_{id} variables, which is important.

Definition 151
For a Markov Decision Process, the **balance equations** state that for every $i \in \Omega$,

$$\sum_{d \in D(i)} \pi_{id} = \sum_i \sum_{d \in D(i)} \pi_{id} p(j | i, d).$$

37.2 *Average reward*

So how can we use this to optimize our average award? Recall that we are in state i and make decision d, we gather reward r_{id}. So our long-run average expected reward can be found using the long-run portion of time spent in each state making each decision:

$$\lim_{t \to \infty} \frac{r_{X_1, D_1} + \cdots + r_{X_t, D_t}}{t} = \sum_i \pi_{id} r_{id}.$$

(The formal proof of this is beyond the scope of this course, but utilizes a version of the Ergodic Theorem.)

Because the π_{id} are the long-run percentage of time spent in state i making decisions d, when we sum over all states and decisions, they must add to 1.

$$\sum_i \sum_{d \in D(i)} \pi_{id} = 1.$$

And of course, they must all be positive: $\pi_{id} \geq 0$.

Combining all of these constraints (the balance equations, the nonnegativity, the sum to 1) with the objective function, we have created a linear program which we can then optimize to find an optimal stationary policy.

Answering the question of the day

Let's look at how this all plays out in the question of the day. Let the states P, A, S, and B be represented by 1, 2, 3, and 4. Let the decision no align be decision 1, and align be decision 2. Then the rewards r_{id} form a matrix:

$$r = \begin{array}{c} \\ P=1 \\ A=2 \\ S=3 \\ B=4 \end{array} \begin{array}{c} \begin{array}{cc} R=1 & \neg R=2 \end{array} \\ \begin{pmatrix} 2500 & 4000 \\ 2500 & 3000 \\ 2500 & 2000 \\ 2500 & 1000 \end{pmatrix} \end{array}$$

The objective function that we are trying to maximize is

$$2500\pi_{11} + 4000\pi_{12} + \cdots + 2500\pi_{41} + 1000\pi_{42}.$$

This maximization is subject to five linear constraints, plus they must all be nonnegative. First, the variables must add to 1.

$$\pi_{11} + \cdots + \pi_{42} = 1$$

Next, we have a balance equation for each of the states.

$$\begin{aligned}
\pi_{11} + \pi_{12} &= 0.8\pi_{11} + 0.8\pi_{12} + 0.8\pi_{21} + 0.8\pi_{31} + 0.8\pi_{41} \\
\pi_{21} + \pi_{22} &= 0.2\pi_{11} + 0.2\pi_{12} + 0.8\pi_{21} + 0.2\pi_{21} + 0.2\pi_{31} + 0.2\pi_{41} \\
\pi_{31} + \pi_{32} &= 0.2\pi_{22} + 0.6\pi_{32} \\
\pi_{41} + \pi_{42} &= 0.4\pi_{32} + \pi_{42}
\end{aligned}$$

and all the variables must be nonnegative.

Letting $x = (\pi_{11}, \ldots, \pi_{41})$, the LP can be written as

$$\max \begin{pmatrix} 2500 & 4000 & 2500 & 3000 & 2500 & 2000 & 2500 & 1000 \end{pmatrix} x$$

subject to

$$\begin{pmatrix} 1 & 1 & 1 & 1 & 1 & 1 & 1 & 1 \\ 0.2 & 0.2 & -0.8 & 0 & -0.8 & 0 & -0.8 & 0 \\ -0.2 & -0.2 & 0.2 & 0.8 & -0.2 & 0 & -0.2 & 0 \\ 0 & 0 & 0 & -0.2 & 1 & 0.4 & 0 & 0 \\ 0 & 0 & 0 & 0 & 0 & -0.4 & 1 & 0 \end{pmatrix} x = \begin{pmatrix} 1 \\ 0 \\ 0 \\ 0 \\ 0 \end{pmatrix}$$

$$x \geq 0.$$

Solving the LP

R contains a package `lpSolve` that interfaces with the open source LP Solver to solve linear and integer programs. To set up our problem, we first load the library, installing the package if necessary.

```
# install.packages("lpSolve")
library(lpSolve)
```

Next we put the vector for the objective function, the matrix and vector for the inequalities, and the type of inequality or equality into variables.

```
f.obj <- c(2500, 4000, 2500, 3000,
           2500, 2000, 2500, 1000)
#f.obj <- c(500, 4000, 500, 3000,
#            500, 2000, 500, 1000)
f.con <- matrix(c(
  1, 1, 1, 1, 1, 1, 1, 1,
  0.2, 0.2, -0.8, 0, -0.8, 0, -0.8, 0,
  -0.2, -0.2, 0.2, 0.8, -0.2, 0, -0.2, 0,
  0, 0, 0, -0.2, 0.4, 1, 0, 0,
  0, 0, 0, 0, 0, -0.4, 0, 1),
  byrow = TRUE, nrow = 5)
f.dir <- rep("=", 5)
f.rhs <- c(1, 0, 0, 0, 0)
```

Now we are ready to solve the LP.

```
soln <- lp("max", f.obj, f.con, f.dir, f.rhs)
soln$solution
```

```
## 0.00000000 0.66666667 0.08333333 0.16666667
## 0.08333333 0.00000000 0.00000000 0.00000000
```

```
soln
## Success: the objective function is 3583.333
```

So how do we figure out our policy from this? Recall that $\pi_{id} = \pi_i q_i(d)$ and $\pi_i = \sum_{d \in D(i)} \pi_{id}$. Using this with

$$x^* = (0, 2/3, 1/12, 1/6, 1/12, 0, 0, 0),$$

for instance, we get that $\pi_2 = 1/12 + 1/6 = 3/12 = 1/4$. Overall, we get that

$$(\pi_1, \pi_2, \pi_3, \pi_4) = (2/3, 1/4, 1/12, 0, 0).$$

Now we can solve for the $q_i(d)$. For instance,

$$\pi_{21} = \pi_2 q_2(1) \Rightarrow 1/12 = (1/4)q_2(1),$$

so $q_2(1) = 1/3$.

Now we know $q_1(1)\pi_1 = \pi_{11} = 5/6$, so $q_1(1) = 1$. Similarly, we can calculate

i	d	$q_i(d)$
1	1	0
1	2	1
2	1	1/3
2	2	2/3
3	1	1
3	2	0.

$$q_1(1) = 1, \; q_1(2) = 0, \; q_2(1) = 0, \; q_2(2) = 1.$$

Therefore, the optimal policy is

State P	Never realign
State A	Realign with probability $1/3$
State S	Always realign
State B	Always realign.

Note that the last state will never be reached with this policy unless the printer starts in that state, so we choose to realign at that point.

Problems

37.1 Suppose that there are three states $\{1, 2, 3\}$. For states 1 and 2 there are two decisions $\{a, b\}$, and in the third state there are three decisions $\{a, b, c\}$. Say

$$\pi_{1,a} = 0.2, \pi_{1,b} = 0.2, \pi_{2,a} = 0.1, \pi_{2,b} = 0.25, \pi_{3,a} = 0.05, \pi_{3,b} = 0.1.$$

What is $\pi_{3,c}$?

37.2 Suppose there are two states $\{1, 2\}$ and two decisions for each state $\{a, b\}$ with

$$\pi_{1,a} = 0.3, \ \pi_{1,b} = 0.1, \ \pi_{2,a} = 0.05.$$

What is $\pi_{2,b}$?

Part IX

Introduction to Quasi-Monte Carlo

Chapter 38

Reducing variance from simulation

Question of the Day

Suppose that I wish to estimate $\mathbb{E}[U_i^2]$ where U_i are iid $\textsf{Unif}([0,1])$ random variables. Is there a better way than just using

$$\frac{U_1^2 + \cdots + U_1^2}{n}?$$

Summary

- **Quasi-Monte Carlo (QMC)** algorithms use random variables that are identically distributed but not necessarily independent to build faster algorithms for estimation.

- For U uniform over $[0,1]$, $1-U$ is an **antithetic random variable**. Since U and $1-U$ are negatively correlated, this can reduce variance of estimates in some simulations.

- A **randomly shifted grid** can generate uniforms by taking a grid of equally separated values, and then shifting it a random amount. The result is a set of values that are all uniformly distributed, but more evenly spaced than would be expected by chance.

Since the earliest computers, generating random variables has been considered one of the longest operations. Today it requires much more time to generate a random variate than to calculate something like a cosine or natural logarithm, while additions and multiplications are even faster.

So it is not unusual to try to get the most out of the random variables that we do use. Recall that if we use

$$\hat{a} = \frac{m(U_1) + \cdots + m(U_n)}{n}$$

to estimate $a = \mathbb{E}[m(U)]$, then the standard deviation in the result will be $\text{SD}(m(U))/\sqrt{n}$. So we can improve the estimate by making the standard deviation smaller.

38.1 Antithetic random variables

One of the simplest (and yet very effective) approaches is whenever a random variable $U_i \sim \textsf{Unif}([0,1])$ is used, to also use $1 - U_i$. This takes advantage of the following simple fact.

Lemma 4
If $U \sim \textsf{Unif}([0,1])$, then $1 - U \sim \textsf{Unif}([0,1])$ as well.

Definition 152
If $U \sim \textsf{Unif}([0,1])$, then the pair $(U, 1-U)$ form **antithetic random variables.**

For the question of the day,

$$\frac{U_1^2 + \cdots + U_1^2}{n}$$

and

$$\frac{(1-U_1)^2 + \cdots + (1-U_1)^2}{n}$$

are both unbiased estimators of $\mathbb{E}[U_1^2]$. Therefore, their average is also an unbiased estimator of $\mathbb{E}[U_1^2]$.

Another way to view this is to let

$$W_i = \frac{U_i^2 + (1-U_i)^2}{2}.$$

Then $\mathbb{E}[W_i] = \mathbb{E}[U_i^2]$.

Note that if U is larger, $1 - U$ is smaller. So averaging the antithetic pair $[U^2 + (1-U)^2]/2$ gives a result that is closer to the true average than either alone. We can analyze this precisely by considering the variance of the original estimate versus the variance of the antithetic estimate.

Let $Y = U_i^2$. Then the variance of Y is

$$\begin{aligned}
\mathbb{E}[Y^2] - \mathbb{E}[Y]^2 &= \mathbb{E}[U_i^4] - \mathbb{E}[U_i^2])^2 \\
&= (1/5) - (1/3)^2 \\
&= 0.08888\ldots
\end{aligned}$$

On the other hand, the variance of W is

$$\begin{aligned}\mathbb{E}[W^2] - \mathbb{E}[W]^2 &= \mathbb{E}[((U^2 + (1-U)^2)/2)^2] - \mathbb{E}[W]^2 \\ &= \mathbb{E}[((2U^2 - 2U + 1)/2)^2] - \mathbb{E}[W]^2 \\ &= (1/4)[2\mathbb{E}[U^2] - 2\mathbb{E}[U] + 1] - (1/3)^2 \\ &= (1/4)[2/3] - (1/3)^2 \\ &= (1/6) - (1/3)^2 \\ &= 0.05555\ldots\end{aligned}$$

Recall a formula from probability theory.

Fact 56
For random variables X and Y with finite variance,

$$\mathbb{V}((X+Y)/2) = \frac{\mathbb{V}(X) + \mathbb{V}(Y)}{2} + \text{Cov}(X, Y).$$

So if X and Y have negative covariance (as U^2 and $(1-U)^2$ do) then the variance of the average will be smaller. Otherwise, if the covariance is positive then the result will be worse than before!

38.2 Quasi Monte Carlo

We can take this idea one step further by using *quasi Monte Carlo* methods.

Definition 153
A **quasi Monte Carlo** (QMC) uses random variables that are identically distributed but not independent to build faster algorithms for estimation.

Define the fractional part function as follows.

Definition 154
The **fractional part function** is defined as

$$\text{fpf}(x) = x - \lfloor x \rfloor.$$

So for example, $\text{fpf}(1.32) = 0.32$, $\text{fpf}(4) = 0$, $\text{fpf}(\sqrt{2}) = 0.4142\ldots$.

A nice fact about uniforms over $[0, 1]$ is that if you add any constant and take the fractional part, you are left once more with a uniform over $[0, 1]$.

Fact 57
If $U \sim \textsf{Unif}([0, 1])$ and $c \in \mathbb{R}$, then $\text{fpf}(U + c) \sim \textsf{Unif}([0, 1])$.

Note that this means that for any n, and a single uniform $U \sim \mathsf{Unif}([0,1])$,

$$U, \text{fpf}(U + 1/n), \text{fpf}(U + 2/n), \ldots, \text{fpf}(U + (n-1)/n),$$

are all uniform over $[0, 1]$!

We have taken a single random draw and managed to create n different uniforms from them. This gives us an estimate of $\mathbb{E}[U_1]$:

$$\hat{a}_{\text{QMC}} = \sum_{i=0}^{n-1} \frac{\text{fpf}(U + i/n)^2}{n}$$

For example, if $U = .72\ldots$ and $n = 4$, then our estimate would be

$$\hat{a}_{\text{QMC}} = \frac{0.72\ldots^2 + 0.97\ldots^2 + 0.22\ldots^2 + 0.47\ldots^2}{4}.$$

How well does this perform? It is much more difficult to analyze the error in this method than the previous approaches. Remember that for the pure Monte Carlo average, the error is

$$\Theta(1/\sqrt{n}),$$

where the constant factor is $\text{SD}(m(U))$.

For the QMC approach, the error is

$$O\left(\frac{\ln(n)}{\sqrt{n}}\right)$$

which can be much smaller for large n.

Example 59
The basic MC approach for $\mathbb{E}[U^2]$ gives a standard deviation of $0.08888\ldots$ divided by the square root of n. By simulating the QMC approach 1000 times, we find that the standard deviation for QMC is about as follows.

n	standard deviation QMC	standard deviation MC
10	$0.0394\ldots$	$0.0281\ldots$
100	$0.00414\ldots$	$0.00888\ldots$
1000	$0.000414\ldots$	$0.00281\ldots$

Note the standard deviation for MC goes down as $\sqrt{n}$ while that of QMC goes down by n. So for even moderate values of n, the QMC will be better. It will also be faster, because while it does $\Theta(n)$ additions and subtractions, it only needs 1 uniform random draw, while MC uses n uniform draws.

Problems

38.1 If $U \sim \mathsf{Unif}([0,1])$, then $Y = -\ln(U) \sim \mathsf{Exp}(1)$. Let $W = -\ln(1-U)$.

a) What is the distribution of W?

b) Find $\mathbb{E}[Y]$ and $\mathbb{V}(Y)$.

c) Find $\mathbb{E}[(W+Y)/2]$.

d) Find $\mathbb{V}((W+Y)/2)$.

38.2 Suppose for $U \sim \mathsf{Unif}([0,1])$, $Y = \sqrt{U}$, and $W = \sqrt{1-U}$.

a) What is the distribution of W?

b) Find $\mathbb{E}[Y]$ and $\mathbb{V}(Y)$.

c) Find $\mathbb{E}[(W+Y)/2]$.

d) Find $\mathbb{V}((W+Y)/2)$.

38.3 Suppose $p \in (0,1)$. Let $U \sim \mathsf{Unif}([0,1])$, $X = \mathbb{1}(U \leq p)$, $Y = \mathbb{1}(1-U \leq p)$. What is

$$\text{SD}((X+Y)/2)?$$

38.4 Continuing the last problem.

a. What value(s) of p makes the standard deviation as small as possible, and how small can it be?

b. What value(s) of p makes the standard deviation as large as possible, and how large can it be?

Part X

Extras

Chapter 39

Worked problems

1.1 Which of the following are logical statements?

a) The capital of Iowa.

b) $4 > 6$.

c) $(\mathbb{1}(4 > 6) = 1)$.

d) The temperature at which water boils.

Solution

Parts $\boxed{\text{b and c}}$ are statements that are either true or false (actually both false), making them logical statements.

1.3 Evaluate the following.

a) $\mathbb{1}(3 = 4)$.

b) $\mathbb{1}(3 < 4)$.

c) $\mathbb{1}(4 < 3)$.

Solution

a) $\boxed{0}$.

b) $\boxed{1}$.

c) $\boxed{0}$.

1.5 Given the density f_X of a random variable X, state whether X is discrete or continuous.

a) $f_X(2) = 0.3,\ f_X(4) = 0.7$.

b) $f_X(x) = \mathbb{1}(x \in [0, 1])$.

c) $f_X(0) = 1/3,\ f_X(1) = 1/3,\ f_X(2) = 1/3$.

d) $f_X(x) = \exp(-x)\mathbb{1}(x \geq 0)$.

Solution

a) Here $\mathbb{P}(X = 2) = 0.3$ and $\mathbb{P}(X = 4) = 0.7$, so this is $\boxed{\text{discrete}}$.

b) This is a continuous function, so the random variable is $\boxed{\text{continuous}}$.

c) Here X is uniform over the set $\{0, 1, 2\}$, so is $\boxed{\text{discrete}}$.

d) Here X is exponential with rate 1, and so is $\boxed{\text{continuous}}$.

1.7 Suppose $X \sim \mathsf{Exp}(0.1)$.

a) Find $\mathbb{P}(X > 10)$.

b) Find $\mathbb{P}(X \leq 10)$.

Solution

a) This is

$$\begin{aligned}\mathbb{P}(X > 10) &= \int_{10}^{\infty} 0.1 \exp(-0.1x)\mathbb{1}(x \geq 0)\,dx = \exp(-1) \\ &= \boxed{0.3678}.\end{aligned}$$

b) This is

$$\begin{aligned}\mathbb{P}(X \leq 10) &= \int_{0}^{1} 00.1 \exp(-0.1x)\mathbb{1}(x \geq 0)\,dx = 1 - \exp(-1) \\ &= \boxed{0.6321}.\end{aligned}$$

2.1 Suppose A occurs with probability 0.3, B occurs with probability 0.7, and both occur with probability 0.2.

a) Find $\mathbb{P}(A|B)$.

b) Find $\mathbb{P}(B|A)$.

Solution

a) This will be

$$\mathbb{P}(A|B) = \frac{\mathbb{P}(AB)}{\mathbb{P}(B)} = \frac{0.2}{0.7} = \frac{2}{7} = \boxed{0.2857\ldots}.$$

b) This will be

$$\mathbb{P}(B|A) = \frac{\mathbb{P}(AB)}{\mathbb{P}(A)} = \frac{0.2}{0.3} = \frac{2}{3} = \boxed{0.6666\ldots}.$$

2.3 Suppose $D \sim \mathsf{Unif}(\{1, \ldots, 100\})$.

a) Find $\mathbb{P}(D = 1 | D \leq 60)$.
b) Find $\mathbb{P}(D \leq 60 | D = 1)$.

Solution

a) By the property of conditional uniforms, $[D|D \leq 60] \sim \mathsf{Unif}(\{1, \ldots, 60\})$, so $1/60 = \boxed{0.01666\ldots}$.
b) By the property of conditional uniforms, $[D|D = 1] \sim \mathsf{Unif}(\{1\})$, so $1/1 = \boxed{1}$.

2.5 Let $X \sim \mathsf{Exp}(0.2)$.

a) What is the distribution of $[X - 3|X > 3]$?
b) What is $\mathbb{P}(X > 5|X > 3)$?

Solution

a) By the memoryless property, this is $\boxed{\mathsf{Exp}(0.2)}$.
b) By the survival function of exponentials, this if $\exp(-0.2 \cdot (5 - 3)) = \boxed{0.6703}$

2.7 Let (B_1, B_2, B_3) be the first three draws from a stream of iid random variables where $\mathbb{P}(B_i = 1) = 0.3, \mathbb{P}(B_i = 0) = 0.7$ (write $B_i \sim \mathsf{Bern}(0.3)$ as this is a Bernoulli distribution.)

a) What is $\mathbb{P}(B_1 = 1, B_2 = 1)$?
b) Find $\mathbb{P}(B_1 + B_2 + B_3 = 1)$.

Solution

a) Since the B_i are iid, and the first i stands for independent,

$$\mathbb{P}(B_1 = 1, B_2 = 1) = \mathbb{P}(B_1 = 1)\mathbb{P}(B_2 = 1) = (0.3)(0.3) = \boxed{0.09000}.$$

b) There are three ways this can happen, $(1, 0, 0), (0, 1, 0), (0, 0, 1)$. Each way happens with probability $(0.3)(0.7)^2$ so the overall chance is $3(0.3)(0.7)^2 = \boxed{0.4410}$.

3.1 Suppose customer 5 enters service at time 7.1 and finishes service at time 9.6. What is customer 5's service time?

Solution

This will be $9.6 - 7.1 = \boxed{2.500}$.

3.3 Suppose three customers, a, b, and c arrive to a queue in that order.

a) Under a FIFO queue discipline, in what order are the customers served?

b) Under a LIFO queue discipline, in what order are the customers served?

Solution

a) In FIFO, the customers are served in the order they arrive, so $\boxed{(a, b, c)}$.

b) LIFO, the last customer to arrive is served first, so $\boxed{(c, b, a)}$.

3.5 If the first three interarrival times are $A_1 = 0.4$, $A_2 = 1.34$, and $A_3 = 0.013$, what are the first three arrival times?

Solution

The first three times will be

$$T_1 = A_1 = \boxed{0.4000}$$
$$T_2 = A_1 + A_2 = \boxed{1.740}$$
$$T_3 = A_1 + A_2 + A_3 = \boxed{1.753}$$

3.7 For interarrival times that are uniform over $[0, 2]$ hours, what is the arrival rate?

Solution

The average of $X \sim \text{Unif}([0, 2])$ is just $(0 + 2)/2 = 1$. Remembering the units, that makes the expected time between arrivals 1 hours, and so the arrival rate is $1/[1 \text{ hour}]$, or $\boxed{1/\text{hour}}$.

4.1 Suppose $\mathbb{E}[X] = 4.2$ and $\mathbb{E}[Y] = 5.6$. What is $\mathbb{E}[2X - 4Y]$?

Solution

Using linearity of expectations,

$$\mathbb{E}[2X - 4Y] = 2\mathbb{E}[X] - 4\mathbb{E}[Y] = 2(4.2) - 4(5.6) = \boxed{-14}.$$

4.3 Find the infimum of the following sets.

a) $S_1 = \{1, 2, 3\}$.

b) $S_2 = \{1, 2, 3, \ldots\}$.

c) $S_3 = \{x : x > 0, x < 5\} =]0, 5[$.

Solution

a) Since this set is finite, it is just the minimum value $\boxed{1}$.

b) Here 1 is a lower bound and is the largest lower bound, so $\boxed{1}$.

c) Here 0 is a lower bound (since for all x in S, $x > 0$) and any $s > 0$ bigger than 0 is not a lower bound since $s/2$ is smaller and in S_1. So $\boxed{0}$.

4.5 Say that interarrival times for a $G/G/2$ queue have density $20x^3(1-x)\mathbb{1}(x \in [0,1])$ when measured in minutes. Lower bound the expected number of customers to arrive in the first ten minutes.

Solution

The average interarrival time is

$$\begin{aligned}\mathbb{E}[A_i] &= \int_{-\infty}^{\infty} x20x^3(1-x)\mathbb{1}(x \in [0,1])\,dx \\ &= 2/3,\end{aligned}$$

hence $\lambda = 3/2$, and the lower bound is

$$(3/2)(10) - 1 = \boxed{14}.$$

4.7 Suppose interarrival times for a $G/G/2$ queue are 1 minute with probability 0.3, 2 minutes with probability 0.6, and 3 minutes with probability 0.1.

a) Lower bound the expected number of customers to arrive in the first hour.

b) Lower bound the expected number of customers to arrive in the first two hours.

Solution

The expected interarrival time is

$$(1)(0.3) + (2)(0.6) + (3)(0.1) = 1.8,$$

so the arrival rate is 1.8/min.

a) One hour is 60 minutes, so this is $(60/1.8)(1) - 1 \approx \boxed{32.33}$.

b) Note that two hours is 120 minutes, so this is

$$(120/1.8) - 1 \approx \boxed{65.66}.$$

5.1 If P is a Poisson process of rate 2.5 per second over $[0, \infty)$, what is the chance that there are at most 3 points of P in the first 2 seconds?

Solution

Multiplying the rate (2.5 per second) times the length of the interval (2 seconds) gives 5. Hence the number of points of P in the first two seconds is Poisson distributed with parameter 5. Let

$$N = \#(P \cap [0, 2])$$

denote the number of arrivals in the first two seconds. Then

$$\begin{aligned}\mathbb{P}(N \leq 3) &= \mathbb{P}(N = 0) + \mathbb{P}(N = 1) + \mathbb{P}(N = 2) + \mathbb{P}(N = 3) \\ &= \exp(-5)\left[\frac{5^0}{0!} + \frac{5^1}{1!} + \frac{5^2}{2!} + \frac{5^3}{3!}\right] \\ &\approx \boxed{0.2650}.\end{aligned}$$

5.3 Consider an $M/G/2$ queue with arrival rate 3 per minute.

a) What is the average number of arrivals in the first minute?
b) What is the chance that there are at least 3 arrivals in the first minute?
c) What is the chance of no arrivals in the first 1.5 minutes?

Solution

a) Since the arrival rate is 3 per minute, this average is just $\boxed{3}$.
b) Here the knowledge that the number of arrivals will be Poisson distributed with parameter $(3/\text{min})(1\text{ min}) = 3$ is needed. For $N_{[0,1]}$ denoting the number of arrivals in the first minute,

$$\begin{aligned}\mathbb{P}(N_{[0,1]} \geq 3) &= 1 - \mathbb{P}(N_{[0,1]} \leq 2) \\ &= 1 - \mathbb{P}(N_{[0,1]} = 0) - \mathbb{P}(N_{[0,1]} = 1) - \mathbb{P}(N_{[0,1]} = 2) \\ &= 1 - \exp(-3)[1 + 3 + 3^2/2!] \\ &= \boxed{0.5768\ldots}.\end{aligned}$$

c) This is the chance that the first arrival occurs after time 1.5. Since the first arrival has an exponential distribution of rate 3, this is

$$\exp(-3 \cdot 1.5) = \boxed{0.01110\ldots.}$$

5.5 If the interarrival times between customers are modeled as iid $\text{Exp}(8.4/s)$, how many seconds (on average) are there between customer arrivals?

Solution

The average of an exponentially distributed random variable is one over the rate parameter, so $1/[8.4/\text{s}] \approx \boxed{0.1190\text{ s}}$.

5.7 For an $M/G/2$ queue of arrival rate λ, what is the distribution of the time of the third customer arrival?

Solution

The first M tells us that the arrival distribution is λ. Hence the time of the third arrival is the sum of three independent exponential random variables, making it $\text{Erlang}(3, \lambda)$.

6.1 A queuing network's overall rate is limited by what type of server?

Solution

$\boxed{\text{Bottleneck.}}$

6.3 An entry ramp to the freeway uses a stoplight that lets traffic on at a rate of 2 cars every 3 seconds. If there are 24 cars waiting to get on the freeway, on average how long are you going to have to wait?

Solution

Cars are entering the freeway at rate 2 per 3 seconds, or (2/3) per second. Hence the time to enter the freeway will be $24/(2/3 \text{ per s}) = \boxed{36 \text{ s}}$.

6.5 In the previous problem, what are the bottleneck servers?

Solution

In part (a), the servers were in parallel, so both $\boxed{\text{Server 1 and Server 2}}$ are bottlenecks.

In part (b), the servers were in series, so only $\boxed{\text{Server 2}}$ is the bottleneck.

6.7 What is the capacity of the network in the previous problem? [In other words, what is the overall service rate of this network.]

Solution

Server 1 and 2 are in parallel, so their service rates add to give a $10 + 7$ per minute. Next is Server 3 in series, so the overall rate is the minimum of their service rates, so $\min\{17, 15\} = 15$. So the overall rate is $\boxed{\text{15 per minute.}}$

7.1 The long term time customers spend waiting in a $G/G/5$ queue is 15 minutes, and the average long term queue length is 18.4.

a) What is the arrival rate to this queue?

b) What is the expected time between arrivals in this queue?

Solution

a) Here $L = 18.4$, and $W = 15$ minutes, so the arrival rate is

$$\frac{18.4}{15 \text{ min}} = \boxed{1.226/\text{min}}.$$

b) The expected time between arrivals is just the multiplicative inverse of the arrival rate, or

$$\frac{15 \text{ min}}{18.4} = \boxed{0.8152 \text{ min}}.$$

7.3 A cafeteria has several queues (for food gathering and payment). If the average number of customers in the cafeteria is 20.3 during the lunch hour (call this time $[0, 1]$ hours), and each customer spends an average of ten minutes in the cafeteria, what is λ_1?

Solution

Little's law for finite times says that $\lambda_t W_t = L_t$. Given the average number of customers is $L_1 = 20.3$ and $W_1 = 1/6$ hour, then

$$\lambda_1 = \frac{20.3}{1/6 \text{ hour}} = \boxed{121.8 \text{ per hour}}.$$

7.5 Let $n(s)$ denote the number of customers in a queuing system. Suppose that the system starts with 2 customers. Customer 1 finishes service at time 0.8, Customer 3 arrives at time 1.4, Customer 4 arrives at time 1.8, Customer 2 finishes service at time 3.3, and Customer 3 immediately enters service but does not finish before time 5.

Draw a graph of $n(s)$ for $s \in [0, 5]$.

Solution

This looks as follows.

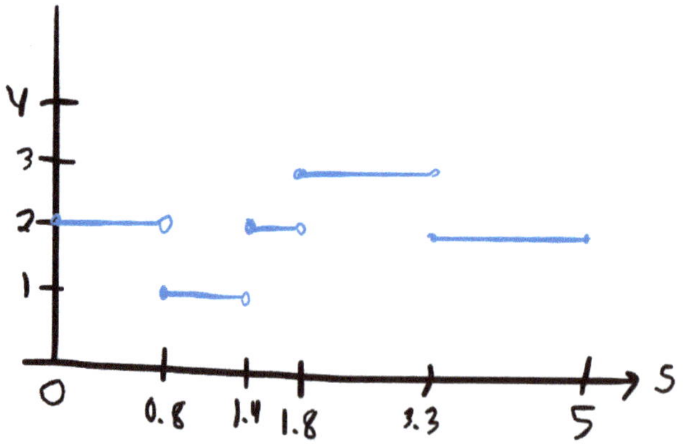

7.7 Jobs arrive at a computer server at 11.4 per second. If the average number of jobs waiting at any moment is 14.2, what is the average amount of time a job waits before being served?

Solution

Here $L = 14.2$ and $\lambda = 11.4$ per second, so

$$W = \frac{L}{\lambda} = \frac{14.2}{11.4/s} = \boxed{1.245 \text{ sec}}.$$

8.1 The capacity utilization is usually denoted by what symbol?

Solution

$\boxed{\rho}$

8.3 For a $G/G/4$ queue with capacity utilization 65%, what is the long run idle time?

Solution

This will be $1 - 0.65 = 0.35 = \boxed{35\%}$.

8.5 Suppose a $G/G/4$ queue has arrival rate 4 per min, and the average service time for a single server is 0.8 minutes. What is the capacity utilization for the queue?

Solution

There are 4 servers, and each server has rate $1/0.8$ minutes. So

$$\rho = \frac{\lambda}{\mu \cdot s} = \frac{4/\text{min}}{4/0.8 \text{ min}} = \boxed{0.8000}$$

8.7 For a $G/G/s$ queue with arrival rate 4.2 per second and the expected time for a single server to serve a customer of 1.9 seconds, what is the maximum number of servers we can have and still have less than 50% long run idle time?

Solution

Here the service rate for a single server is $1/1.9$ per second. Hence the idle time is

$$1 - \rho = 1 - \frac{4.2}{s/1.9} \leq 0.5,$$

so

$$0.5 \leq (4.2)(1.9)/s \Rightarrow s \leq (4.2)(1.9)/(0.5) = 15.96.$$

Hence there can be at most $\boxed{15}$ servers and still have long run idle time below 50%.

9.1 For an $M/M/1$ queue with arrival rate 3 per minute and service rate 5 per minute, what is the steady state length of the queue?

Solution

Here the capacity utilization is

$$\rho = \frac{3 \text{ min}}{5 \text{ min}} = 0.6.$$

This makes the steady-state length of the queue

$$\frac{\rho}{1-\rho} = \frac{0.6}{1-0.6} = \boxed{1.500}.$$

9.3 For an $M/M/1$ queue with arrival rate 3 per minute and service rate 5 per minute, what is the steady state probability there are two or fewer jobs in the system?

Solution

The long term probability of i jobs in the system is $(1-\rho)\rho^i$. Here $\rho = 3/5$. Therefore, the probability of getting 0, 1, or 2 jobs in the steady state is

$$0.4[1 + 0.6 + 0.6^2] = \boxed{0.7840}.$$

9.5 The help desk from the last problem upgrades to two servers (each has the 25 per hour service rate). Now what is the probability that there are four or more customers in the queue?

Solution

With two servers, the capacity utilization is now

$$\rho = \frac{20}{2 \cdot 25} = 0.4.$$

The steady state distribution for the $M/M/2$ queue is $\pi(0) = (1-\rho)/(1+\rho)$ and $\pi(i) = 2\rho^i(1-\rho)/(1+\rho)$ for $i \geq 1$. So

$$\pi(0) = \frac{1-0.4}{1+0.4} = \frac{6}{14},$$

and

$$\pi(1) = 2(0.4)\frac{6}{14}$$
$$\pi(2) = 2(0.4)^2\frac{6}{14}$$
$$\pi(3) = 2(0.4)^3\frac{6}{14}.$$

Hence the total chance of having four or more customers in the queue is

$$1 - \frac{6}{14}[1 + 0.8 + 0.32 + 0.128] = \boxed{0.03657\ldots}.$$

9.7 Draw a graphical model of the continuous time Markov chain that models the $M/M/3$ queue with arrival rate λ and single server service rate μ.

Solution

When there is one job in the queue, one server is working and the service rate is μ. When there are two jobs, two servers are working in parallel, and the service rate is 2μ. When there are three jobs, three servers are working in parallel, and the service rate is 3μ. So the CTMC looks like this.

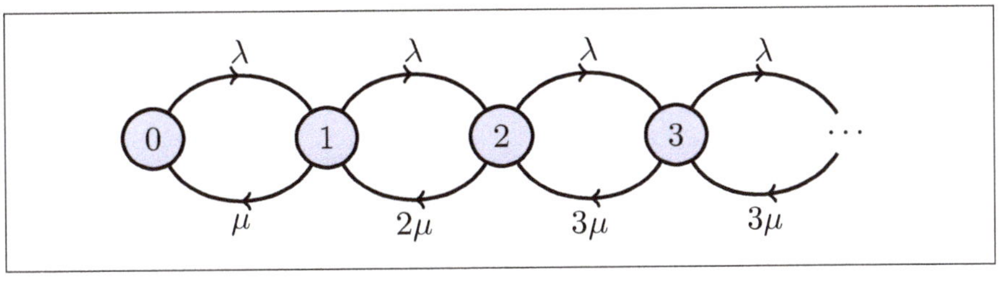

10.1 Suppose that data are stored in $X_1, X_2, \ldots, X_n$.

a) The function $M = \max(X_1, \ldots, X_n)$ is an example of a ______________.

b) For $(X_1, X_2, X_3) = (4.2, 5.1, -1.6)$, find M.

Solution

a) This is a function of data, so is a $\boxed{\text{statistic}}$.

b) For this data, the maximum value is $\boxed{5.1}$.

10.3 Try out the following commands in R, and record the final result.

```
a <- c(4.2, 5.1, -1.6)
mean(a)
```

Solution

The result is

```
[1] 2.566667
```

10.5 Write an R command to put the following data

$$(2.3, 1.7, 2.3, 0.6)$$

into a vector named `data`.

Solution

The command to use is

```
data <- c(2.3, 1.7, 2.3, 0.6)
```

10.7 Consider data $\{2.3, 1.7, 2.3, 0.6\}$.

a) Find the sample average by hand.
b) Find the sample average using R.
c) Find the sample standard deviation using R.

Solution

a) This is
$$\frac{2.3, 1.7, 2.3, 0.6}{4} = \boxed{1.725}.$$

b) It can be found in R using

```
x <- c(2.3, 1.7, 2.3, 0.6)
mean(x)
```

```
## [1] 1.725
```

c) This can be found with

```
sd(x)
```

```
## [1] 0.801561
```

So the answer is $\boxed{0.8015}$.

11.1 In an event representation graph, what do nodes represent?

Solution

The nodes of an ERG represent $\boxed{\text{events}}$.

11.3 In the $G/G/1$ queue above:

a) What event(s) can the Enter event schedule?
b) What event(s) can the Start event schedule?

Solution

a) Enter can schedule $\boxed{\text{Enter, Start}}$.
b) Start can schedule $\boxed{\text{Leave}}$.

11.5 Events change the ______________ of the system in a Discrete Event Simulation.

Solution

Events change the [state] of the system.

11.7 Suppose in the DES for the $G/G/1$ queue above, $t_a \sim \text{Unif}([0, 4])$ and $t_s \sim \text{Unif}([1, 2])$ are both in terms of minutes

a) What is the arrival rate?

b) What is the service rate?

c) What is the capacity utilization?

Solution

a) The average of a uniform over an interval is the arithmetic average of the endpoints. So $(4 + 0)/2 = 2$ minutes. Hence the arrival rate is $\boxed{0.5000 \text{ per min}}$.

b) Here the average service time is $(1 + 2)/2 = 3/2$ minutes. Therefore, the service rate is $\boxed{0.6666\ldots \text{ per min}}$.

c) The capacity utilization is the arrival rate divided by the service rate, so $(1/2)/(1/1.5) = \boxed{0.7500}$.

12.1 When an event executes, it can change the state, cancel existing events, or ______________ new events.

Solution

Executing events has the possibility of [scheduling] new events.

12.3 If event A executes at time 1.4 and rolls that event B is to be scheduled 2.3 time later, when is event B scheduled for?

Solution

The time event B will be scheduled for will be $1.4 + 2.3 = \boxed{3.700}$.

12.5 Before the next event is executed, the clock needs to be ______________.

Solution

The clock needs to be [advanced].

12.7 Deadlock occurs when if either A or B goes first, the other event will not have the ______________ it needs to execute properly.

Solution

Deadlock occurs when [resources] are not being properly released.

13.1 True or false: strings must always be enclosed in single quotes.

Solution

False, strings can be enclosed in either single or double quotes.

13.3 In R Markdown, mathematics can be included using the ______________ typesetting system.

Solution

R Markdown uses LaTeX to typeset mathematics.

13.5 True or false: the YAML header of an R Markdown file is at the beginning of the file.

Solution

This is true.

13.7 True or false: functions can be assigned to variables in R.

Solution

This is true.

14.1 A data type that is a table that holds extra information is called what in the tidyverse?

Solution

This is called a tibble.

14.3 The command `slice(1, A)` returns the ______________ row of the tibble `A`.

Solution

This would return the first row.

14.5 The function to sort the rows of a tibble with respect to a variable is called ______________.

Solution

This is the arrange command.

14.7 What function adds a new row to a tibble?

Solution

This is the `add_row` function.

15.1 Consider the following code.

```
ta <- function() return(rexp(1, rate = 4.3))
```

If function `ta` is the distribution of interarrival times, the distribution the service time is a general distribution, and there are 3 servers, what is the notation for this queue?

Solution

Because the interarrivals are exponential, this would be a $\boxed{M/G/3}$ queue.

15.3 True or false: resetting the seed to the same value at start of two simulations will result in the same random choices.

Solution

This is $\boxed{\text{true}}$.

15.5 Running the following code would get output close to what value?

```
mean(runif(100000))
```

Solution

This will output a result close to the mean of a uniform over 0 to 1, so will be about $\boxed{0.5000}$.

15.7 Suppose the queue length statistics are stored in a tibble `df` with columns named `queue_length` and `time_spent`. Write code to create a bar plot of this data where the bars are filled with blue color and the outline of the bars is black using the classic theme.

Solution

This can be done with

```
statistics |>
  ggplot() +
    geom_bar(aes(x = queue_length, y = time_spent),
             stat = "identity", color = "black",
             fill = "blue") +
    theme_classic()
```

16.1 A graph where the nodes are partitioned into two sets, and edges must have their head and tail in different sets, is called ______________.

Solution

This kind of graph is called $\boxed{\text{bipartite}}$.

16.3 The following questions are about unweighted Petri Nets.

a) Transitions fire when there at least _______ token(s) in all input places.
b) True or false: every state is reachable in a Petri Net.
c) True or false: A Petri Net is allowed to fire any enabled transition.
d) True or false: A Petri Net can be represented by a labeled bipartite graph.

Solution

a) This is [1] for basic Petri Nets.
b) This is [F].
c) This is [T].
d) This is [T].

16.5 An inhibitor arc ______________ a transition from firing when the source place is occupied.

Solution

Such an arc [prevents] the transition from firing.

16.7 If the transition fires after a random amount of time, the Petri Net is called ______________.

Solution

This is a [stochastic] Petri Net.

17.1 True or false: higher utility is good.

Solution

[True.] Utility measures the desirability of a result, making a higher utility result better.

17.3 True or false.

a) Decision variables are variables that you control.
b) State variables can be either variables that you control or variables that you do not control.

Solution

a) [True.] This is the definition of decision variables.
b) [False.] State variables are always outside of your control.

17.5 Suppose the utility of outcome s_1 is 4, while the utility of outcome s_2 is 4.2. Which outcome is preferred?

Solution

The second outcome has higher utility, so it is preferred.

17.7 Consider the following payoff matrix:

	a_1	a_2	a_3	a_4
Θ_1	4	2	0	6
Θ_2	2	6	0	5
Θ_3	1	3	7	3

a) What decision should you make using the Maximin approach?

b) What decision should you make using the Maximax approach?

c) What decision should you make using the Laplace Principle of Insufficient Reason approach?

Solution

a) The vector of minima of the columns is $(1, 2, 0, 3)$, so $\boxed{a_4}$ should be made here.

b) The vector maxima of the columns is $(4, 6, 7, 6)$, so $\boxed{a_3}$ should be made here.

c) The sums of the columns are $(7, 11, 7, 14)$, so using Laplace's approach $\boxed{a_4}$ should be made.

17.9 Consider the following payoff matrix:

	a_1	a_2	a_3	a_4
Θ_1	4	2	0	6
Θ_2	2	6	0	5
Θ_3	1	3	7	3

a) What decision should you make using the Hurwicz principle? [For every $\alpha \in [0, 1]$, state what decision is made.]

b) What decision should be made using the Savage minimum regret principle?

Solution

a) Hurwicz depends on the value of α. The Hurwicz measure is

$$\begin{aligned} h &= \alpha \begin{pmatrix}4 & 6 & 7 & 6\end{pmatrix} + (1-\alpha)\begin{pmatrix}1 & 2 & 0 & 3\end{pmatrix} \\ &= \begin{pmatrix}3\alpha+1 & 4\alpha+2 & 7\alpha & 3\alpha+3\end{pmatrix}. \end{aligned}$$

Graphing over $\alpha \in [0, 1]$ gives the idea of which is best:

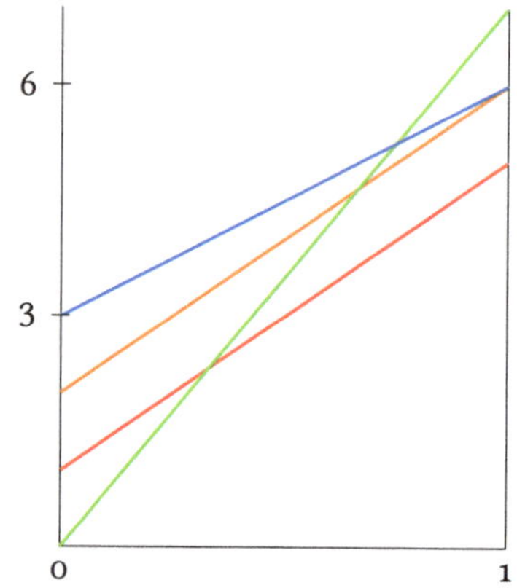

For all $\alpha \in [0, 1]$ $3\alpha + 1 < 4\alpha + 2$. Also $4\alpha + 2 \leq 3\alpha + 3$ since the inequality holds at $\alpha = 0$ and $\alpha = 1$. That leaves 7α and $3\alpha + 3$. Note

$$7\alpha - (3\alpha + 3) = 4\alpha - 3$$

which is nonnegative when $\alpha \geq 3/4$ and nonpositive when $\alpha \leq 3/4$. Hence the decision that should be made is:

$$\boxed{a_4 \text{ when } \alpha \in [0, 0.7500], \text{ and } a_3 \text{ when } \alpha \in [0.7500, 1].}$$

b) To work out the Savage decision, remember that for a given state of nature i and decision j, for payoff $A(i, j)$, the regret is then

$$r_{ij} = \left[\max_{j'} A(i, j')\right] - A(i, j).$$

In other words, it is the best decision payoff for that particular state of nature minus the payoff actually achieved.
This gives the following matrix:

	a_1	a_2	a_3	a_4
Θ_1	2	4	6	0
Θ_2	4	0	6	1
Θ_3	6	4	0	4

The maximum of each column is

$$\begin{pmatrix}6 & 4 & 6 & 4\end{pmatrix}$$

so the decisions that minimize this maximum regret are $\boxed{a_2 \text{ and } a_4}$.

17.11 Consider the following payoff matrix:

	a_1	a_2	a_3	a_4
Θ_1	4	2	0	6
Θ_2	2	6	0	5
Θ_3	1	3	7	3

Research indicates that Θ_1 and Θ_2 each have a 20% chance of occurring, while Θ_3 has a 60% chance. What decision maximizes expected utility?

Solution

The expected utility of the payoff matrix is

$$(0.2)(\text{row 1}) + (0.2)(\text{row 2}) + (0.6)(\text{row 3}) = \begin{pmatrix} 1.8 & 3.4 & 4.2 & 4.0 \end{pmatrix}.$$

So once again, $\boxed{a_3}$ emerges as the winner!

18.1 True or false: Regret is the negative of utility.

Solution

$\boxed{\text{False.}}$ Regret is the difference between the payoff and the best possible payoff given a strategy.

18.3 For each of the following, say whether or not this vector is part of the probability simplex.

a) $(0.3, 0.5, 0.2)$
b) $(0.3, 1.2, -0.5)$
c) $(0.1, 0.1, 0.2)$
d) $(1 - \epsilon, \epsilon/2, \epsilon/2)$ for $\epsilon \in [0, 0.1)$.

Solution

a) $\boxed{\text{True}}$
b) $\boxed{\text{False}}$
c) $\boxed{\text{False}}$
d) $\boxed{\text{True}}$

18.5 Suppose that an actor's preferences for lotteries are complete, transitive, continuous, and independent with utility function U.

a) Suppose for lotteries L and M, $U(L) \leq U(M)$. What can be said about the preferences between L and M?

b) Suppose for lotteries L and M, $U(L) < U(M)$. What can be said about the preferences between L and M?

Solution

a) This would make $\boxed{L \preceq M}$.

b) This would make $\boxed{L \prec M}$.

18.7 If lotteries are transitive, and for lotteries A, B, and C, $A \preceq B$ and $B \preceq C$ what can be said about the preference between A and C?

Solution

By transitivity, $\boxed{A \preceq C}$.

19.1 If $u(x) = \sqrt{x}$ and the payoff is $X \sim \text{Unif}([0,1])$, what is the average utility?

Solution

$2/3 \approx \boxed{0.6666}$.

19.3 Suppose $N = 0.4L + 0.6M$, and $X \sim \text{Bern}(0.4)$ is used to determine which of the two lotteries is played in the mixture. If $X = 1$, which lottery is played instead of N?

Solution

The lottery $\boxed{L}$ is played with probability 0.4, the same probability that $X = 1$.

19.5 True or false: for u a utility function, $3u + 6$ gives the same preferences as u.

Solution

$\boxed{\text{True}}$. Note that $u(A) < u(B)$ if and only if $3u(A) + 6 < 3u(A) + 6$, so preferences are preserved by the affine function with positive coefficient on the u.

19.7 Suppose f is an affine function with $f((1,1)) = (4,2)$, $f((1,2)) = (5,3)$.

a) Using the usual rules for scaling and adding vectors in $\mathbb{R}^2$, what does $0.4(1,1) + 0.6(1,2)$ equal?

b) Find $f((1,1.6))$.

Solution

a) Here

$$(0.4)(1,1) + (0.6)(1,2) = \boxed{(1.000, 1.600)}.$$

b) Let $x_1 = (1,1)$ and $x_2 = (1,2)$, $p_1 = 0.4$ and $p_2 = 0.6$. Then $p_1x_1 + p_2x_2 = (1, 1.6)$. So

$$\begin{aligned} f((1,1.6)) &= f(p_1x_1 + p_2x_2) \\ &= p_1 f(x_1) + p_2 f(x_2) \\ &= 0.4(4,2) + 0.6(5,3) \\ &= \boxed{(4.600, 2.600)}. \end{aligned}$$

20.1 Avatar Pharmaceuticals is thinking about whether or not to pursue a new product. Not pursuing the product costs nothing. If they do pursue the product and it is successful, there is a 30% chance that it will make 1.2 million dollars, but if it is a failure it will cost the company 0.3 million dollars. If money is treated as utility, what should Avatar do to maximize their utility?

Solution

Let $D1$ denote the decision to pursue or not pursue, and $R1$ be the random choice of whether it is successful or failure given pursuit. Then the expected utility of pursuit is

$$(0.3)(1.2) + (0.7)(-0.3) = 0.15,$$

which is greater than the expected utility of non-pursuit, which is 0. Hence the decision should be to $\boxed{\text{pursue the product.}}$

20.3 A business is testing out a new wind turbine design. It would take \$10 000 000 to develop the design fully. If demand for green energy is good (20%) the business stands to make 30 million dollars, but if it is medium (50%) they will only make 12 million, and if it is bad (30%), they will only make 2 million.

a) Draw the decision tree for this problem.

b) What decision should the business make?

Solution

a) As with most of these situations, there are several equivalent ways to describe the decision tree. One possibility is:

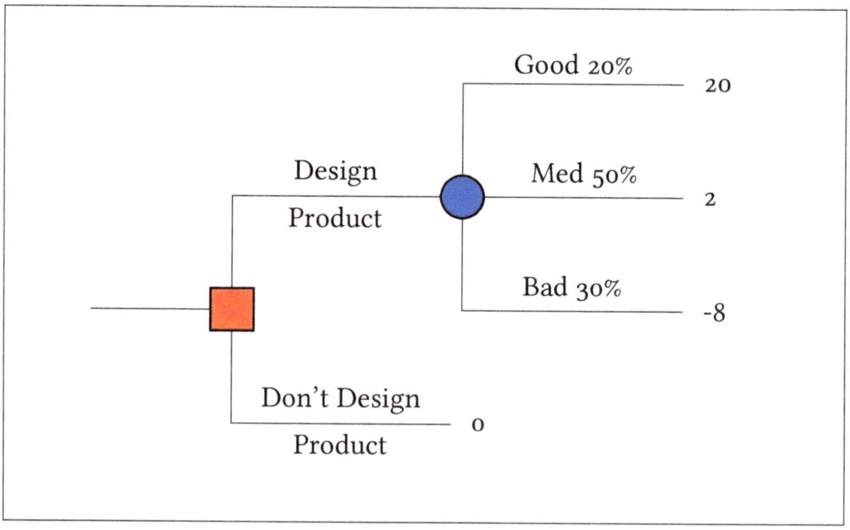

where the values are measured in millions of dollars.

b) Reducing the tree means taking the random outcome branch and replacing it with its expected value:

$$(0.2)(20) + (0.5)(2) + (0.3)(-8) = 2.6$$

which gives

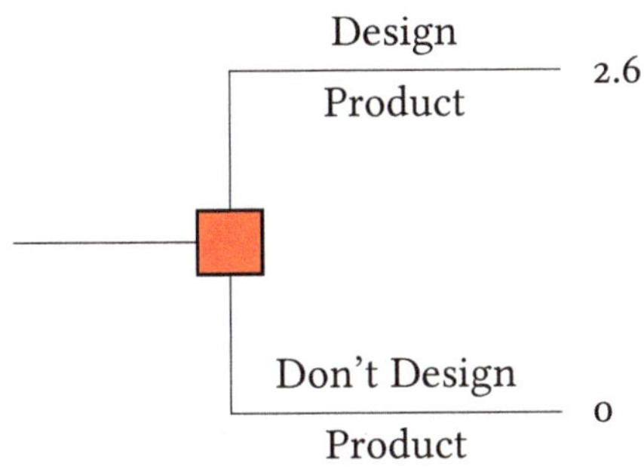

At this point the decision to Design the product results in more expected utility than not designing the product, so the optimal design is to Design the product.

20.5 After working with a consultant, Bender Incorporated has built the following decision tree. What decisions at D_1 and D_2 would maximize expected utility? (Write *up* or *down* for each of the two decisions.)

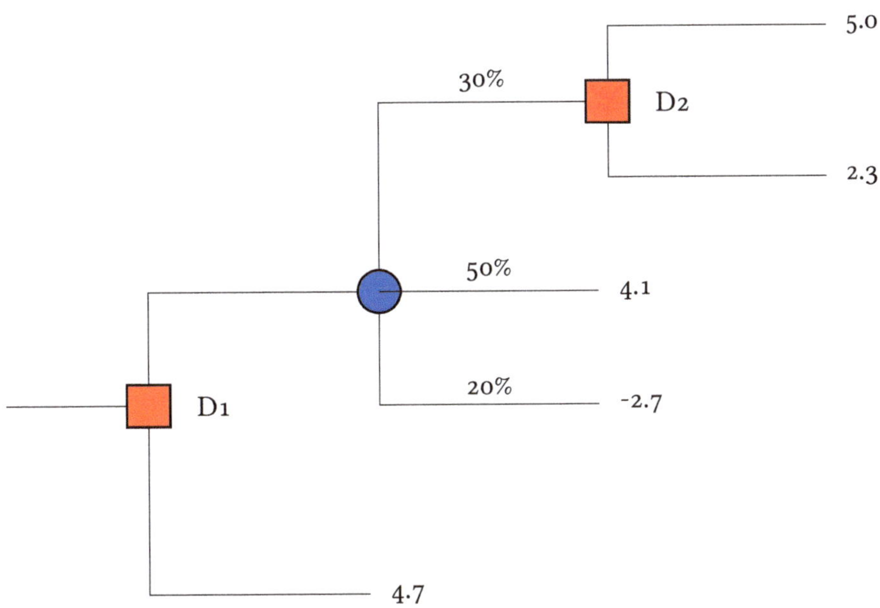

Solution

Start with D_2: since each outcome is fixed, the decision should be *up* since $5.0 > 2.3$.

Then the expected outcome at the only random node is

$$(0.3)(5) + (0.5)(4.1) + (0.2)(-2.7) = 3.01.$$

This is worse than 4.7, so the decision for D_1 is down. To summarize:

Node	Decision
D_1	down
D_2	up

20.7 Suppose that a venture capital (VC) firm has an opportunity to either buy into an IPO for an SSD maker or wait and see how the product performs. If they wait, the SSD maker might sell out its shares, and the VC firm will not be able to invest. The result will be making nothing, and this happens with probability 50%.

If shares remain, then there is a further 35% chance that the shares will be reduced in price, leading to a 23 million dollar windfall. But with 65%, the VC firm will make nothing.

On the other hand, if the VC makes its decision right away, then it must immediately make the next decision whether to buy or not to buy. If it decides to not buy, then again it makes nothing. If it decides to buy, there is an expected 60% chance that it still makes the 23 million dollar windfall, but now with 40% the VC firm loses 5 million dollars.

Draw a decision tree with $D1$ being the first decision to buy or not buy and $D2$ being the second decision to buy in or not buy in.

Solution

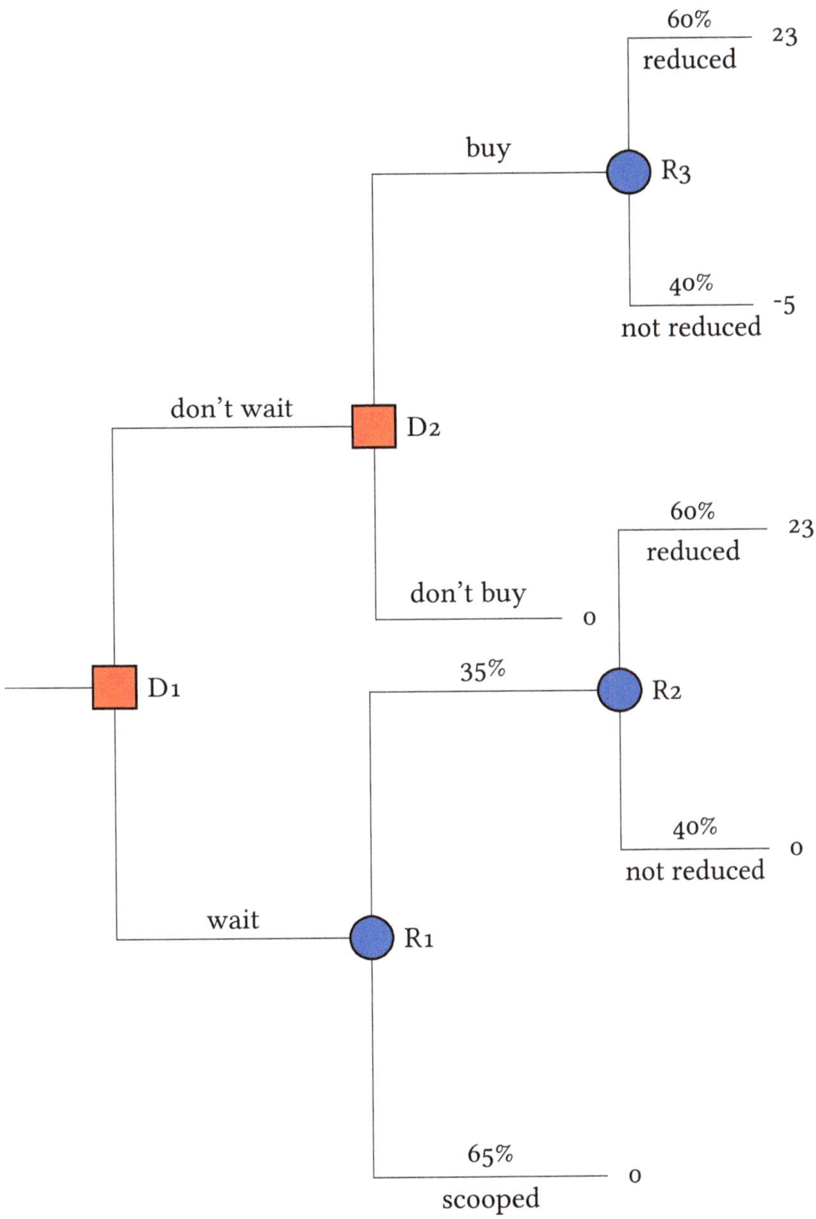

21.1 A survey question reads

Over 80% of U.K. members surveyed favored greater government expansion. What percentage of U.K. voters do you believe also favored expansion?

This question is an example of what type of problem in psychological decision making?

Solution

This is an example of $\boxed{\text{anchoring}}$. In general, you should avoid having numbers in your survey questions unless absolutely necessary.

21.3 A company has seen market data that has a good outcome four quarters in a row. They assume that a bad quarter must be coming. This is an example of what fallacy?

Solution

Assuming that an alternate outcome is due is the $\boxed{\text{Gambler's fallacy}}$.

21.5 Consider lottery N where everyone participating wins 100 dollars, and lottery M where 81% win 100 dollars, 2% win nothing, and the remaining 17% win 250 dollars. Among those surveyed, there is a clear preference for lottery N over lottery M.

In lottery R, 81% win nothing, but 19% win 100 dollars. In lottery S, 83% win nothing, but 17% win 250 dollars. Among those surveyed, there is a clear preference for lottery S with lottery R.

Prove that these choices are not compatible with any utility function.

Solution

If expected utility maximization was being used, then there exists utilities $U(0)$, $U(100)$, and $U(250)$. The expected utility is then used to determine preferences.

The expected utility for each lottery are

$$\begin{aligned}
\mathbb{E}_N[U] &= U(100) \\
\mathbb{E}_M[U] &= 0.81U(100) + 0.02U(0) + 0.17U(250) \\
\mathbb{E}_R[U] &= 0.81U(0) + 0.19U(100) \\
\mathbb{E}_S[U] &= 0.83U(0) + 0.17U(250)
\end{aligned}$$

Then

$$\mathbb{E}_S[U] - \mathbb{E}_R[U] = 0.02U(0) + 0.17U(250) - 0.19U(100),$$

and

$$\mathbb{E}_N[U] - \mathbb{E}_M[U] = 0.19U(100) - 0.02U(0) - 0.17U(250).$$

Note that one is the negative of the other. If expected utility was being used to determine preferences, then both would be positive, which cannot happen. Therefore, the users in the survey are not using expected utility maximization.

21.7 Consider a lottery A with outcomes of 25 dollars and 5 dollars with probabilities 60% and 40$ respectively. Similarly, lottery B is always worth 10 dollars. If an actor prefers to play B to A, show that this is incompatible with any affine utility function, that is, one of the form $U(m) = am + b$ for any positive constant a and m the monetary amount.

Solution

Let U be an affine utility function. Then

$$\mathbb{E}_A[U] = 0.6(25a + b) + 0.4(5a + b) = 17a + b$$

and

$$\mathbb{E}_B[U] = 10a + b$$

Since $a > 0$, $17a + b > 10a + b$, so the user would prefer lottery A if they were using this utility function.

In fact, they prefer B to A, so they cannot be using utility maximization with an affine utility function to make their choice.

22.1 Suppose that $\mathbb{E}[X] = 4.3$ and $\mathbb{E}[Y|X] = 2X$. What is $\mathbb{E}[Y]$?

Solution

By the Fundamental Theorem of Probability, this is

$$\mathbb{E}[Y] = \mathbb{E}[\mathbb{E}[Y|X]] = \mathbb{E}[2X] = 2\mathbb{E}[X] = \boxed{8.600}.$$

22.3 Suppose $T \sim \mathsf{Exp}(\lambda)$, where $\lambda \sim \mathsf{Unif}([1, 5])$.

a) What is $\mathbb{E}[T|\lambda]$?

b) What is $\mathbb{E}[T]$?

Solution

a) This is $\boxed{1/\lambda}$.

b) Using the Law of the Unconscious Statistician, this is

$$\int_1^5 \frac{1}{4}\frac{1}{s}\,ds = (1/4)(\ln(5) - \ln(1)) = \boxed{0.4023\ldots}.$$

22.5 An investor believes there is a 30% chance of tariffs being enacted on aluminum soon. If the tariffs are put in place, then purchasing stock in an aluminum mining company will result in a \$2 000 000 profit. if the tariffs are not put in place, then the investor will lose \$500 000.

a) Draw the decision tree for this problem.

b) Should the investor invest?

c) What is the EVPI for $I = \mathbb{1}$(tariffs are enacted)?

Solution

a) The decision tree looks like this:

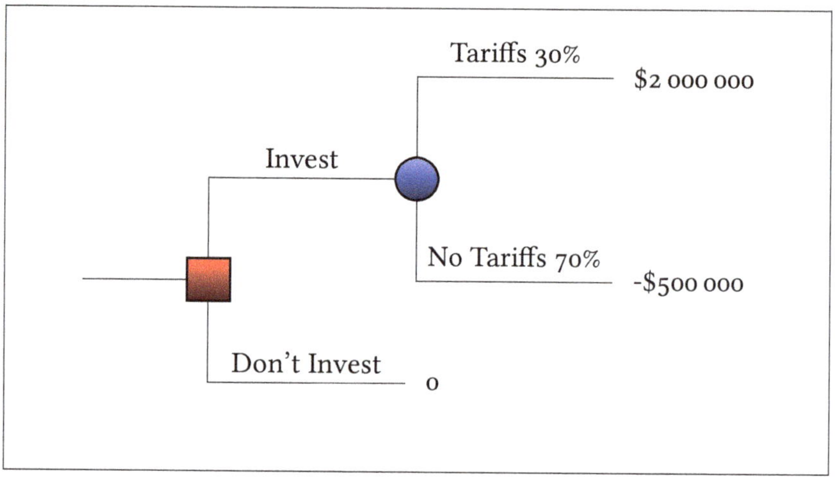

b) To determine that, we have to deconstruct the tree. The random node subtree can be replaced with its expected utility:

$$(2 \cdot 10^6)(0.3) + (-0.5 \cdot 10^6)(0.7) = 250\,000,$$

Since $250\,000 > 0$, the expected utility hypothesis decision is to $\boxed{\text{invest}}$.

c) Now the random value comes first in the decision tree:

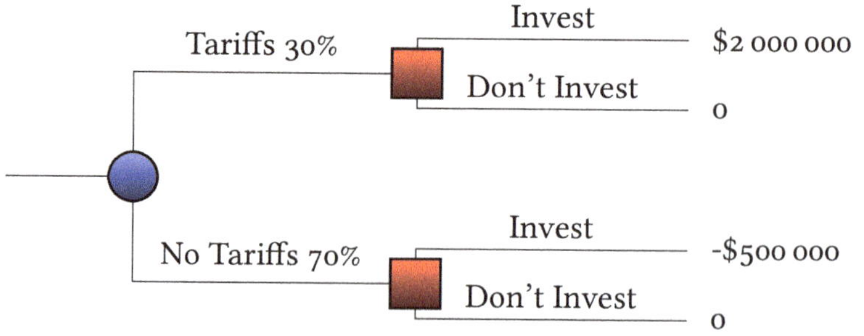

For the top path we always invest, and for the bottom one we do not. Hence the decision tree reduces to

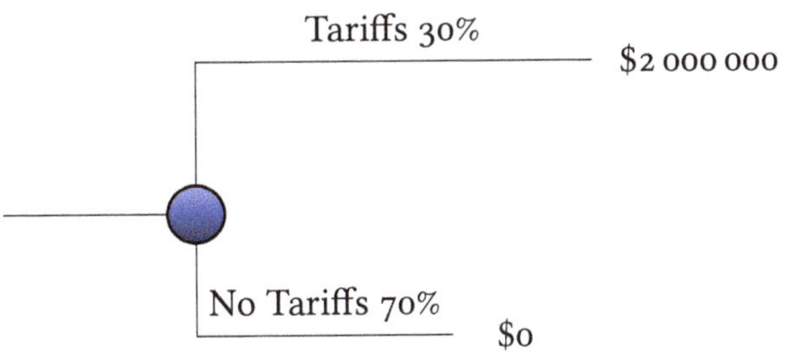

Therefore, the value of this tree is

$$(2 \cdot 10^6)(0.3) = 0.6 \cdot 10^6.$$

Hence the EVPI is

$$(0.6 - 0.25) \cdot 10^6 = \boxed{\$350\,000}.$$

22.7 In mathematical finance a *call option* with strike price K returns $S - K$ if a stock ends a time period with value S that is greater than or equal to K, or nothing otherwise. That is, the payoff of the call as a function of K is

$$P = \max(S - K, 0)$$

a) For a stock modeled as $S \sim \mathsf{Unif}([75, 150])$ and a strike price of $K = 110$, what is $\mathbb{E}[P]$?

b) If the call costs \$50 to purchase, should the call be bought? (Use expected utility maximization with utility equal to monetary value.)

Solution

a) Here

$$\mathbb{E}[P] = \int_{75}^{150} \frac{1}{75} \max(s - 110, 0)\, ds = \int_{110}^{150} \frac{1}{75}(s - 110)\, ds = \boxed{10.66\ldots}.$$

b) Given a cost of \$50 dollars, the expected return is negative and so the decision should be $\boxed{\text{not to buy.}}$

23.1 A new disease is spreading! Vaccinations are guaranteed to prevent 90% of infections but have a 1% chance of causing nausea. Among those infected, 3% will require hospitalization.

a) Write this using a positive frame for the vaccination.

b) Write this using a negative frame for the vaccination.

Solution

a) The vacination program will keep 97.3% of the population out of the hospital, but cause 1% of the population nausea. Not vaccinating will lead to 3% needing hospitalization.

b) The vacination program will still end up with 0.3% of the population going to the hospital, and 1% of the population will experience nausea. Not vaccinating only results in 3% hospitalization.

23.3 In 2007, a contest for best pie gave \$100 to each of the three top finishers. In 2008, they gave \$500 to first place, \$300 to second place, and \$150 to third place. Would you rather have won third place in 2007 or 2008?

Solution

There is no right answer to this question! From a purely utilitarian point of view, the 2008 third place winner received \$150, more than the third place winner of 2007. However, given that the higher finishers earned more money, the third place winner of 2008 might regret not doing better, and so might actually be more unhappy with their reward than the third place finisher of 2007.

23.5 Suppose that (unknown to the player) there are two envelopes one with \$10 and one with \$5. The player is allowed to open one envelope, then has the choice to stay or switch to the other.

The player decides to use the following strategy: randomly generate a Cauchy random variable and take the absolute value. This gives a random variable X with density

$$f_X(x) = \frac{4}{\tau(1+x^2)}\mathbb{1}(x \geq 0).$$

The player then plans to open one envelope uniformly at random and see the value x of money inside. The player then generates X. If $X \leq x$, the player keeps the envelope, otherwise they switch. What is the chance that they end up with the \$10 envelope?

Solution

If $X \leq 5$ they always keep whatever envelope they choose, and if $X > 10$ they always switch. Therefore they have a $1/2$ chance of winning the game. If $X \in (5, 10]$ they switch if they have the smaller envelope, so they always win. Hence the overall probability is

$$\begin{aligned}
\mathbb{P}(\text{win}) &= (1/2)\mathbb{P}(X \leq 5) + \mathbb{P}(X \in (5,10]) + (1/2)\mathbb{P}(X > 10) \\
&= (1/2) + (1/2)\mathbb{P}(X \in (5,10]) \\
&= (1/2)\left[1 + \int_5^{10} \frac{4}{\tau(1+x^2)}\,dx\right] \\
&= 0.5 + \arctan(255/1288)/\tau = \boxed{0.5311\ldots}.
\end{aligned}$$

23.7 Suppose that $X \sim \text{Unif}(\{1, 2, 3, 4\})$, and two envelopes are presented, one with X dollars, and one with $2X$ dollars. You are allowed to select one envelope, look inside, and then switch if you'd like.

You decide to randomly choose a continuous uniform W over $[0, 10]$. If the amount in the envelope is smaller than W, switch, otherwise keep your envelope. What is the chance that you end with the larger dollar amount?

Solution

There is a $1/2$ chance that the money is in the smaller envelope, in which case there are four values, each with probability $1/4$. For instance, if you see 3 dollars, then you switch if $3 \leq W$, which happens with probability $(10 - 3)/(10 - 0) = 0.7$.

Overall the probability of switching is

$$(0.25)(9/10) + (0.25)(8/10) + (0.25)(7/10) + (0.25)(6/10) = 0.75.$$

If you picked the largest envelope with values $\{2, 4, 6, 8\}$, the chance of switching would be

$$(0.25)(8/10)+(0.25)(6/10)+(0.25)(4/10)+(0.25)(2/10) = 5/10 = 0.50.$$

Hence the chance of winning the bigger envelope with this strategy is:

$$(0.5)(0.75) + (0.5)(1 - 0.5) = \boxed{0.6250}.$$

24.1 Suppose a user has $p = (0.2, 0.2, 0.3, 0.3)$ for a four answer multiple choice test question. Of the four choices, which maximizes the chance that the answer is correct?

Solution

Both $\boxed{\text{answer 3 and answer 4}}$ have the highest probability of being correct.

24.3 Suppose a user has $p = (0.2, 0.2, 0.25, 0.35)$ for a four answer multiple choice test question. The test taker is allowed to write a probability vector (m_1, m_2, m_3, m_4) as the answer. If the reward for answering correctly is $U(m_X) = m_X$, where X is the correct answer, then what is the choice of probability vector m that maximizes the expected utility?

Solution

The expectation maximizing choice is to put all the probability on $\boxed{\text{answer 4}}$, the answer with the highest probability given by the user.

24.5 Suppose a user has $p = (0.2, 0.2, 0.25, 0.35)$ for a four answer multiple choice test question. The test taker is allowed to write a probability vector (m_1, m_2, m_3, m_4) as the answer. If the reward for answering correctly is $U(m_X) = \ln(m_X)$, where X is the correct answer, then what is the choice of probability vector m that maximizes the expected utility?

Solution

Under these circumstances, the way to maximize utility is just to use the probability beliefs, so

$$\boxed{(0.2, 0.2, 0.25, 0.35)}$$

24.7 Suppose the economy either does well, medium, or poorly next quarter. An expert believes the chance of each outcome is 40%, 30%, and 30% respectively. Let X be the true answer. Find the value of $m \in [0, 1]^3$ that maximizes $\mathbb{E}[U_i(m)]$, where

a) the utility function is

$$U_1(m) = m(X),$$

b) or the utility function is

$$U_2(m) = \ln(m(X)).$$

Solution

a) Here $U(m) = m(X)$, so pick the response with the highest probability, put a 1 there. So the answer is

$$\boxed{(1, 0, 0)}.$$

b) Since $U(m) = \ln(m(X))$, we use the real probabilities,

$$\boxed{(0.4000, 0.3000, 0.3000)}.$$

24.9 The set of points (x, y) such that $x^2 + y^2 = 1$ forms a closed, bounded set. Find the maximum value of $x + y$ subject to $x^2 + y^2 = 1$ using Lagrange multipliers.

Solution

Because it is closed and bounded with no boundary, the optimal value exists and is attained at a critical point where

$$\nabla(x + y) = \lambda \nabla(x^2 + y^2)$$

for a constant λ. Taking partial derivatives gives

$$(1,1) = \lambda(2x, 2y).$$

If x or y is 0 then there is no solution for λ. So assume $x \neq 0$ and $y \neq 0$. Then

$$\frac{1}{2x} = \frac{1}{2y} = \lambda,$$

which means $x = y$.

The only two points satisfying both $x = y$ and $x^2 + y^2 = 1$ are $x = y = 1/\sqrt{2}$ and $x = y = -1/\sqrt{2}$. Since

$$\frac{1}{\sqrt{2}} + \frac{1}{\sqrt{2}} = \sqrt{2},$$

and

$$-\frac{1}{\sqrt{2}} - \frac{1}{\sqrt{2}} = -\sqrt{2},$$

the maximum value is $\sqrt{2} = \boxed{1.414\ldots}$.

25.1 What is $\log_2(1/8)$?

Solution

Since $2^{-3} = 1/2^3 = 1/8$, this is $\boxed{-3}$.

Another way to find it is $\ln(1/8)/\ln(2) = -3$.

25.3 True or false: The Shannon entropy is always nonnegative.

Solution

$\boxed{\text{True}}$. The Shannon entropy is the sum of positive things ($f_X(s)$) times positive things (negative the natural logarithm of probabilities).

25.5 What is the Shannon entropy of $X \sim \mathsf{Unif}(\{0,1\})$?

Solution

Using the formula for Shannon entropy:

$$\begin{aligned} H(X) &= -\mathbb{E}[\log_2(f_X(X))] \\ &= (1/2)(-\log_2(1/2)) + (1/2)(-\log_2(1/2)) \\ &= (1/2)(-(-1)) + (1/2)(-(-1)) \\ &= \boxed{1}. \end{aligned}$$

25.7 Consider the code from $\{a, b, c\}$ to $\{0, 01, 10\}$ defined as

$$f(a) = 0,\ f(b) = 01,\ f(c) = 10.$$

Is f uniquely encodable?

Solution

No, since `01001` could have come from either `acb` or `bab`.

25.9 Suppose $X_1, \ldots, X_n$ are iid $\mathsf{Bern}(0.7)$. For a given code/compression scheme, what is the minimum number of bits on average needed to encode a length n sequence?

Solution

Each bit has entropy $-[0.7\ln(0.7) + 0.3\ln(0.3)] = 0.8812909$. So by the Shannon source coding Theorem, any code uses a minimum of $\boxed{0.8812n}$ bits on average.

26.1 True or false: Decision theory can be used to analyze two-person games.

Solution

$\boxed{\text{False.}}$ Decision theory involves one person against a state of nature. We assume that nature is random (unknown), but that it is not actively striving against us!

26.3 True or false: In the Prisoner's Dilemma, cooperation can be undermined by self-interest.

Solution

This is $\boxed{\text{true}}$.

26.5 Suppose that 3 players are making decisions that affect the payoff. The payoff function has how many inputs?

Solution

Because each player gets a decision, this has $\boxed{3}$ inputs.

26.7 Consider the following payoff matrix, where each of two players is deciding between strategies a_1 and a_2.

		Player 1	
		a_1	a_2
Player 2	a_1	$(0, -1)$	$(4, -2)$
	a_2	$(-3, 4)$	$(3, 2)$

a) If Player 1 is self-interested, what decision will they make?

b) If Player 2 is self-interested, what decision will they make?

Solution

a) No matter what Player 2 does, Player 1 does better by switching to $\boxed{a_1}$.

b) No matter what Player 1 does, Player 2 does better by switching to $\boxed{a_2}$.

27.1 Fill in the blank: If the outcomes of a game all satisfy for entry

$$(a_1, a_2, \ldots, a_n)$$

that

$$a_1 + a_2 + \cdots + a_n = 0,$$

call it a(n) ____________ game.

Solution

This is a $\boxed{\text{zero sum}}$ game.

27.3 Consider a zero-sum game with payoff matrix:

		Player II a	b
Player I	a	-6	2
	b	4	-3

Answer the following questions about the strategic form of this two person zero sum game.

a) What is X?

b) What is Y?

c) What is the payoff function A?

Solution

a) This is the set of strategies for Player I, so $\boxed{a, b}$.

b) This is the set of strategies for Player II, so $\boxed{a, b}$.

c) This is the function that gives the payoffs, so

$$A(a, a) = -6$$
$$A(a, b) = 2$$
$$A(b, a) = 4$$
$$A(b, b) = -3.$$

27.5 Consider the zero-sum game with entries

		Player II	
		1	2
Player I	1	−5	5
	2	5	−5

If Player I plays strategy 1 with probability 40% and strategy 2 with probability 60%, then what strategy should Player II use to maximize expected utility for Player II?

Solution

Note that the value in the matrix is the utility that Player II gives to Player I, so they are trying to make this as small as possible.

If Player II uses strategy 1, then the expected utility for Player I is

$$(0.6)(-5) + (0.4)(5) = -1.$$

If Player II uses strategy 2, then the expected utility for Player I is

$$(0.6)(5) + (0.4)(-5) = 1.$$

So to minimize the utility for Player I (and maximize the utility for Player II), Player II should play strategy $\boxed{1}$.

27.7 Consider the game with entries

		Player II	
		1	2
Player I	1	−5	5
	2	5	−5

What is the value of this game?

Solution

By inspection, the strategy $(1/2, 1/2)$ for both Player I and II gives an expected payoff of 0, regardless of what the other player chooses. Hence the value of this game is $\boxed{0}$.

28.1 If a Player has a 50% chance of playing a, and a 50% chance of playing b, this is what type of strategy?

Solution

This is a $\boxed{\text{mixed}}$ strategy.

28.3 Consider the following payoff matrix.

		Player 2		
		a	b	c
Player 1	a	$(-3,-4)$	$(-1,2)$	$(2,-3)$
	b	$(-1,2)$	$(3,-2)$	$(0,0)$

Show that this is not a zero sum game.

Solution

If Player 1 and Player 2 both choose a, then the outcome is $(-3,-4)$. Since these entries add to -7 rather than 0, this is not a zero sum game.

28.5 Consider the following payoff matrix.

		Player 2		
		a	b	c
Player 1	a	$(-3,-4)$	$(-1,2)$	$(2,-3)$
	b	$(-1,2)$	$(3,-2)$	$(0,0)$

Show that no pure strategies for the players form a Nash equilibrium.

Solution

Look at each of the six pure strategies:

- From (a,a), Player 1 wants to move to b.
- From (a,b), Player 2 wants to move to b.
- From (a,c), Player 2 wants to move to b.
- From (b,a), Player 2 wants to move to b.
- From (b,b), Player 2 wants to move to a.
- From (b,a), Player 1 wants to move to a.

Therefore, none of the six pure strategies is also a Nash equilibrium.

28.7 Consider the following payoff matrix.

		Player 2	
		a	b
Player 1	a	$(-2,-3)$	$(2,2)$
	b	$(1,1)$	$(0,0)$

Find three Nash equilibria.

Solution

Suppose that Player 1 chooses b and Player 2 chooses a. Then neither player can switch their strategy without decreasing their expected payoff. Therefore, the pure strategy $\boxed{(b, a)}$ is a Nash equilibrium.

Similarly, the pure strategy $\boxed{(a, b)}$ is also a Nash equilibrium.

Finally, consider if there is a mixed strategy.

Suppose Player 1 chooses a with probability p, and b otherwise. The expected return for Player 2 is then:

$$\mathbb{E}[\text{Payoff for Player 2}|\text{Player 2 plays } a] = -3p + (1-p) = 1 - 4p$$
$$\mathbb{E}[\text{Payoff for Player 2}|\text{Player 2 plays } b] = 2p + 0(1-p) = 2p.$$

By setting $1 - 4p = 2p$ or $p = 1/6$, it can be shown that Player 2 will always have a expected return above $1/3$, regardless of their strategy!

Player 2 can do something similar. If they play a with probability q and b with probability $1 - q$, then the return for Player 1 is

$$\mathbb{E}[\text{Payoff for Player 1}|\text{Player 1 plays } a] = -2q + 2(1-q) = 2 - 4q$$
$$\mathbb{E}[\text{Payoff for Player 1}|\text{Player 1 plays } b] = q + 0(1-q) = q.$$

Then $2 - 4q = q$ gives $q = 2/5$ as the crossover point. Therefore, there is a Nash equilibrium at

$$\boxed{(1/3, 2/3), (2/5, 3/5)}.$$

or

$$\boxed{(0.3333, 0.6666), (0.4000, 0.6000)}$$

truncated at four sig figs.

29.1 An algorithm with a random output is a ____________ algorithm.

Solution

This is a $\boxed{\text{Monte Carlo}}$ algorithm.

29.3 Show that $n^3 + n^2 \in O(n^3)$ by explicitly finding C and n that satisfies the definition.

Solution

Let $C = 2$, $N = 1$. Let $n \geq N = 1$. Then

$$n^3 + n^2 \leq n^3 + n^3 = 2n^3.$$

29.5 Given that $n^3 + n^2 \in O(n^3)$ and $n^3 + n^2 \in \Omega(n^3)$, what else can be said about the order of $n^3 + n^2$?

Solution

Having a function both in big-O and big-Omegea gives that it is in big-Theta. That is,

$$\boxed{n^3 + n^2 \in \Theta(n^3)}.$$

29.7 Show that $5n \in o(n \ln(n))$ by explicity finding an N value such that for all $C > 0$ and $n \geq N$, $5n \leq n \ln(n)$.

Solution

Let $C > 0$. Then to get $5n \leq Cn \ln(n)$, it is necessary to choose N so that $C \ln(N) \geq 5$, or $N \geq \exp(5/C)$. So let $N = \text{ceiling}(\exp(5/C))$. Let $n \geq N$. Since $\ln(n)$ is an increasing function,

$$Cn \ln(n) \geq Cn \ln(N) \geq 5n,$$

and the proof is complete.

29.9 Suppose there is an array with n elements which contains value a in exactly one position.

A randomized algorithm for finding where this value is located does the following: choose uniformly at random a position from 1 up to n. Search that position. If found, quit. Otherwise, start over and independently choose again until the value is found.

What is the expected number of steps needed to find the value?

Solution

There is a $1/n$ chance of finding the value at each step of the algorithm. Therefore the number of steps is geometrically distributed with parameter $1/n$. The expected value of a geometric random variable is one over the parameter, so the expected number of steps is $\boxed{n}$.

30.1 Find the sample median of $8, 4, 4, 5, 3$.

Solution

The order statistics of this data are

$$3, 4, 4, 5, 8$$

and so the sample median is $\boxed{4}$.

30.3 For $x = (8, 4, 4, 5, 3)$, answer the following.

a) What would `QuickSort(x)` return?

b) What would `QuickSelect(x, 2)` return?

c) What would `QuickSelect(x, 4)` return?

Solution

a) This would sort the items into $\boxed{(3, 4, 4, 5, 8)}$.

b) This would find the second smallest item, so $\boxed{4}$.

c) This would fin the fourth smallest item, so $\boxed{5}$.

30.5 Suppose $\mathbb{E}[T(n)] \leq \mathbb{E}[T(n-1)] + 2$ and $\mathbb{E}[T(0)] = 0$. Prove by induction that $\mathbb{E}[T(n)] \leq 2n$.

Solution

The base case is $\mathbb{E}[T(0] = 0 \leq 2(0) = 2$, so is satisfied.

Assume $\mathbb{E}[T(n)] \leq 2n$. Then

$$\begin{aligned}\mathbb{E}[T(n+1)] &\leq \mathbb{E}(T[n]) + 2 \\ &\leq 2n + 2 \\ &\leq 2(n+1),\end{aligned}$$

completing the induction.

30.7 A recursive algorithm when presented with input of size $n \geq 2$, makes one call of size $n-1$ and another of size $n-2$. If the input is size 0 or 1, then 1 operation is needed. Prove by strong induction that the running time is at most α^n where $\alpha = (1+\sqrt{5})/2$.

Solution

Let $R(n)$ be the running time on an input of size n.

The statement holds for $n = 0$ and $n = 1$.

Assume it holds for $n \geq 2$. Then

$$\begin{aligned}R(n) &= R(n-1) + R(n-2) \\ &\leq \alpha^{n-1} + \alpha^{n-2} \\ &\leq \alpha^{n-1} + (1/\alpha)\alpha^{n-1} \\ &\leq (1 + 1/\alpha)\alpha^{n-1}.\end{aligned}$$

Note that

$$\begin{aligned}1+1/\alpha &= 1+\frac{2}{1+\sqrt{5}}\\ &= 1+\frac{2-2\sqrt{5}}{(1+\sqrt{5})(1-\sqrt{5})}\\ &= 1+\frac{2-2\sqrt{5}}{-4}\\ &= \frac{1}{2}(1+\sqrt{5})\\ &= \alpha.\end{aligned}$$

Combining gives

$$R(n) \leq \alpha \cdot \alpha^{n-1} = \alpha^n,$$

and the induction is complete.

31.1 True or false: A BPP algorithm might return the correct answer $1/2$ of the time.

Solution

$\boxed{\text{False.}}$ A BPP algorithm has to be right at least $2/3$ of the time.

31.3 An RP algorithm is run twice and the output is the logical OR of the two runs. What is the largest chance that it made an error?

Solution

The largest chance of making an error in one run is $1/2$, so the largest chance of making an error in two runs is $(1/2)^2 = \boxed{0.2500}$.

31.5 A BPP algorithm is run 5 times and the majority winner is taken. What is the largest chance that it made an error?

Solution

The chance a single run is wrong is at most $1/3$. There would need to be at least three runs with the wrong outcome to make the majority incorrect. Using the probabilities of a binomial random variable, this is

$$\binom{5}{3}\left(\frac{1}{3}\right)^3\left(\frac{2}{3}\right)^2+\binom{5}{4}\left(\frac{1}{3}\right)^4\left(\frac{2}{3}\right)^1+\binom{5}{5}\left(\frac{1}{3}\right)^5\left(\frac{2}{3}\right)^0.$$

This comes out to be $17/81 = \boxed{0.2098\ldots}$.

31.7 How many times must an RP algorithm be run to guarantee that the chance of failure is at most 1%?

Solution

The chance of failure after running k times is at most $(1/2)^k$. Hence to have $(1/2)^k \leq 0.01$ requires $k \geq \lg(100) = 6.643\ldots$. Hence $\boxed{k = 7}$ times suffices.

32.1 Consider the following optimization problem.

$$\begin{aligned} \max\ & x_1^2 + x_2^2 \\ \text{subject to}\ & x_1 + x_2 \leq 4 \\ & x_1 \geq 0 \\ & x_2 \geq 0 \end{aligned}$$

Is this a linear program?

Solution

$\boxed{\text{No}}$, since the objective function has an x_1^2 term, which is not a linear function. The x_2^2 term also disqualifies it from being a linear program.

32.3 Suppose $\mathcal{U} = \{1, 2, 3, 4\}$,

$$\begin{aligned} S_1 &= \{1, 2\} \\ S_2 &= \{3, 4\} \\ S_3 &= \{1, 2, 3, 4\}. \end{aligned}$$

a) Does $\{S_1, S_2\}$ cover $\mathcal{U}$? (That is, does the union of S_1 and S_2 equal $\mathcal{U}$?)

b) Is there a smaller set cover?

Solution

a) $\boxed{\text{Yes}}$ it does, because $\{1, 2\} \cup \{3, 4\} = \{1, 2, 3, 4\}$..

b) $\boxed{\text{Yes}}$, $S_3 = \{1, 2, 3, 4\}$ is by itself a set cover.

32.5 Suppose $\mathcal{U} = \{1, 2, 3, 4, 5\}$,

$$\begin{aligned} S_1 &= \{1, 2\} \\ S_2 &= \{3, 4\} \\ S_3 &= \{2, 3, 4, 5\}. \end{aligned}$$

a) Write the problem of finding the smallest set cover as an integer program.

b) What is the linear relaxation of this IP?

Solution

a) This can be done using x_1, x_2, x_3, where x_i indicates if S_i is part of the set cover.

$$\begin{aligned} \min x_1 + x_2 + x_3 \\ x_1 \geq 1 \\ x_1 + x_3 \geq 1 \\ x_2 + x_3 \geq 1 \\ x_2 + x_3 \geq 1 \\ x_3 \geq 1.(x_1, x_2, x_3) \in \{0, 1\}^3. \end{aligned}$$

b) The linear relaxation just changes $\{0, 1\}$ to $[0, 1]$.

$$\begin{aligned} \min x_1 + x_2 + x_3 \\ x_1 \geq 1 \\ x_1 + x_3 \geq 1 \\ x_2 + x_3 \geq 1 \\ x_2 + x_3 \geq 1 \\ x_3 \geq 1.(x_1, x_2, x_3) \in [0, 1]^3. \end{aligned}$$

32.7 Consider the IP

$$\begin{aligned} \max x_1 + x_2 \\ (1/2)x_1 + x_2 \leq 1 \\ 3x_1 + x_2 \leq 2 \\ (x_1, x_2) \in \{0, 1\}^3. \end{aligned}$$

The linear relaxation would be

$$\begin{aligned} \max x_1 + x_2 \\ (1/2)x_1 + x_2 \leq 1 \\ 3x_1 + x_2 \leq 2 \\ (x_1, x_2) \in [0, 1]^3. \end{aligned}$$

The optimal solution to this is

$$(x_1, x_2) = (2/5, 4/5).$$

a) If randomized rounding was then used to generate a solution from the original IP, what would the expected objective value be?

b) What is the chance that the $(1/2)x_1 + x_2 \leq 1$ constraint is satisfied?

Solution

a) This would be (by linearity of expectations) $(2/5) + (4/5) = \boxed{1.200}$.

b) For this constraint satisfied as long as both x_1 and x_2 are not both 1. This happens with probability

$$1 - \frac{2}{5} \cdot \frac{4}{5} = \frac{17}{25} = \boxed{0.6800}.$$

33.1 Consider data

time	sales
0	4.3
1	3.7
2	7.2
3	4.5
4	6.1.

Estimate the baseline average.

Solution

This would be

$$\frac{4.3 + 3.7 + 7.2 + 4.5 + 6.1}{5} = \boxed{5.160}.$$

33.3 Continuing the last problem, find the $n = 2$ and $n = 3$ moving averages for this data.

Solution

To four sig figs, this would be

time	sales	$n = 2$ MA	$n = 3$ MA
0	4.3		
1	3.7	4	
2	7.2	5.450	5.066
3	4.5	5.850	5.133
4	6.1	5.300	5.933.

33.5 For $U \sim \text{Unif}([0, 1])$, find $\text{MAD}(u)$.

Solution

The mean of U is 0.5, so this is

$$\begin{aligned}\mathbb{E}[|U-1/2|] &= \int_{-\infty}^{\infty} |u-1/2|\mathbb{1}(u \in [0,1])\,du \\ &= \int_0^{1/2} 1/2 - u\,du + \int_{1/2}^{1} u - 1/2\,du \\ &= -u^2/2|_0^{1/2} + u^2/2|_{1/2}^{1} \\ &= -(1/8) + 1/2 - 1/8 \\ &= 1/4 = \boxed{0.2500}\end{aligned}$$

33.7 For X an integrable random variable, prove that $\text{MAD}(X) = \text{MAD}(X + a)$ for any constant a.

Solution

For X integrable and a a constant,

$$\begin{aligned}\text{MAD}(X+a) &= \mathbb{E}[|X+a-\mathbb{E}[X+a]|] \\ &= \mathbb{E}[|X+a-\mathbb{E}[X]-a|] \\ &= \mathbb{E}[|X-\mathbb{E}[X]|] \\ &= \text{MAD}(X).\end{aligned}$$

34.1 Suppose a prediction for y_1 was $\hat{y}_1 = 10$. If $\alpha = 0.4$ with simple exponential smoothing, what would the prediction $\hat{y}_2$ be if y_1 turned out to have value 12.

Solution

The error here was $12 - 10 = 2$, so the prediction would be

$$\hat{y}_2 = 10 + (0.4)(2) = \boxed{10.80}.$$

Another way to find it is to use $(0.6)(10) + (0.4)(12) = 10.80$.

34.3 The California milk per cow from organic herds is summarized in the following table (drawn from https://www.californiadairymagazine.com/read/adtrack/2017/0717/2016cdfamilkreport.pdf accessed 2024-04-15.) It also includes predictions made using simple exponential smoothing with $\alpha = 0.6$ using $\hat{y}_1 = y_0$.

Year	Annual Milk per cow (pounds)	pred
2012	14904	NA
2013	15204	14904.00
2014	15480	15084.00
2015	16284	15321.60
2016	15816	15899.04

Find an estimate of the mean absolute deviation of the error.

Solution For the year 2013, the absolute error between the true value and the prediction is $|15204 - 14904| = 300$. Similary, the errors for the other three years are $|15480 - 15084|$, $|16284 - 15321.60|$, and $|15816 - 15899.04|$. The sample average of these four values is

$$\boxed{435.4}.$$

34.5 Continuing the California cows data from earlier, here are the predictions for $\alpha = 0.6$ and $\alpha = 0.4$. Which would be chosen as the better value of α using MAD to make the decision.

Year	Annual Milk per cow (pounds)	$\alpha = 0.4$	$\alpha = 0.6$
2012	14904	NA	NA
2013	15204	14904.00	14902.00
2014	15480	15084.00	15024.00
2015	16284	15321.60	15206.40
2016	15816	15899.04	15637.44

Solution

The MAD estimate for the two α values are:

α	MAD estimate
0.6	435.36
0.4	503.04

So based on these estimates, go with $\boxed{\alpha = 0.6}$.

34.7 Domestic U.S. data for passengers scheduled to fly month by month in 2000 is as follows. (Drawn from `transtats.bts.gov/TRAFFIC` on 2024-04-15.)

Period	Scheduled
January 2000	41540
February 2000	43714
March 2000	52977
April 2000	50344
May 2000	52309
June 2000	54673
July 2000	55568
August 2000	54474
September 2000	46363
October 2000	50920
November 2000	49632
December 2000	47051

Using $\hat{\ell}_0 = 40000$ and $\hat{m}_0 = 3000$ together with Holt's method with $\beta = 0.1$ and $\alpha = 0.5$, predict the number of passengers for March 2001.

Solution

Filling in the table using Holt's method gives

Period	Scheduled	$\hat{\ell}$	$\hat{m}$
January 2000	41540	42270.00	2927.000
February 2000	43714	44455.50	2852.850
March 2000	52977	50142.68	3136.283
April 2000	50344	51811.48	2989.535
May 2000	52309	53555.01	2864.934
June 2000	54673	55546.47	2777.587
July 2000	55568	56946.03	2639.784
August 2000	54474	57029.91	2384.193
September 2000	46363	52888.55	1731.638
October 2000	50920	52770.09	1546.629
November 2000	49632	51974.36	1312.393
December 2000	47051	50168.88	1000.605

This makes the final prediction three months into the future:

$$50168.88 + (3)(1000.605) = 53170.69,$$

or $\boxed{53170}$ to four sig figs.

35.1 The cost per unit when demand is higher than inventory is the ______________ cost.

Solution

This is called the understocking cost.

35.3 True or false: the function $f(x) = x^2$ is convex.

Solution

True. Since $f(x)$ is twice differentiable, and $[f(x)]'' = 2 \geq 0$ for all x, this is a convex function.

35.5 Suppose that a Christmas tree seller can obtain trees for $13.50 and that they sell in the local market for an average of $110.00. Any trees left over after Christmas require payment of $5.15 for disposal. If demand is modeled as a negative binomial distribution with parameters 1000 and 0.42, what is the optimal number of trees for the lot to buy?

Solution

The profit made from each tree is $110 - 13.50 = 96.50$, while the cost associated with an extra tree is $13.50 + 5.15 = 18.65$. Hence $c_o = 18.65$ and $c_u = 96.50$. Therefore, we want to order an amount q such that $\mathbb{P}(D \leq q) = 96.50/(96.50 + 18.65) = 0.8380\ldots$. Using `qnbinom((96.50 / (96.50 + 18.65), 1000, 0.42)` gives 1437, so that is how many trees should be ordered.

36.1 A strategy that tells the distribution of choices for each state in a Markov Decision Process is called a(n) ________.

Solution

This is a policy.

36.3 Suppose $\beta = 1/2$ and the reward is $r_{X_t,d_t} = 5$ for every value of X_t and d_t. What is the discounted reward of the policy.

Solution

Since every reward is 5, this is

$$\sum_{i=1}^{\infty} (0.5)^{i-1} 5 = 5/(1 - 1/2) = \boxed{10}.$$

36.5 Suppose with a particular policy that r_{X_t,d_t} converges to uniform over $\{1, 2, 3, 4\}$ as t goes to infinity. What will the long term average reward be?

Solution

The average reward converges to $(4 + 1)/2 = \boxed{2.500}$, so that is what the long-term average reward will be as well.

37.1 Suppose that there are three states $\{1, 2, 3\}$. For states 1 and 2 there are two decisions $\{a, b\}$, and in the third state there are three decisions $\{a, b, c\}$. Say

$$\pi_{1,a} = 0.2, \pi_{1,b} = 0.2, \pi_{2,a} = 0.1, \pi_{2,b} = 0.25, \pi_{3,a} = 0.05, \pi_{3,b} = 0.1.$$

What is $\pi_{3,c}$?

Solution

Since the $\pi_{i,d}$ have to add up to 1, and the remaining $\pi_{i,d}$ add to 0.9, $\pi_{3,c} = \boxed{0.1000}$.

38.1 If $U \sim \mathsf{Unif}([0, 1])$, then $Y = -\ln(U) \sim \mathsf{Exp}(1)$. Let $W = -\ln(1 - U)$.

a) What is the distribution of W?
b) Find $\mathbb{E}[Y]$ and $\mathbb{V}(Y)$.
c) Find $\mathbb{E}[(W + Y)/2]$.
d) Find $\mathbb{V}((W + Y)/2)$.

Solution

a) Since U and $1 - U$ have the same distribution, so do Y and W. Hence $\boxed{W \sim \mathsf{Exp}(1)}$.
b) Mean and variance for a standard exponential random variable are both 1, so $\boxed{\mathbb{E}[Y] = \mathbb{V}(Y) = 1}$.
c) Since W and Y have the same distribution, they both have the same mean of 1, and

$$\mathbb{E}[(W + Y)/2] = (1 + 1)/2 = \boxed{1}.$$

d) From the rules for variance,

$$\mathbb{V}\left(\frac{W + Y}{2}\right) = \frac{1}{4}[\mathbb{V}(W) + \mathbb{V}(Y) + 2\operatorname{Cov}(W, Y)].$$

Both W and Y have variance 1, so we only need their covariance.

$$\begin{aligned}
\operatorname{Cov}(W, Y) &= \mathbb{E}[WY] - \mathbb{E}[W]\mathbb{E}[Y] \\
&= \mathbb{E}[\ln(U)\ln(1 - U)] - 1 \\
&= \int_0^1 \ln(u)\ln(1 - u)\, du - 1 \\
&= -0.6944\ldots
\end{aligned}$$

Hence the overall variance is $\boxed{0.1775}$.

38.3 Suppose $p \in (0,1)$. Let $U \sim \mathsf{Unif}([0,1])$, $X = \mathbb{1}(U \leq p)$, $Y = \mathbb{1}(1-U \leq p)$. What is

$$\mathrm{SD}((X+Y)/2)?$$

Solution

Suppose $p \leq 1/2$. This if $U \leq p$ then $X = 1$ and $Y = 0$. If $p < U \leq 1-p$ then $X = 0$ and $Y = 0$. If $1 - p > U$ then $X = 0$ and $Y = 1$. So for $W = (X+Y)/2$, $\mathbb{P}(W = 1/2) = 2p$ and $\mathbb{P}(W = 0) = 1 - 2p$. So

$$\mathrm{SD}(W) = \sqrt{2p(1/2)^2 - p^2} = \sqrt{p(1/2 - p)}.$$

For $p \geq 1/2$, $\mathbb{P}(W = 1) = 2p - 1$ and $\mathbb{P}(W = 1/2) = 2 - 2p$. Hence

$$\mathrm{SD}(W) = \sqrt{(1)^2(2p-1) + (1/2)^2(2-2p) - p^2} = \sqrt{(1-p)(p-1/2)}$$

Altogether, the standard deviation is

$$\boxed{\sqrt{p(1/2-p)}\mathbb{1}(p \leq 1/2) + \sqrt{(1-p)(p-1/2)}\mathbb{1}(p > 1/2)}.$$

www.ingramcontent.com/pod-product-compliance
Lightning Source LLC
LaVergne TN
LVHW071340210926
848486LV00003B/196

* 9 7 9 8 9 9 2 7 9 0 6 0 3 *